*I dedicate this book to all experimenters
of photography, especially to those who
are dedicated to FoTotempismo.*

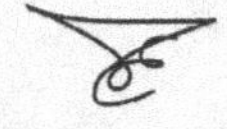

Enzo Trifolelli

Enzo Trifolelli

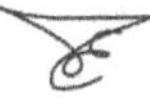

FoTotempismo

the Gesture in photography

between Technique and Art

Vol. I

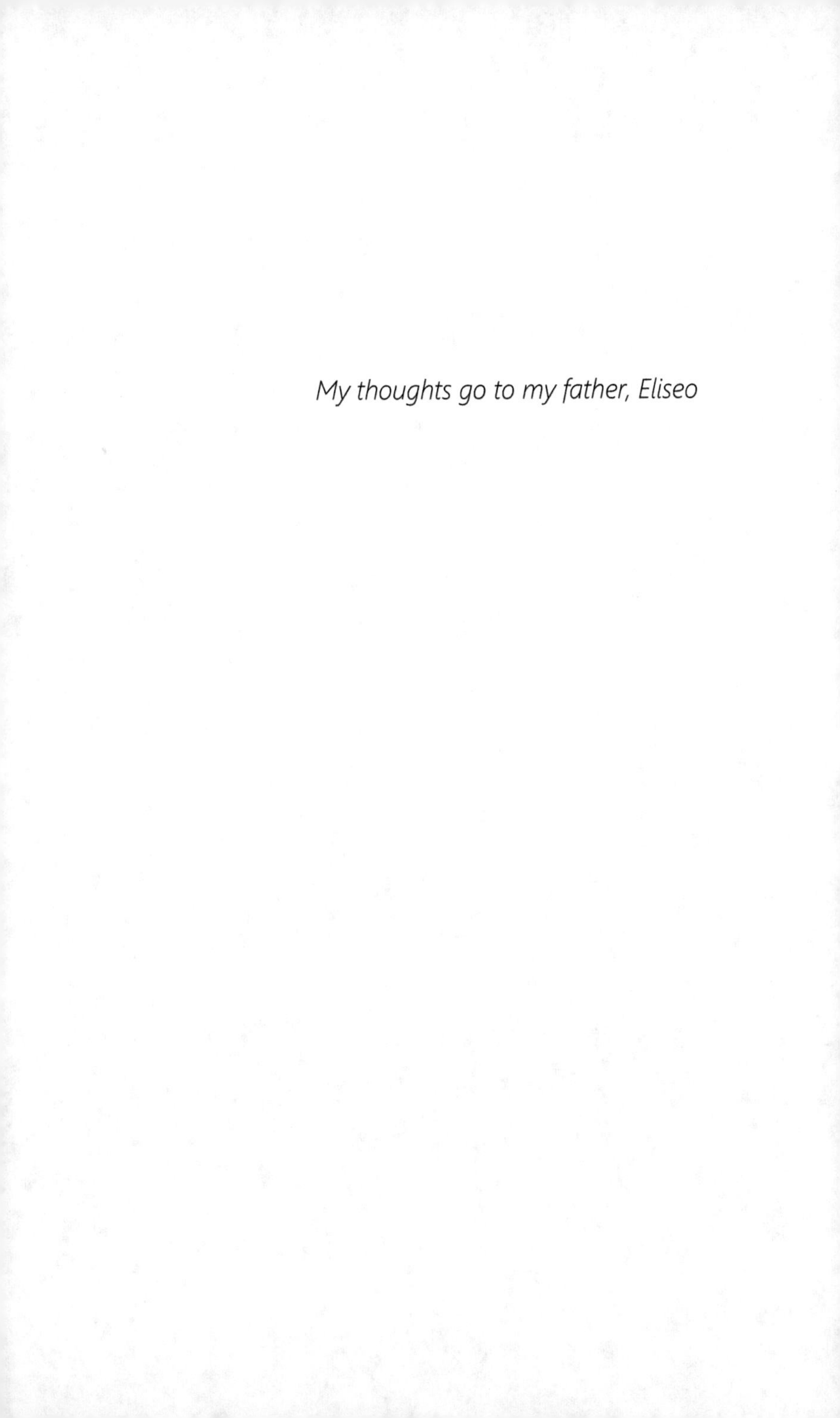

My thoughts go to my father, Eliseo

Preface

There is nothing in the world that does not aspire to become something more, and Enzo Trifolelli's photography arises as one of the possible outcomes of such an aspiration from the image fixed on a flat surface.

In fact, the author decided to take upon himself the efforts and responsibilities of a complex challenge: the formulation of a concept and a shooting technique that would allow both the depth effect of the third dimension (spatial) and the passing of a particular passage of a temporal flow to return to photography.

The optical procedure behind the study, which comprises in moving the camera in space during a single shutter aperture, betrays glimpses of potential communicative vigour. The author has bestowed the name 'FoTotempismo' on this procedure, which derives from the theory that animates it.

Before the registration of light takes place, it is necessary for the photographer to designate an element of visible reality, but neither the dimensions of one nor the space-time dilation are significant; therefore the freedom of interpretation is absolute and can act from the microscopic to the macroscopic, both in terms of breadth and duration.

Not even the quality of the subject matter is an inhibiting factor: the method is equally applicable to portraits as to panoramas, to shots of objects to snapshots of actions or events; that which takes on an unconditional and inalienable importance is only the operator's intellectual approach in acting in creative symbiosis with the device at their disposal.

Carlo Gallerati
(Gallerati Gallery, Rome)

The exploration of Space-Time with FoTotempismo
the Gesture that generates the Sign

from concept
... to photography

Painting is what I did, photography is what I have continued to do since 1972. It is perhaps through images that I can express myself best, grasping the essence of the moment, to convey moods, my feelings.

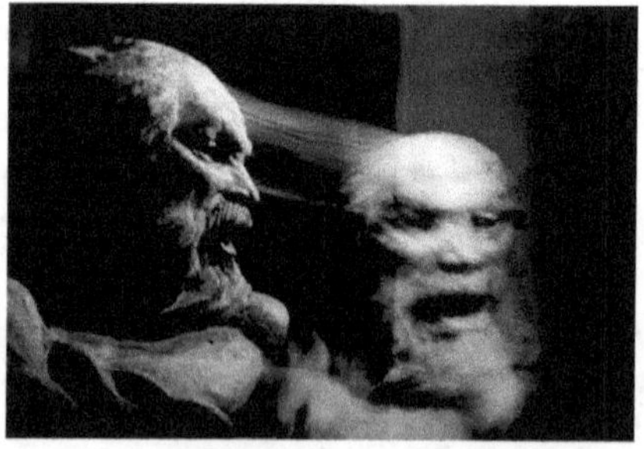

FoTotempismo (*Reprimand of the Eternal Father on the World*)

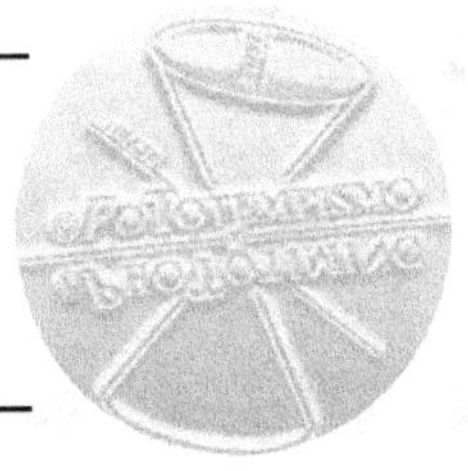

I explored how to communicate aesthetics and concepts with images made with the brush, with the spatula …leaving a 'Sign' with my 'Gesture'. Then, afterwards I returned with other experiences, with other feelings, and then again with other tools. At the same time and from the very beginning, the camera appeared to be a mysterious, magical tool, which when manipulated, as I did not yet know how, created images, reproductions of 'reality'. A reality that left me with a feeling of something impalpable, elusive, something aware of what had passed, the past that is, that no longer existed. Still, fascinating. I was still a child but then finally at 14 my father Eliseo gave me the camera, a Voigtländer, with which I started taking photographs. It was 1965. From the very beginning, my photographic compositions comprised pictorial components, through which I explored and researched various techniques with my first camera and photographic images. And the exploration continued in the dark room experimenting with alternative types of film to the standard, to represent through 'Photography' those emotions I felt every day. Then suddenly the first digital camera appeared, and another impulse pervaded me: it was FoTotempismo.

Photography

The reflections described below originate from one of the simplest observations made by ordinary people, or perhaps 'heroes/heroines' who, expressing themselves through photography defined it as *"a non-artistic practice"*.

Of course, seeing the photographs in the various exhibitions or published in the weeklies, in specialized magazines, or even seen in the vastness of the multimedia world proposed by internet portals, one can only agree with them. In almost all cases, the subject of the photograph is its essence, while the photographer captures the context from a personal point of view, just like 'any' person can do, not only a photographer. In other cases the photos themselves create the scene and only rarely comprise 'Artistic' content, which, in any case varies in only small nuances from a photographic practice that has now reached high expressive saturation. Hence the research, the study and the effort to accentuate what photography has always had, more or less latently – the artistic. It certainly isn't due to criticism made by those 'common' observers that photography has travelled with 'us' to look for the artistic component. This was all already unconsciously present in 'us', and photography was only a stimulus and a way to provide the user with

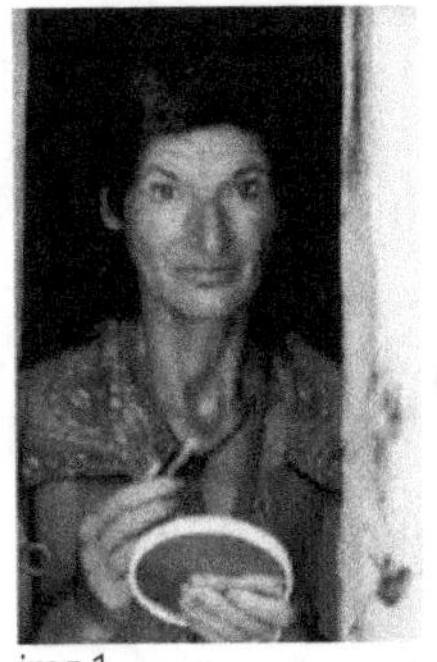
img.1

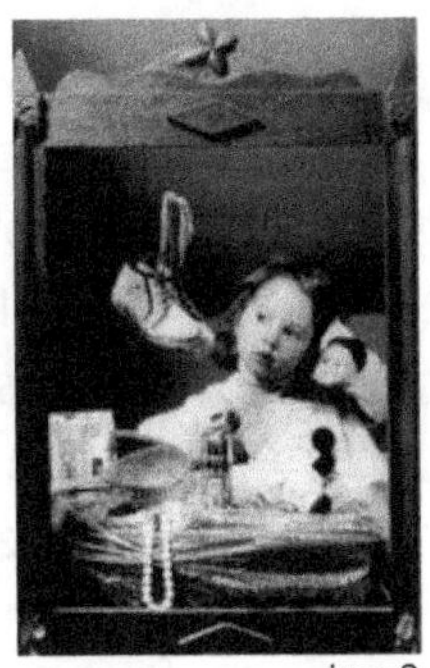
img.2

Portraits

Landscape

img.3

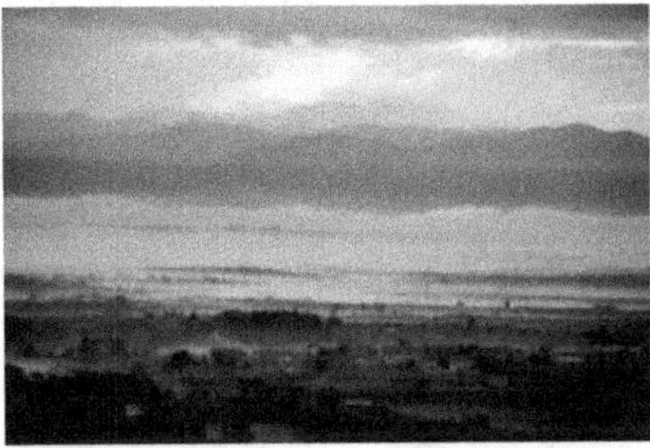

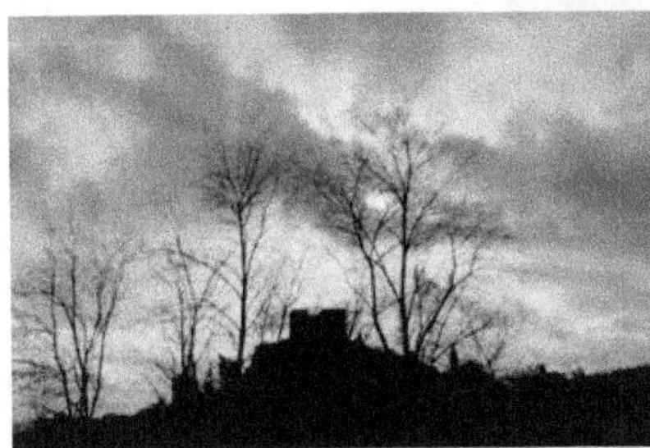
img.4

Landscape

photographic images, whose analyses can lead one to reflect on photographic art. The path that led from the photographic image obtained by mechanical means as a representation of reality, up to the use of the camera to compose an expression of thought, as if it were a pen, a brush, or another tool, today more than ever, has proved its awareness of having fully achieved the goal of being elevated to an expression of art.

In photography, two types of artistic expression can be distinguished, the classic iconic and the indexical, where the author documents the circumstance, subject, capturing an attitude, an atmosphere, a feeling or a particular moment, of which history is now full and even abused, and that of creative and artistic research.

In the first, the determining component of the content is the subject presented and the entirety of the image; the component produced by the shot has its own value, a supplement to the subject, where, in any case, the author can give an interpretation. In the second type, the camera is used as if it were a tool to engrave on the sensor 'signs' of lights, shadows and colours to express the author's message and state of mind to externalize a need with a 'Gesture'.

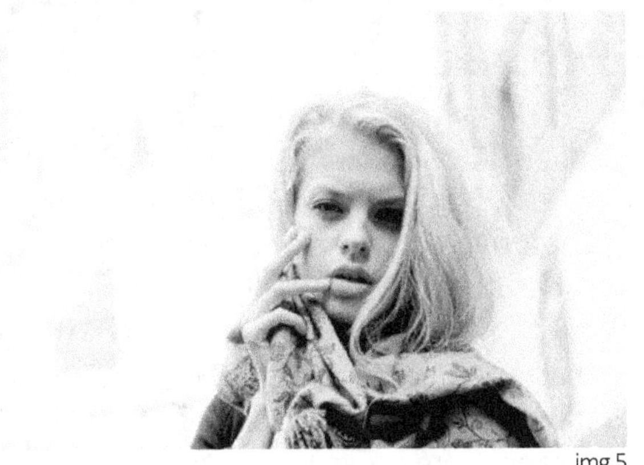

img.5

Portrait

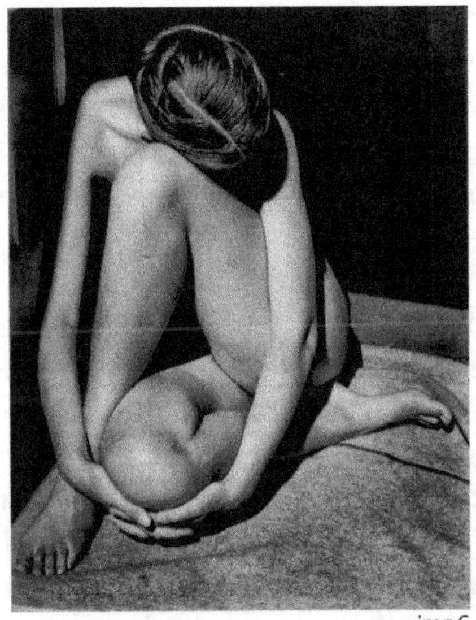

img.6

Edward Weston, (1886-1958) Nude (1936)

photography as
the captured image

Capturing an image with film or a photosensitive sensor is then like partially possessing the subject, the event, the memory, the expression, the concept and all that was photographed. Capturing is an innate ancestral instinct, now evolved and expressed today by many means: from prose to theatre, from painting to photography, from sculpture to digital-art, and so on, with infinite other forms of expression and ways of doing and of being. In any case, these are systems that are always aimed at capturing the subject, the idea, the concept, the attention, until you succeed in capturing the impalpable and then propose it in your own way.

It's true, sometimes you want to capture the very intangible and sometimes the subject wants to be penetrated to use this thirst that the photographer, the writer or the journalist has, to communicate their mood or intimate thought. It has now become all one, subject and chronicler, who together lead the expression thus packaged towards society, transmitting their thoughts. At the beginning, photography was just a technical means of reproduction of reality, as were other forms of expression: 'painting', 'sculpture' and others, defined today as art. As we mastered the ability to use the chisel, the brush, and writing, we gradually mastered the photographic technique; photography too travelled through

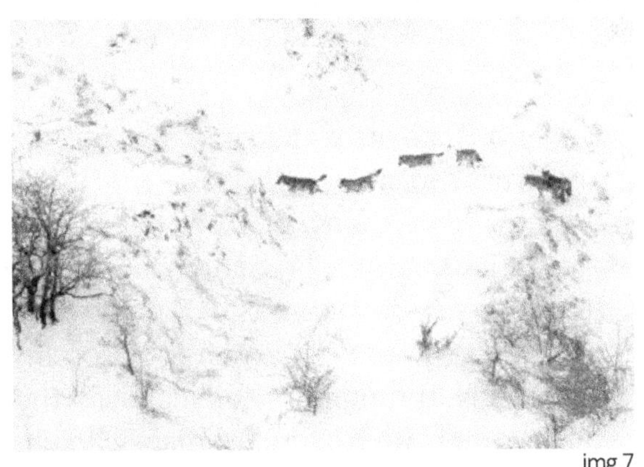

img.7

Giuliano Zappi, Wolves

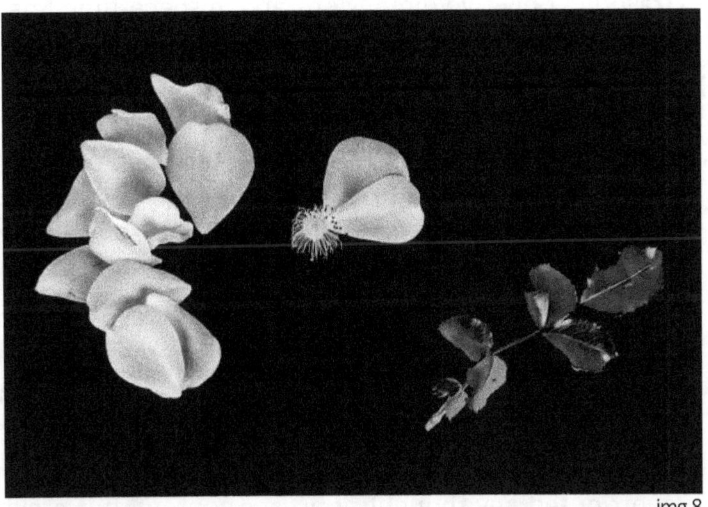

img.8

Gianpiero Ascoli, Defloration

its various stages to become an expression of thought and artistic form.

It is now more than a hundred years since photography moved in the direction of artistic expression and, apart from the experimentalists, it was the Bragaglia brothers who made an enormous contribution in this direction, expressing through Photodynamism the added value that a simple photographic image can offer.

Certainly the mechanical device 'lets us take pictures' and without any need to think on the part of the user, but in this case the result is a cold representation of reality, made worse by the fact that the image is also portrayed in only two dimensions and in space-time 'made cold' in that instant; introducing also distortions, aberrations, disturbances and alterations that only worsen that perfection, which is the original.

The mechanical eye of the camera is so cold, unmoved, monocular and without vitality, and yet it manages to register what the human eye, controlled by the mind, sees and elaborates differently. In this way photographs give the illusion that the camera registers wonderful conditions that are not the usual and therefore defined as 'beautiful', indeed spectacular, only because they are different from the processing of the human eye-mind.

In this case the cold operation of the camera has not contributed any thought or artistic content, but provided merely a technical function.

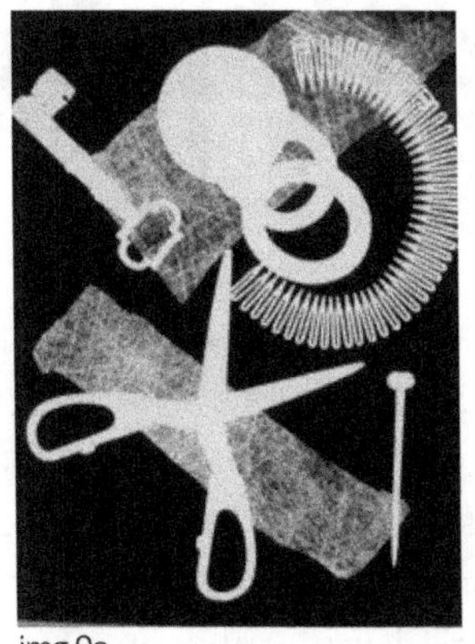
img.9a

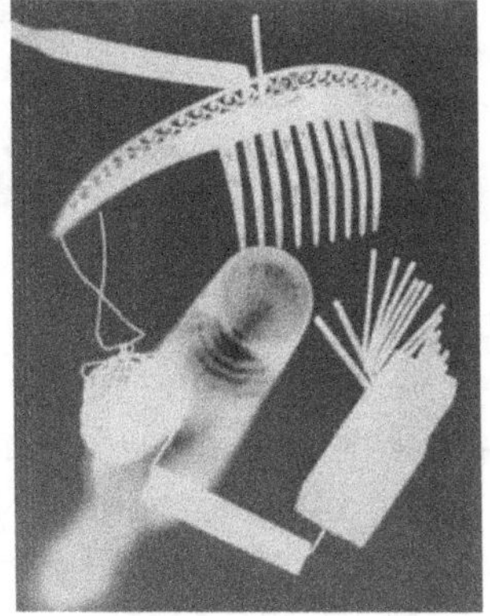
img.9b

Man Ray (1890-1976), Rayographs

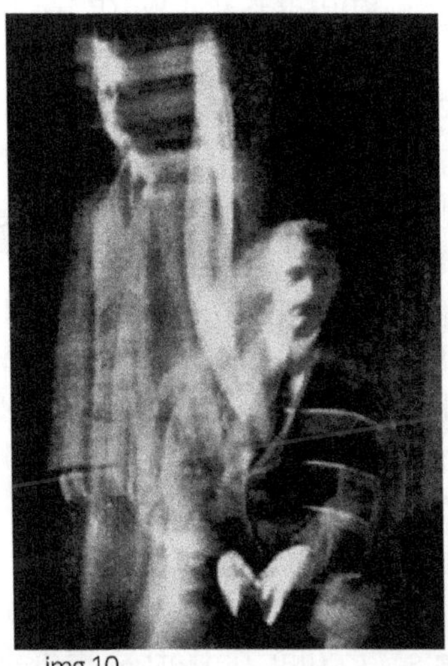
img.10

*Anton Giulio Bragaglia (1911),
Man rising*

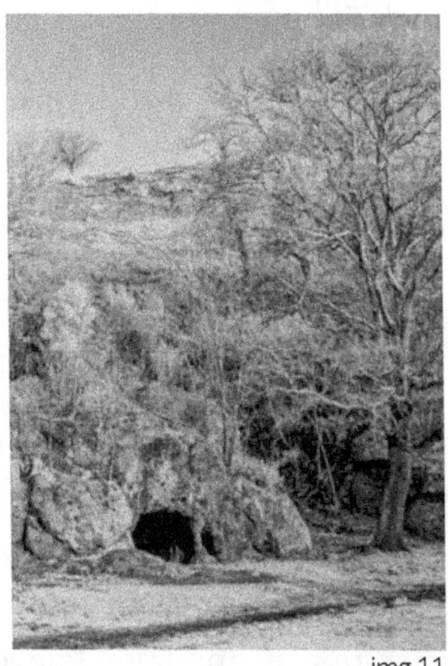
img.11

*Marco Scataglini (2018),
Infrared landscape*

It is from this point that one goes further and the debate between documentary photography, in whatever form: landscape, street, architectural, portrait, journalism and others, and photography as an artistic expression arises. A photograph can be considered artistic where the component that constitutes it is not only contemplative, but where there is also relevant reflective weight. In this case, the technical contribution is taken for granted and the added value is given by the author who packages the image by creating it with the camera as if it were tool at the total disposition of the artist's pre-established idea. In this case, the photographic work does not originate from the spectacular given by the randomness represented then in the image, but from the image and the concept already present in the mind of the author, which are activated through the mechanical means of shooting, using the camera or other systems. The message that the work conveys must be complete with both aesthetic content and concept. Aesthetically it must meet all the requirements that make it a harmonious graphical representation according to the now consolidated principles of composition, such as: thirds, strong lines, diagonals, circular patterns, radials, arabesque, the golden ratio and so on. The message of thought is all that the author wants to communicate,

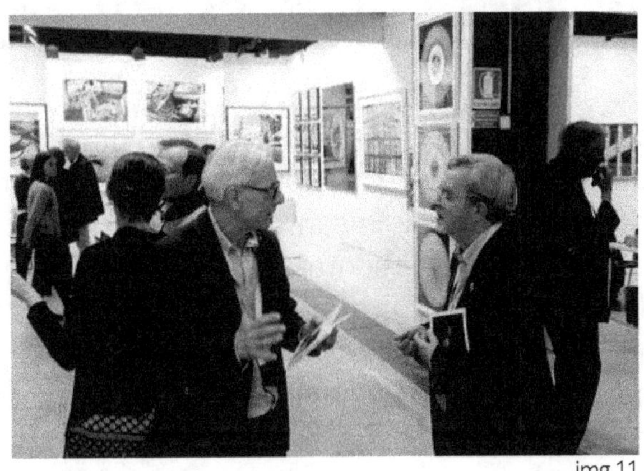

img.11

Documentary photography (Milan: MIA Photo Fair 2016)

through and with, the support of the image: emotions, feelings, conditions, and everything that forms part of their cultural baggage.

For these reasons, the way the subject itself is represented is crucial, using the means of shooting as an eye manipulated by the author in all its possible variations. Clarification is mandatory; to have a photographic work of art, the 'process' regards only the means of shooting, obtaining the image during the shot itself and not subsequently in post-production, where the latter must be limited only to optimizing it. Other methodologies merely generate graphics with the help of a photographic image. Certainly all photographic expressions can be traced back to artwork, but the art that is sovereign in photography originates from the sensor during the shot, the rest is something else, still and in any case possible artistic expressions, but difficult to define as a pure expression of photographic art.

Photography as a means of communication and documentary expression of any category, has achieved today a completeness of such high level, thanks to over a hundred years of life, which has perhaps expressed almost exhaustively everything it could express according to current knowledge.

Today we do nothing but replicate what has already been done and digital facilitation enables almost everyone to emulate even the great masters of photography. Our predecessors have handed down their experience to us in volumes of works, books, treatises, plus equipment and materials to make it easy to achieve their results.

Certainly today we have learned well and we can easily reach what were their goals, we have even surpassed them, but we must not be complacent and stop at the consolidated results. Even today we pause over the pleasant result of a sunset, over a line stolen from nature, or a furtive shot. In these cases we must be aware that these results have already been achieved and that we are not contributing anything additional, sometimes they are just simply inspired replicas of those who took these photographs before us. These are not the photographs you wish to examine, consider, or use as new ways to communicate or to transmit new feelings and thoughts. These images have no added

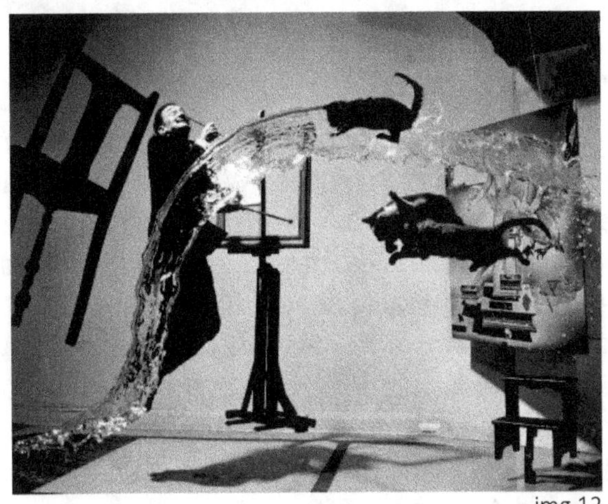

img.12

Philippe Halsman, Salvador Dalì

value compared to what is known and what nature already has, indeed, as already mentioned, they can only worsen what the scene has intrinsically.

Much effort is put into photographic works by authors attempting to transmit their thoughts and ideas into their creations, which often result aesthetically unsatisfying or, indeed inharmonious. These works, perhaps due to their informative content which is not easily identifiable, indeed too personal and hermetic, penetrate neither the mind of the observer nor the mind of the communications expert or evolved observer. Often the author closes themself in a self-created labyrinth, curling up on themself, making Pindaric flights and seeing in their work the 'beauty' understood only by themself. The result thus obtained is information which must be explained to the observer by the author, thus confirming the failure of the message addressed to that audience. When these explanations must also be provided to experienced critics or observers, then either the message has not been transmitted, or the language is not suitable or new. Photography must give an emotion and transmit a message to the observer without any further explanation. It is clear that also photography, being a language, must be used with those who know this language. The more sophisticated the means of expression, the more limited is the audience of observers that the message can reach. It is exceptional when the message reaches every level and all users, (*fig.1*) even at different levels of penetration and stratification; like many fairy tales which can be told in a simple way while expressing concepts so deep that, unwittingly stimulating the unconscious, can be appropriated.

Other considerations need to be made when an artistic concept goes beyond the known and the academic, where everything is encoded and tested. In these circumstances the concept is explained as innovation, where no literature and information is available, except those provided by the author who had the intuition for a new expressive concept.

Very often in the world of criticism and academia, after having examined the abstraction and attempted to restore it to patterns previously and even historically known, and failing however to satisfy this innovation in its entirety, one provides all those connections and interactions of the historically conceptualized aspects by expanding them with new explorations and considerations, thus inserting them into the world of criticism and academia.

When a message, an image, gives layered information that satisfies all levels of knowledge, then it is a message that has achieved its purpose.

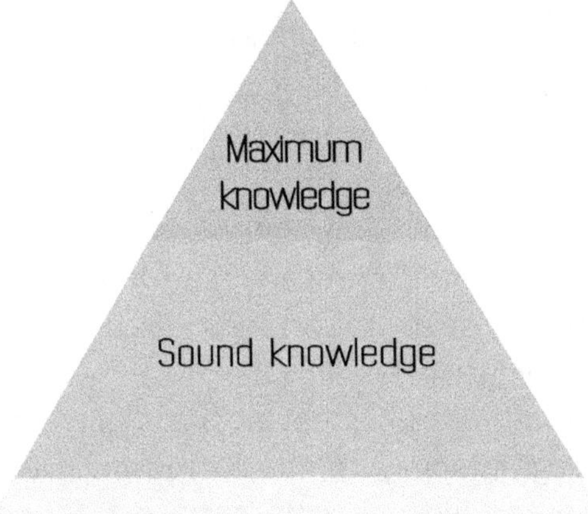

fig.1

Pyramid of reading a message, an image

Unlike what the Bragaglia brothers did, despite the difficulties of the early 1900s, today doing research for new artistic expressions is easier thanks to more advanced technology, but at the same time more difficult as demands have evolved. In the early years of the last century the photographic field was 'unexplored' and for this reason every simple idea was pure innovation (img.15, 20, 21). The Bragaglias, however, immediately understood the importance of the representation of movement in a photographic image (img.14), where previously subjects were always represented as static; they defined this innovation as 'Photodynamism'. Simultaneously and subsequent to Photodynamism there were experiments but no more intuitions of such importance, excepting, of course, Panning by Ernst Hass (img.16).

Even if there was a great desire to diversify the way of photographing with the increasingly sophisticated means available, all attempts made were simply artifices made available by the now evolved techniques and as such they remain, 'exercises', now accessible even to those who have not evolved photographically. The only variations on the previous artistic insights are interpretations which have evolved into reinterpretations of that guiding thought.

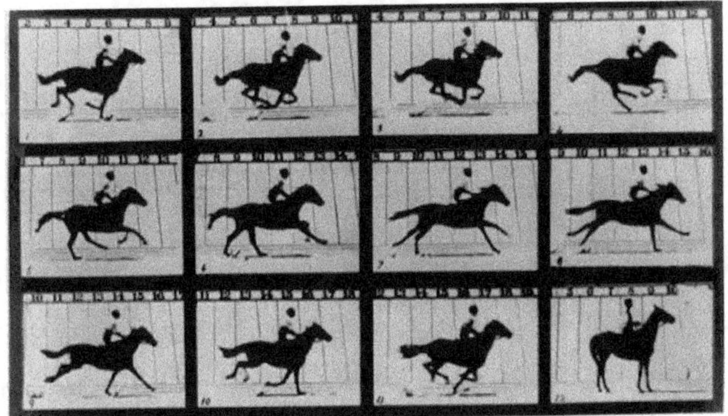

Eadweard Muybridge (1830-1904), Chronophotography

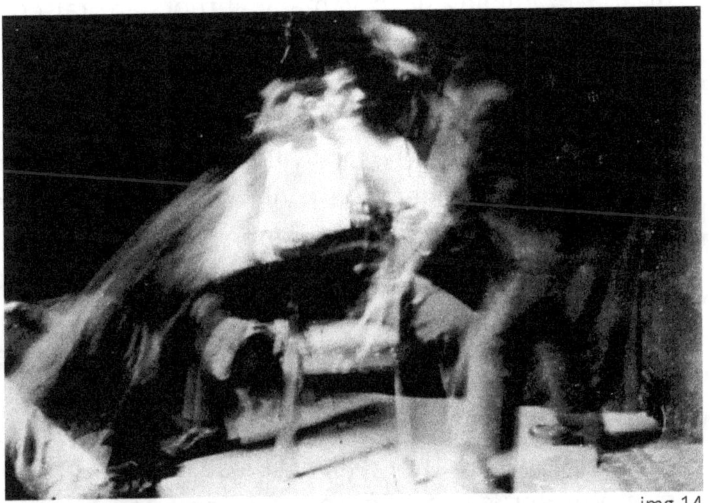

img.14

The Bragaglia brothers, Photodynamism

The special effects given by filters, lights, software, electronic devices and other possibilities offered by evolution, are not elements that can determine an elevated artistic thought in photography. So, one returns to the origins of photography as an expression of art, but only where there is thought. Photography can be elevated to the status of art by combining the contemplative component with the reflective in an appropriate blend to express all the completeness of a work of art. What are these thoughts, these ideas that determine the passage leading from the photograph to be admired to that elevated as a work of art? Examining history, many authors are raised to the level of great interpreters of the shot, expressing themselves at high levels, sometimes maddeningly complete, but also unconsciously imitating other authors, who might very well ignore each other's actions. This consideration confirms the excellent use of the craft of the photographer and less of the artistic contribution to photography. Of course art can also be made by interpreting and revisiting certain thoughts and ideas, but photography is increasingly intertwined with the expression of thought where the word form has taken over from the image, making the image itself support to words, thus making it lose its full expressive role. Without detracting from this form of expression, it is clear that in this case the image has not achieved

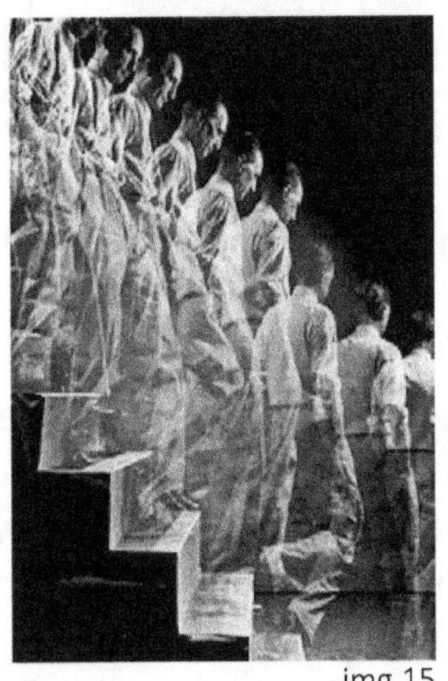

img.15

Marcel Duchamp (1987-1968), Descending a staircase

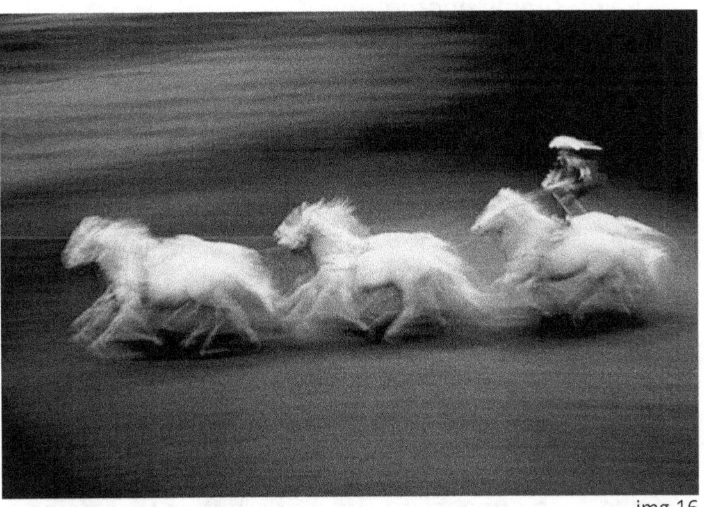

img.16

Ernst Hass, (1890-1968), Panning

the goal of communicating, at least in that specific historical period and to that audience.

Research has always gone through many stages subject to its historical period, and this research has left its mark, that could at times even be the result of simple graphic representations, but because they were created by mechanical means, were often perceived as innovation. In these cases the fame that ensued was limited to the temporal space of that period; the case of **Anton Giulio Bragaglia** is different, who argued:

> *"The photographic image can be elevated to the status of a work of art only when it denies itself of being simply photography".*

His concept makes it clear that his Photodynamism can be a means of artistic expression. This making of art is not simply a trend of the moment but it has traced and is intertwined with a parallel concept in painting (Futurism) reaching the present day without dissolving like a fashion. From the distant beginning of the 1900s to date there has never been such a high artistic intuition in photography, and this has left a void of innovation contrary to what has happened in painting. Art has often used photography as a medium of expression by combining it with paint or collage, obtaining a work with mixed technique of photographic derivation, thus giving a uniqueness to the work, but at that point it is no longer pure photography.

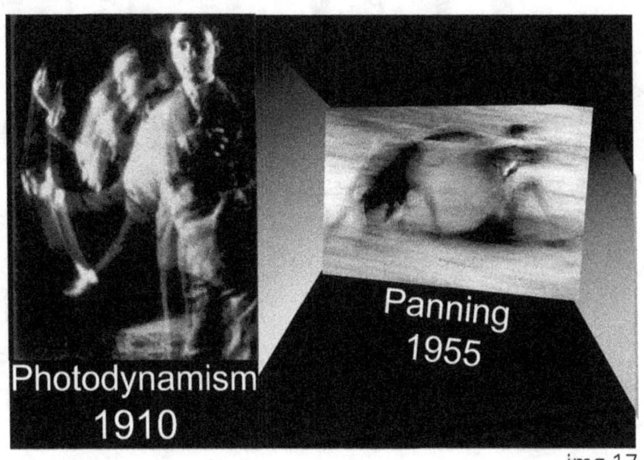

img.17

From Photodynamism to Panning ...

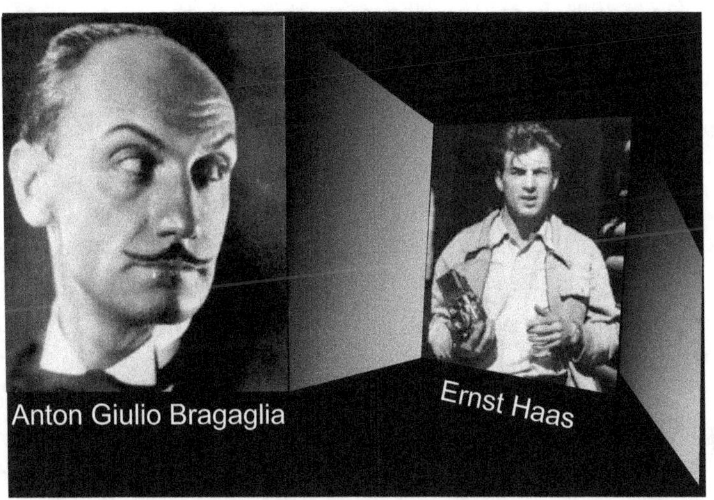

img.18

From the Bragaglia brothers to Ernst Haas ...

Here is Photodynamism as an artistic expression of photography (img.14). Certainly the images of Bragaglia should not be considered a point of arrival of artistic thought in photography, but as an inspiration to fulfill over time. That intuition aimed at revolutionizing the way of photographing, that is, making art with photography finds fertile ground in our days to be explored and enriched with values that can be understood in the concepts of the Bragaglias. Hence many interpretations and reinterpretations have taken shape, among which, in addition to the representation of the dynamism of the subject, there is also the extrapolation of the energy released, both by the subject, in its vibrations, and from the environment that surrounds it, as well as by the author. Thus there is also an energy value in the expression of the subject, as well as the dissolving of matter that dematerializes and re-materializes in the photographed subject. This combination of values is researched and quantified by the author, who endows it with a unique strength which otherwise could not be expressed. The author thus expresses their own feelings and those of the subject, creating an image that is no longer simply a 'photograph' but a work of art. Few artists have managed to interpret such a wide-reaching concept, while other authors have failed to fulfil the concept in its entirety and reinterpretation, not even by using or including diversity from other values. These authors did not succeed in manifesting their intentions through Photodynamism, but they used only a few ingredients from a broader possible expression. In any case, works have always been produced that are not a simple presentation of reality, but rather an interpretation, expressing moods and feelings that otherwise would not have been possible to reveal.

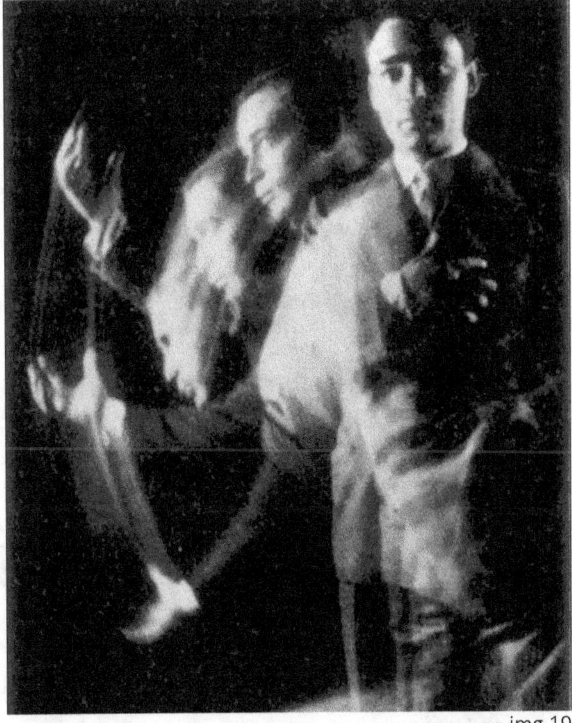

img.19

The Bragaglia brothers, 'The bow' (Photodynamism)

There are many artists, photographers, philosophers, opinion leaders who express their views about photography as an artistic expression, such as:

Man Ray (1890-1976):

"I am not at all interested in being consistent as a painter, an object-maker or a photographer. I can use several different techniques, ... I have never shared the contempt shown by painters for photography: there is no competition involved, painting and photography are two media engaged in different paths. There is no conflict between the two".

Anton Giulio Bragaglia (1890-1960):

"If we reproduce only the trajectory of a movement, then our sensation of it will be still fuller and easier.

Then we will have completely achieved our artistic goal, since a gesture for us is a pure dynamic sensation which, in turn, is nothing other than the effect produced on our sensibility by its trajectory, and hence we can re-experience the dynamic sensation of the gesture and achieve our goal".

"We want to achieve a revolution in photography, through progress: in order to purify, ennoble, and truly elevate photography to an art. 'Movement' and 'life' are the two watchwords; making visible what is not seen superficially, ... for I affirm that we can achieve art with the mechanical means of photography only if we overcome the pedestrian

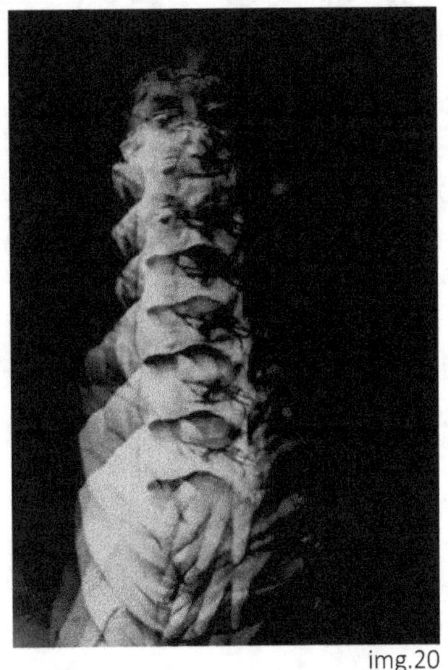

img.20

Man Ray Version of Man Ray (1961), Imogen Cunningham

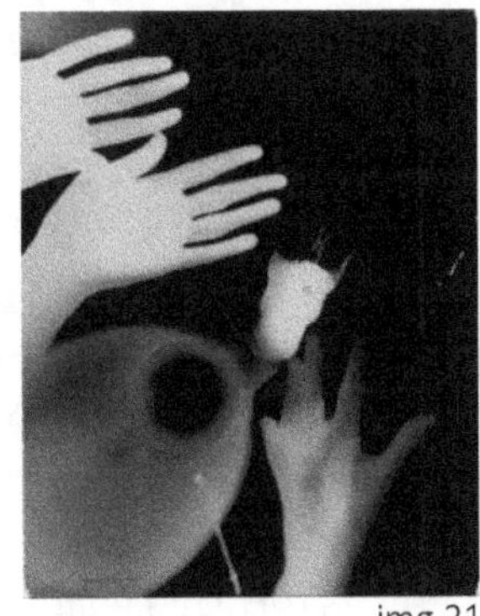

img.21

Man Ray, Rayographs

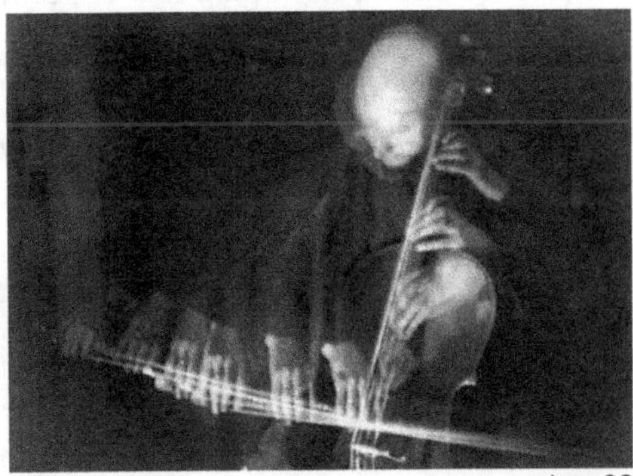

img.22

The Bragaglia brothers, Cellist (1913) Photodynamism

photographic reproduction of the real as something static or caught in a pose in a snapshot. We want to start a revolution, for progress in photography: and this to purify it, ennoble it and truly elevate it to art ... turning away from one's own obscene and brutal static realism, becomes no longer the usual photography, but something much more elevated ... "

Walter Benjamin (189-1940) (img.23) states:

> *"its (artistic) value is always given by the relationship of the photographer with his/her own technique".*

László Moholy-Nagy (189-1946) (img.24) claims:

> *"The enemy of photography is the convention, the fixed rules of 'how to do'. The salvation of photography comes from the experiment. One who experiments has no pre-established ideas about photography. He/she does not believe that photography, as we think of it today, is the repetition and exact transcription of the ordinary view ...".*

Ernst Haas (Vienna, 1921-1986) creator of *Panning* writes:

> *"Bored with obvious reality, I find my fascination in transforming it into a subjective point of view. Without touching my subject I want to come to the moment when, through pure concentration of seeing, the composed picture becomes more made than taken".*

Roland Barthes (1915-1980) (img.26) in his book *The light room* (1980) states that:

"Due to the cancellation of the representation of time in photography, the image gives the subject that feeling of 'death', of an instant, of a time and space that no longer exists".

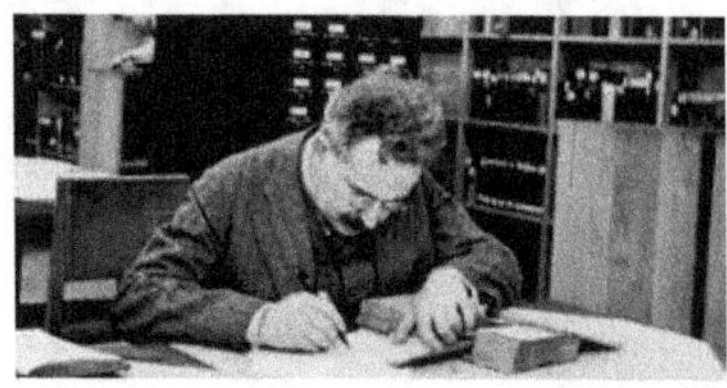

img.23

Walter Benjamin (1892-1940)

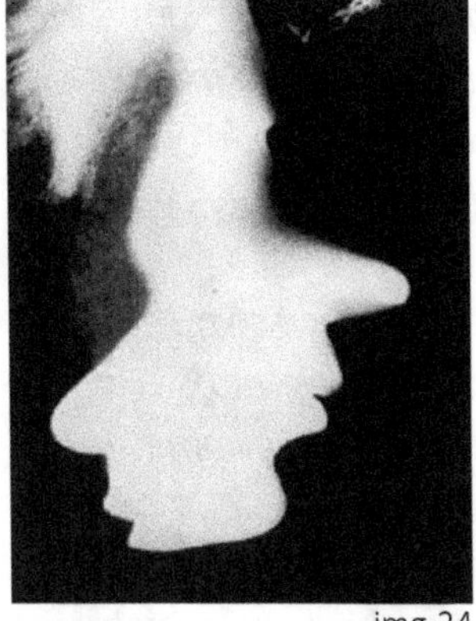

img.24

László Moholy-Nagy, Self-portrait

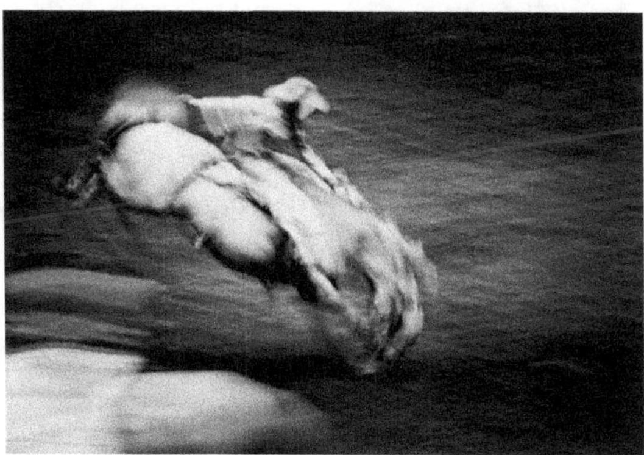

img.25

Ernst Haas, Rodeo

And still in the vein of photographer as artist: the philosopher **Vilém Flusser** (1920-1991) (img.28) in his book *Towards a philosophy of photography*, asserts that:

"Reduced to a minimum, the photographer's intentions are to:

1) Encode their concepts of the world into images

2) Use the camera for this purpose

3) Show photographs as models for experience, knowledge, judgement and action

4) Ensure that these models last over time; that is to make oneself immortal through one's photos ...

The camera's program, reduced to a minimum is to

1) Place its inherent capabilities into the image

2) Use the photographer for this purpose

3) Disseminate the photographs into society for feedback

4) Improve its qualities ..."

"This struggle sees: the machine prevails, with unconscious dictating, giving images only apparently desired by man, and no real freedom of the author. With one exception: the so-called experimental photographers...who are actually aware of the fact that the image, apparatus, program and information are the essential problems to deal with. They [the photographers] are in fact consciously attempting to create unpredictable information, that is, to extract something from the device and to put in the image what does not result from its program (automatisms).

The philosophy of photography must reveal the fact

Rosalind Epstein Krauss (Washington, 30 November 1941), (img.27) art critic, US curator, professor of History of Art at Columbia University, asserts:

> "[Photographic] *art has to take strength from its own specificity that distinguishes it from the pictorial... Photography is not attributable to the statistical dimensions of the history of* [pictorial] *art."*

These considerations are found for the first time in their maximum expression in the fototempistic concept. With its accelerations and decelerations FoTotempismo explores non-linear space and time, bringing out freedom and uniqueness.

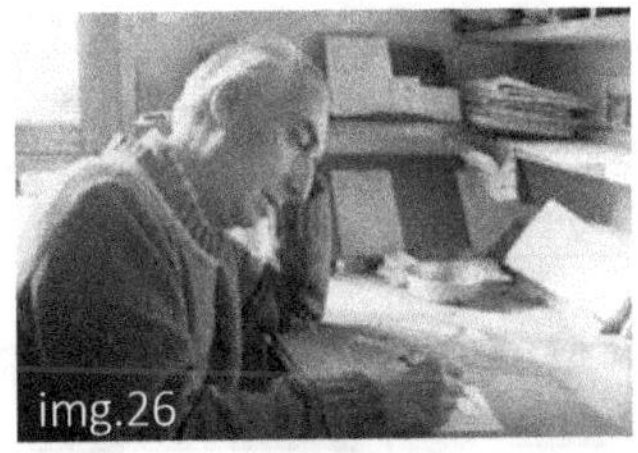
img.26

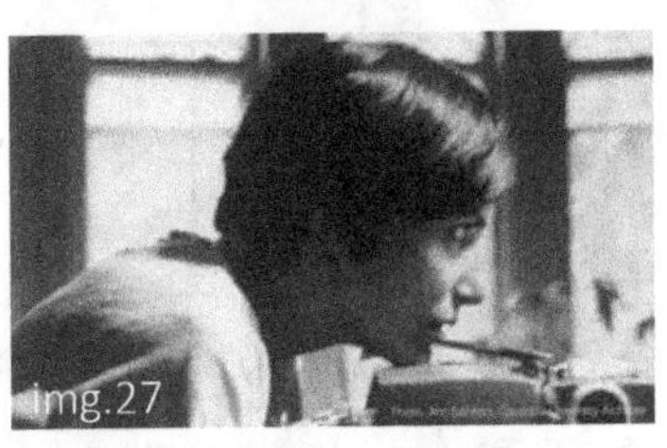
img.27

Rosalind Epstein Krauss (1941)

Roland Barthes (1915-1980)

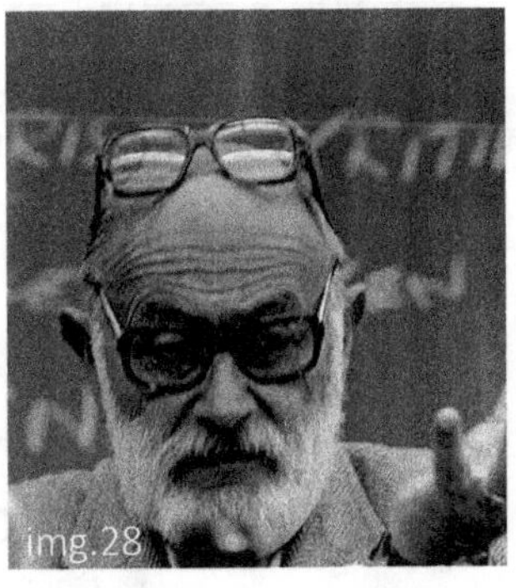
img.28

Vilém Flusser (1920-1991)

new disciplines

space-time

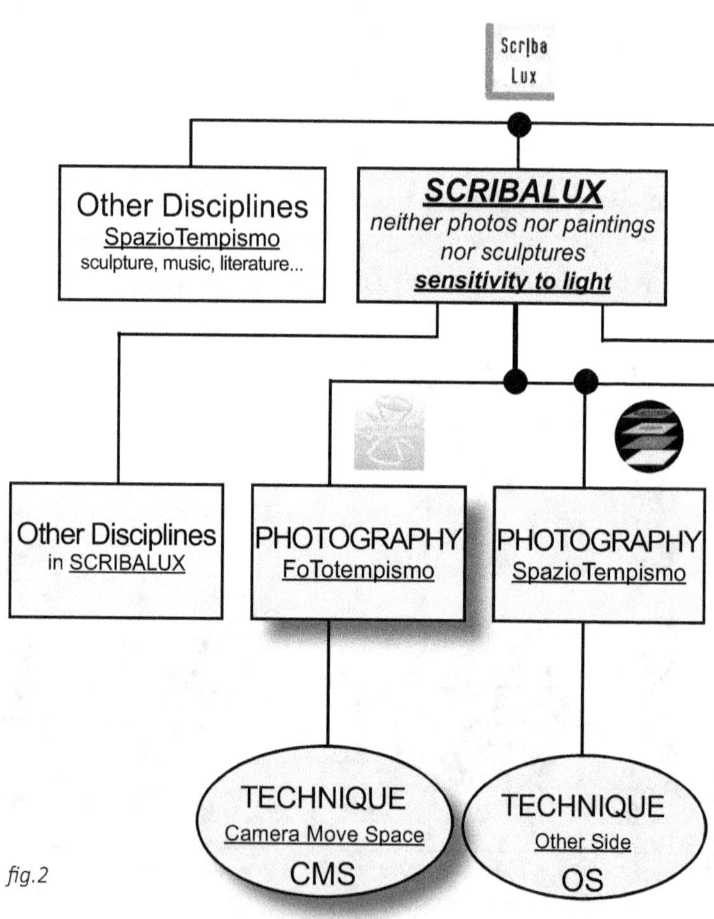

fig.2

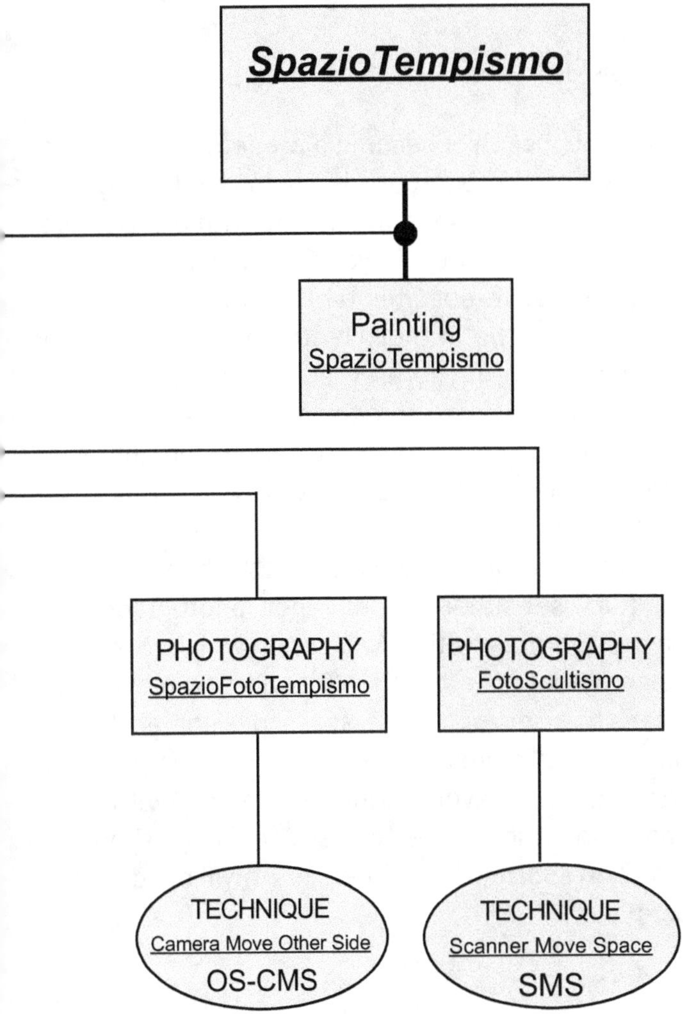

SPAZIO TEMPO

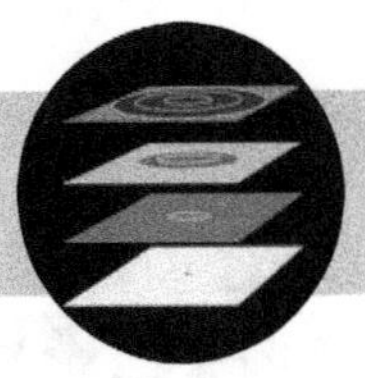

SpazioTempismo

Painting
SpazioTempismo

PHOTOGRAPHY
SpazioFotoTempismo

PHOTOGRAPHY
FotoScultismo

TECHNIQUE
Camera Move Other Side
OS-CMS

TECHNIQUE
Scanner Move Space
SMS

A new discipline

The 'Gesture' has thus become a predominant element in an image of photographic derivation, to the point of involving other disciplines. In this way, with the 'Gesture' photography thus goes beyond simply providing an iconic or indicative documentary imprint of what is in front, therefore the author creates not abstract signs but well-conceived representations; in summary a 'contemporary classic' where the harmony and values of the history of the image are represented, and enhanced by current collective cultural knowledge.

This is how new directions for all disciplines in 'Spatial' representations originate *(fig.2, pag.28)* thanks to the image that is neither painting nor photograph, but which uses photosensitive surfaces on which to impress the 'Sign', generating it with a 'Gesture'. By moving the light-sensitive sensor, in the space designated by the author, there is a need to identify a 'new discipline' of expression; and to avoid misunderstandings with other practices, in which values are scaled, diminished and flattened; in subsequent references, it will be identified as 'Scribalux'.

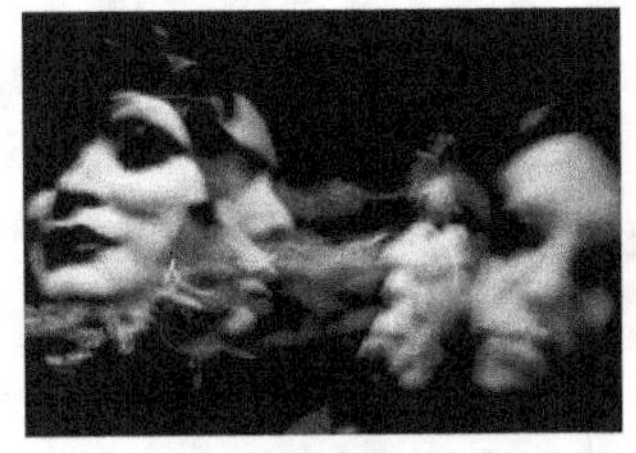

img.29

the 'Gesture' of FoTotempismo

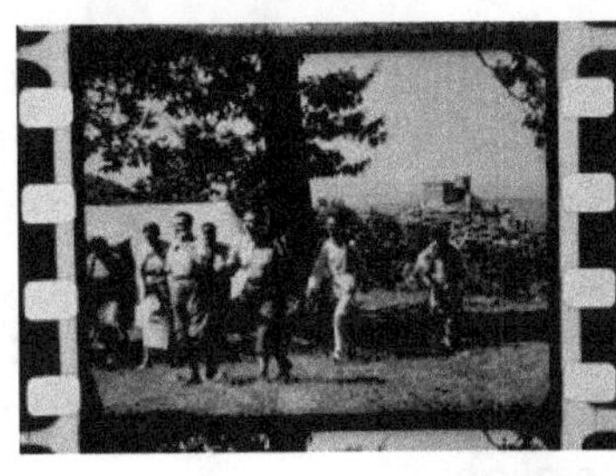

img.30

Documentary photo

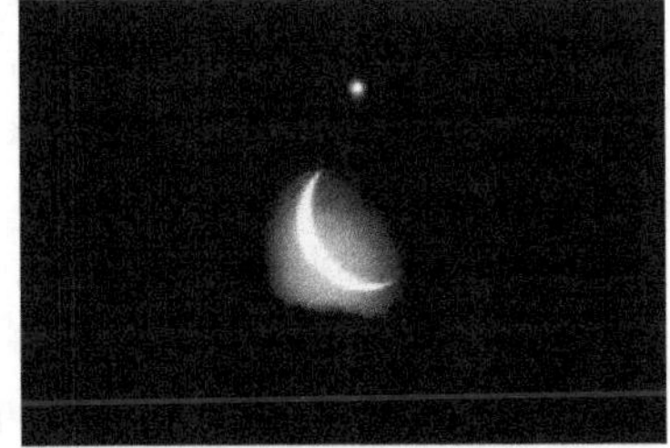

img.31

Iconic photo

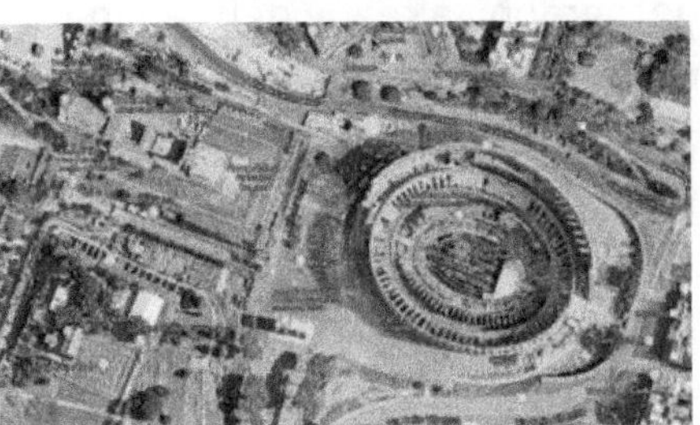

img.32

Indexical photo

ScribaLux

The new term, *Scribalux*, indicates a new discipline for images that are not paintings, drawings, digital-art or photography (img.33).

Scribalux is a new discipline that uses photosensitive surfaces on which to leave the 'Sign' in consequence to a decisive 'Gesture'. The need to identify a new expressive current, originates from the now matured need to use a light sensitive instrument, whatever it may be, which subsequent to the author's gesture, creates the sign, as in other disciplines.

In a broader perspective, dominated by the representation of Space-Time as a current of thought involving other disciplines, which claim to represent the conception of the world according to various sensory and emotional communication 'channels', the cultural current of *SpaceTimism* (*SpazioTempismo*) can be identified (*fig.2*, p. 28).

So also philosophical thought, music, prose, literature, painting, digital-art, sculpture and others, as well as the photography already defined in the new section named in *Scribalux*, are part of it.

This last section, in accordance with the 'Manifesto della Nuova Frontiera Fotografica' (*Manifesto of the New Photographic Frontier*), basically requires that it is obtained in the camera, by means of an exposure and with awareness of the desired result from the moment of shooting.

We want to cross this consolidated border
in order to represent space in time and time
in space ...

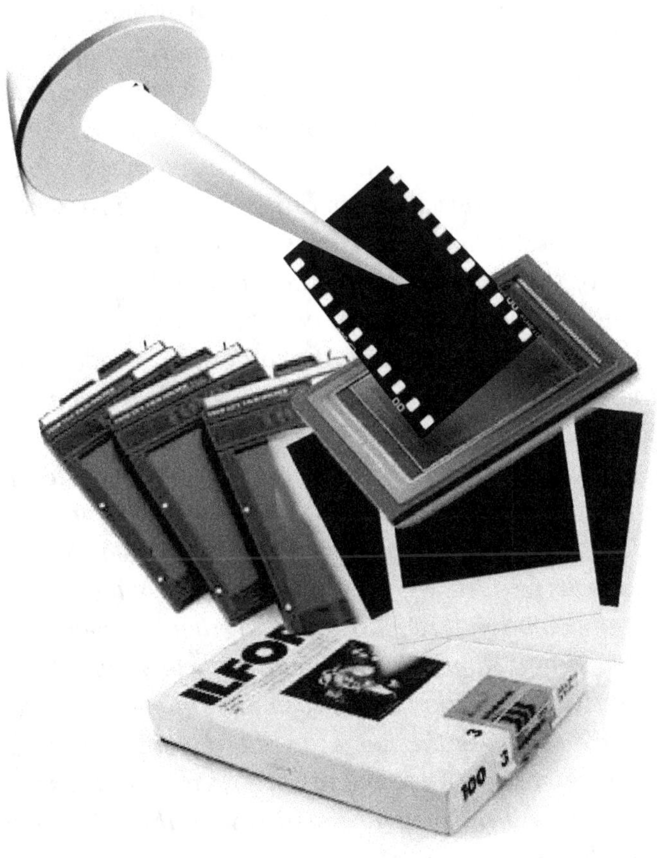

img.33

nuovafrontierafotografica
the Manifesto

Manifesto of the Nuova Frontiera Fotografica

*The **Nuova Frontiera Fotografica Movement** aims to be the starting point of a reflection that, reconnecting with the avant-garde of the 1900s, takes photography back to a world no longer purely indexical but creative, where the camera can be used in the same way as a paintbrush, or in any case as an instrument that leaves a mark, to express what is in the mind and soul of the photographer according to the subject, thus transforming it into a tool capable of overcoming the purely indexical concept of photography. Faced with the great revolution introduced by modern technology and the consequent multiplication of proposed expressions, we manifest our understanding of today's artistic photography in the following key points:*

1. Artistic photography originates from ideas, from emotions and feelings, thus allowing the author to arouse emotional reactions and to stimulate mental associations, to promote responsive behaviours, to elicit fantasy, imagination and dissemination in every area.

2. We reiterate the need for photography to act in its own right, as a means of expression, thus avoiding all those relationships with the other arts which, even today, condition it, moving it further away from other infinite possibilities of expression. Artistic photography must be autonomous.

3. Photography can be carried out on film, on digital sensors or other means using a single exposure, aware from the moment of shooting, that subsequent treatment, in the Dark Room or in the Light Room, is done exclusively for the development of the photo, with interventions that just optimize it without additions or replacements that alter the original intention of the shot.
More radical interventions, photomontages and significant alterations transport photography into the field of graphics or computer art, respectable artistic genres and often practiced simultaneously by some photographers, but totally outside the realm of true photography, as intended by us.

4. We do not wish photography to be a 'hibernation' of the event, thus exhausting its content at first glance, but something that offers the ability to regenerate itself in time and space, represented by the content itself, transformed into emotions.

5. The transposition of the three dimensions onto one flat surface, so far carried out in perspective, must not constitute a limit. We want to cross this consolidated boundary in order to depict space in time and time in space, passing from the infinitesimal to infinity and thus freeing all the imaginative capabilities of our mind.

6. We want photography to have firm roots in its history, but always without forgetting the fundamental innovative function, which must distinguish it, with content linked to originality, to ethics, communication and understanding.

7. Like any other form of expression it must be autonomous with mutual respect, neither dominant nor exploited. In short, it is necessary that photography is simultaneously a manifestation of freedom and of art.

The purpose of this Manifesto, as well as being to propose renewal in the current photographic panorama, which is constantly pushed harder than necessary by marketing and tainted by graphic contributions, is to advertise the idea through all those forms of diffusion permitted by modern technology (internet but not only), in full autonomy compared to the contemporary critical horizon, which up to now and in most cases, in our opinion, is restricted in an immobility contrary to any innovative form and still linked to academic concepts deriving from other arts or, in any case, looking backwards.

Manifesto (img.34) conceived in July 2014 by Enzo Trifolelli, completed with the collaboration of Gianpiero Ascoli, Marco Scataglini and Anna Maria Staccini. Published on 22 July 2017 on the occasion of *SorianoImmagine2017*.

THE MANIFESTO of the 'Nuova Frontiera Fotografica'

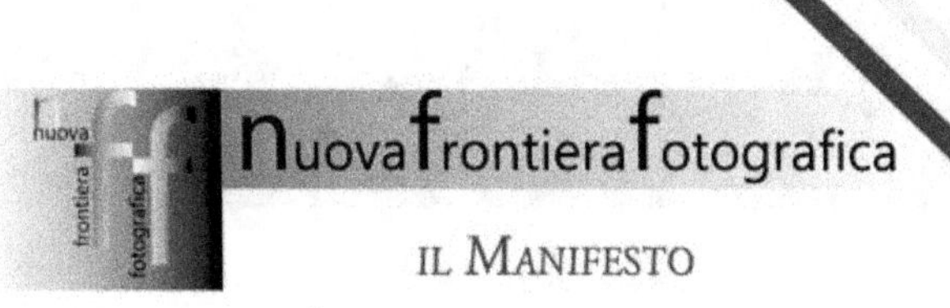

Associazione Culturale IL CASTELLO - *Soriano nel Cimino, 22 Luglio 2017*

Presidente: *Enzo Trifolelli*   Direttore: *Gianpiero Ascoli*

Manifesto della Nuova Frontiera Fotografica

Il Movimento "*Nuova Frontiera Fotografica*" vuole essere il punto di partenza di una riflessione che, riagganciandosi alle avanguardie del '900, riporti la fotografia in un mondo non più puramente indicale ma creativo, dove la macchina fotografica possa essere usata alla stregua di un pennello, o comunque di uno strumento che lasci un segno, per esprimere quello che è nella mente e nell'animo del fotografo rispetto al soggetto, trasformandola così in uno strumento in grado di superare il concetto puramente indicale della fotografia.

Di fronte alla grande rivoluzione introdotta dalla moderna tecnologia e la conseguente moltiplicazione di espressioni proposte, manifestiamo il nostro intendimento sulla fotografia artistica di oggi nei seguenti punti fondamentali:

1.   La fotografia artistica nasce dalle idee, dalle emozioni e dai sentimenti, consentendo così di suscitare reazioni emotive, stimolare associazioni mentali, promuovere comportamenti di risposta, sollecitare la fantasia, l'immaginazione e la diffusione in ogni ambito.

2.   Ribadiamo la necessità che la fotografia agisca nell'ambito che le è proprio, come mezzo di espressione, evitando così tutti quei rapporti con le altre arti che, ancora oggi, la condizionano allontanandola da altre infinite possibilità di espressione. La fotografia artistica deve essere autonoma.

3.   La fotografia può essere eseguita su pellicola, su sensori digitali o altro supporto con un atto espositivo consapevole sin dal momento dello scatto, in modo tale che il successivo trattamento, nella Camera Oscura o in quella Chiara, serva esclusivamente allo sviluppo della foto, con interventi che si limitino a ottimizzarla senza aggiunte o sostituzioni che alterino il senso originario della ripresa. Interventi più radicali, fotomontaggi e alterazioni profonde trasportano la fotografia nel campo della grafica o della Computer Art, generi artistici rispettabili e spesso praticati contemporaneamente da alcuni fotografi, ma totalmente fuori dal campo della vera fotografia come da noi intesa.

4.   Non vogliamo che la fotografia sia una fibernazione dell'evento, esaurendone così il contenuto ad un primo sguardo, ma consenta il rigenerarsi del tempo e dello spazio, rappresentato dal contenuto stesso, trasformato in emozioni.

5.   La trasposizione delle tre dimensioni su una superficie piana, fino ad ora realizzata in maniera prospettica, non deve costituire un limite. Vogliamo oltrepassare questo confine consolidato per poter raffigurare lo spazio nel tempo e il tempo nello spazio, passando dall'infinitesimo all'infinito e liberando così tutte le capacità di immaginazione della nostra mente.

6.   Vogliamo che la fotografia abbia radici ben piantate nella sua storia, ma sempre senza dimenticare la fondamentale funzione innovativa, che la deve contraddistinguere, con contenuti legati all'originalità, all'etica, alla comunicazione e alla comprensione.

7.   Come ogni altra forma di espressione deve essere autonoma nel rispetto reciproco, non dominante né strumentalizzata. Occorre, insomma, che la fotografia sia contemporaneamente manifestazione di libertà e d'arte.

Lo scopo di questo Manifesto, oltre che nella proposta di un rinnovo del panorama fotografico attuale, sempre più stretto da necessità di marketing e contaminato da apporti grafici, è di propagandare l'idea tramite tutte quelle forme di diffusione permesse dalla moderna tecnologia (internet ma non solo), in piena autonomia rispetto all'orizzonte critico contemporaneo, che fino ad ora e nella maggioranza dei casi, a nostro giudizio, è ristretto in un immobilismo contrario a qualsiasi forma innovativa e legato ancora a concetti accademici derivanti da altre arti o, comunque, di retroguardia.

Manifesto ideato nel luglio 2014 da Enzo Trifolelli, con la collaborazione di Gianpiero Ascoli, Marco Scataglini e Anna Maria Staccini. Pubblicato il 22 Luglio 2017 in occasione di SorianoImmagine2017

img.34

Photo in SpazioTempismo and SpazioFotoTempismo

SpazioTempismo and SpazioFotoTempismo

These are expressions of two ways of representing space-time deriving from *Scribalux*: FoTotempismo shown in image 36 and photographic SpaceTime in image 38. A third way was represented even more completely by combining *FoTotempismo* with *SpazioTempismo*, obtaining a higher level of representation of the image on two levels, which had never been depicted so far, called *SpazioFotoTempismo* shown in image 41. Other expressions then find space to be created in the context of *Scribalux*, such as *FotoSculptism*, based on *FoTotempismo*, but carried out with a 3D scanner and currently undergoing exploration by myself.

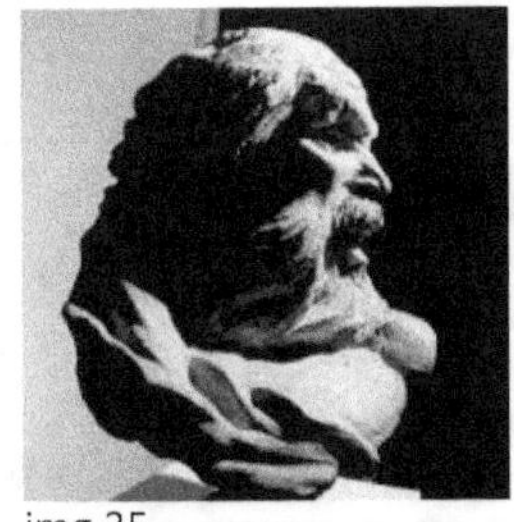

img.35

still image

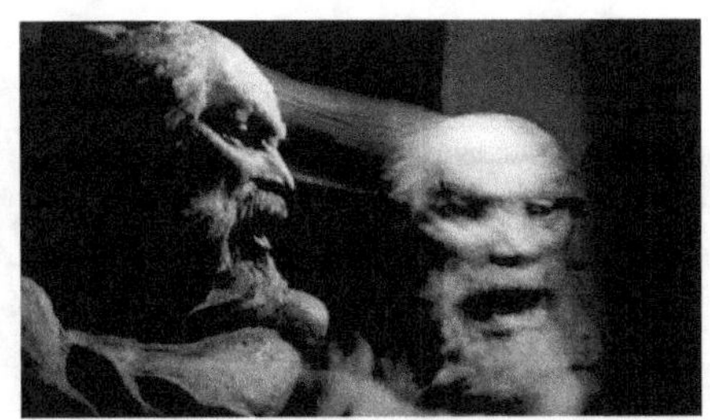

img.36

image in FoTotempismo

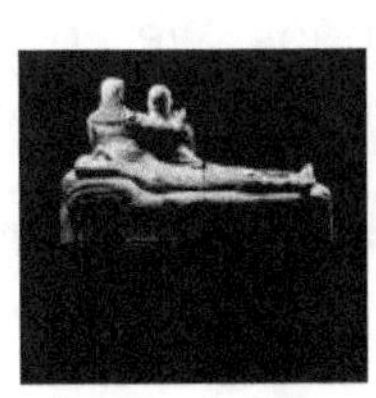

img.37

rear view

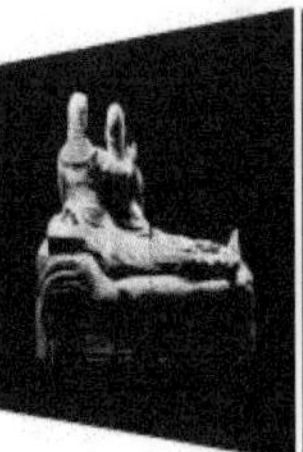

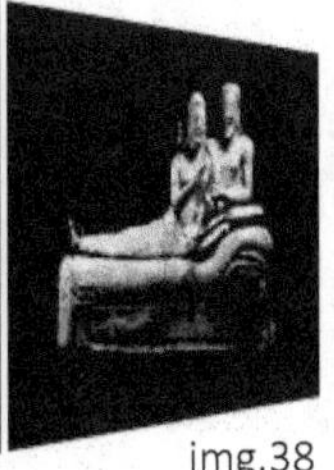

img.38

*image in
SpazioTempismo*

img.39

front view

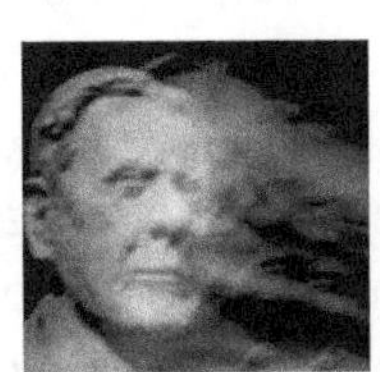

img.40

*FoTotempismo
left view*

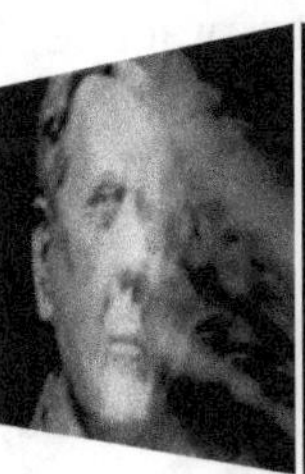

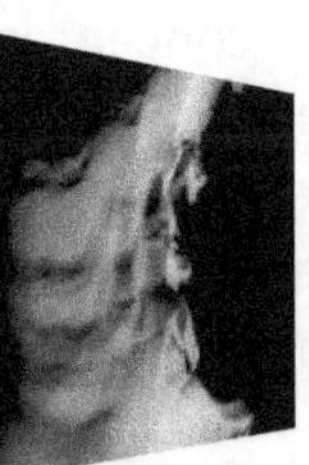

img.41

*Images in
SpazioFotoTempismo*

img.42

*FoTotempismo
right rear view*

With just one shot the 'Gesture' of FoTotempismo becomes the 'Sign'

a new photographic concept

foreword

In the journey undertaken with this book, we go on to explore a new way of photographing that I have named *FoTotempismo*.

FoTotempismo as a photographic concept that investigates the domains of Space-Time and Time-Space.

The aim of this work is not intended to be exclusively informative, but aims also to motivate and stimulate readers to put this concept into practice, by creating photographs that are not only aesthetically pleasing, but with conceptual content organized in such a way as to tell stories, describe events and convey sensations; exactly as with all other means of communication. It will describe how the idea and the need originated, what the concept wishes to express, its relationship with still and conceptual photography, and above all the exploration of the domain space which is inseparable from time.

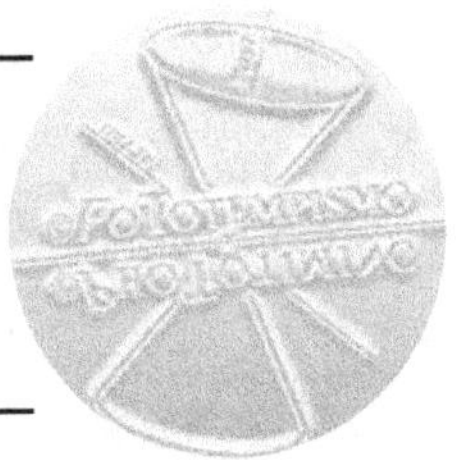

FoTotempismo

The representation of space will lead towards a new consideration that when combined with that of time, already explored in photography, will lead to the emergence of new intellectual developments that have not yet surfaced. Given the recent inception of FoTotempismo, this book cannot be exhaustive in all the facets it presents, however, all the results achieved so far will be presented. On this occasion, interested parties are invited to integrate the evolution of FoTotempismo, both with the images of all the photographic genres, and with the literature.

Some shooting procedures are described and have been implemented, others serve as inspiration but many others will be amateur photographers, professionals and researchers who will propose and implement them. Some sensors and equipment are examined here in order to verify the opportunities that FoTotempismo can capture in the current technical landscape. In addition, the requirements to facilitate the process are indicated, thus opening up a research channel also towards camera manufacturers. With that I hope for an all-round involvement in the intellectual, conceptual and technical advancement of photography.

the origins

how it was conceived

There is nothing born that is not wanted. Desiring is a need that is felt; if then one so wishes, exploration leads to a new birth.

Towards the summer of 2010 I was working on the photo book 'IL PALIO' of Soriano nel Cimino, when, immersed in editing my photographic images, I experienced a satisfaction which is now outdated. Yet those images narrated one of the most beautiful festivals, in such a fascinating way, that state of mind, mood, participation, and even sounds and perfumes could be perceived. Some images capture 'the moment', others are animated, blurred if not in 'Photodynamism'. It was precisely these images that gave me the feeling that the photographic lexicon had stopped. Something was missing but I couldn't understand what it was. And then, towards the end of summer, in one of the many photographic meetings between friends in Soriano, I said: why not photograph the spatiality of the subject?". There was a moment of silence and I felt as though I had said an absurdity, and so the discourse moved on to other things. Certainly the confusion I had in my mind between the conceptual photo and dynamism with the blurring, the moving, the dematerialization of the traces and Photodynamism, continually triggered new thoughts. Thoughts that always led me back

FoTotempismo

to representing photographically multiple perspectives in a single shot. Then after having printed and presented the book 'IL PALIO' in September 2011, in December of the same year I took the first photograph that comprised all the requirements I had hypothesized.

Thus originated '®*FoTotempismo*'.

For the first time with the exploration of space, the author separated the physical view of reality from that which can be observed in a work of art by supporting the qualitative difference between the time of emotions and that of physics, just as in the words of **Pavel Aleksandrovič Florenskij**:

> *"It is entirely possible that physical time has certain characteristics and that the other time has others that we will rediscover in a work of art. We must thus expect different times, constructed according to different typologies, similar to what happens for spaces in a work of art".*

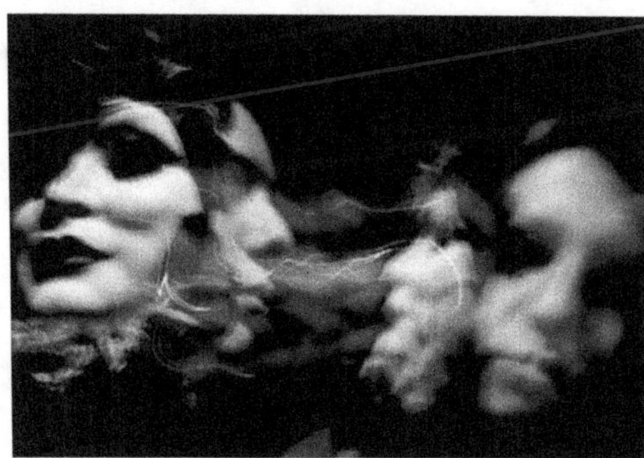

img.43

First portrait in FoTotempismo

the origins

conceptual still photos

The instant image freezes the moment of that portion of reality with which we wish to communicate a situation, a feeling, an emotion, a state of mind.

Photography becomes conceptual the moment in which we wish to transport a message with the image, appropriately 'packaged', that is not only aesthetic but previously formulated and then represented. So this type of photography carries information that can reach the recipient only if the narrative keys are known or available.

The packaging of the concept that then takes shape in the photographic image (img.44-img.48) can be pre-existing naturally, in this case the preparation of the message occurs in the choice of how to photograph the subject, the desired light, the angle, etc. in order to insert the key that is required to communicate the desired message.

Often the author falls into packaging a kind of puzzle, that does everything but communicate.

A sequence, a series, a portfolio, a story with conceptualised images always express an idea, like in other types of photography.

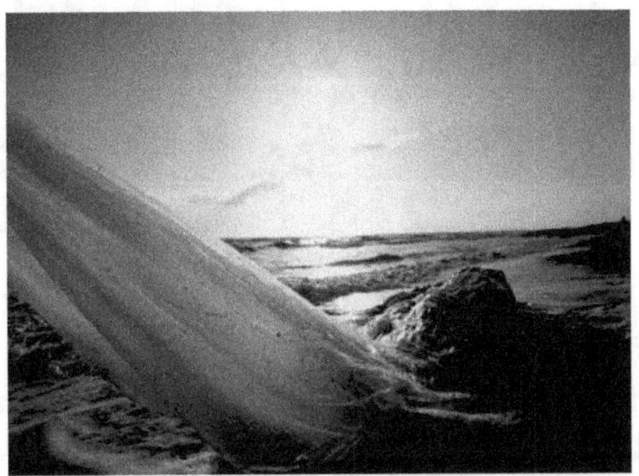

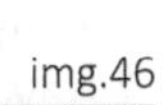
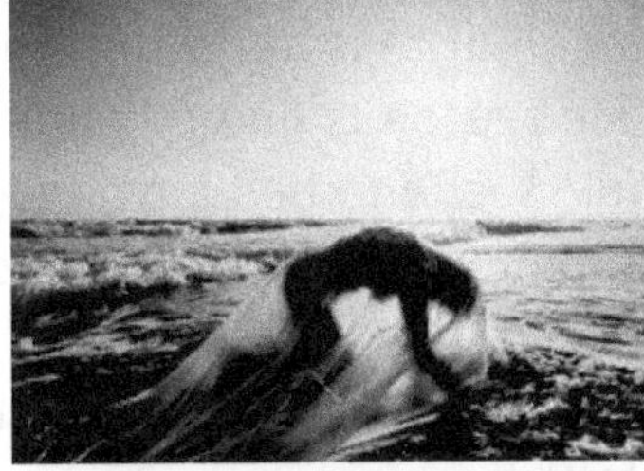
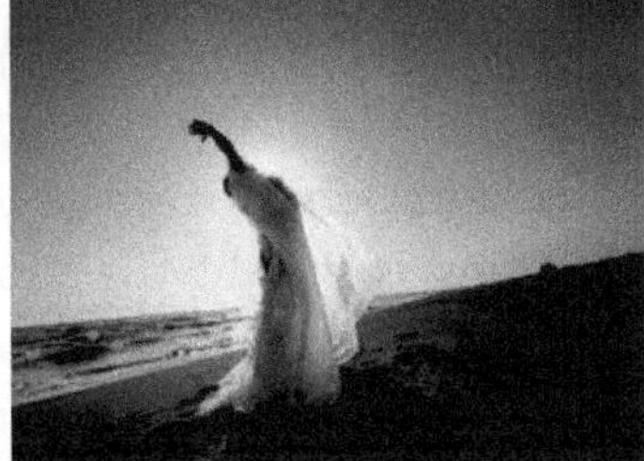

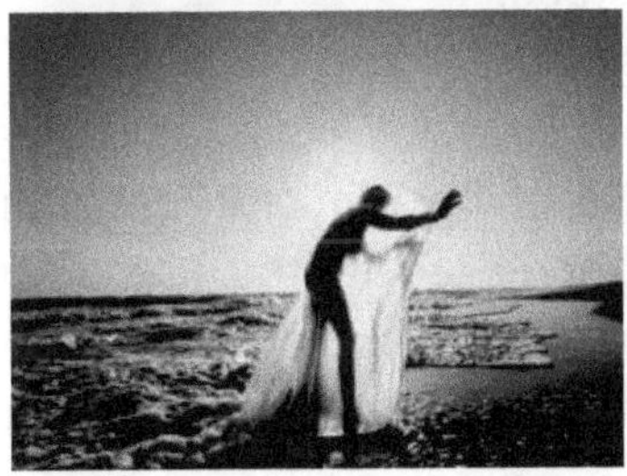
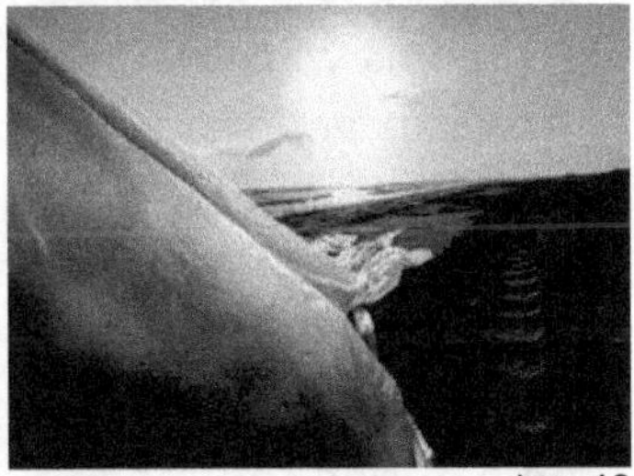

Birth from the sea and indelible traces

In this sequence the 'birth' of life on earth is represented, the praising of a god and the indelible 'footprint' that man will leave in the history of planet Earth.

We now go on to examine 'blurring' which, if appropriately managed and controlled, will be an implication of the 'fototempistic' concept.

The term 'blurred' in photography means an image which is not clear enough to see the details, which can have higher or lower resolution (img.49, img.50). This result is due to two fundamental reasons of instability while taking the shot. One reason is due to camera shake which causes the whole scene to be blurred, the second is due to the movement of the subject, which results in only that being blurred.

Motion blur due to camera movement can be intentional or due to mechanical instability.

Problems with the internal camera components or the lens can generate micromovements, while anchorage instability can be the cause of both micromovements and shake, which can be increased by the use of any long telephoto lenses.

Blurring can also be determined by the shutter opening time during shooting.

In fact, to obtain a clear, distinct image, very short shutter speeds of hundredths or thousandths of a second must be used.

Otherwise, if intentional camera movement (ICM) is required, a 'slower' exposure time is set, generally to the

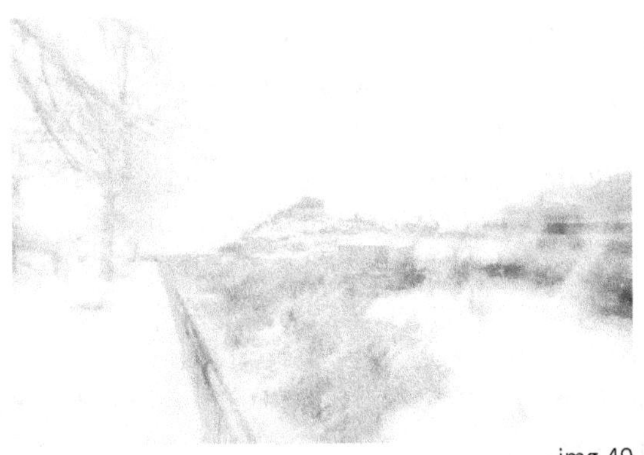

img.49

Winter landscape

img.50

Summer landscape

tenth of a second depending on the speed of movement of the subject and the photographer.

The main aim of these chapters is to deal only with intentional blur due to the movement of the camera desired by the author and thus capturing the movement of the subject.

In this context, movement can range from an image with a brief shift (img.53) up to figurations with such extensive movement that they result in the complete destruction of the subject itself (img.51).

These will be the elements used to arrive at FoTotempismo.

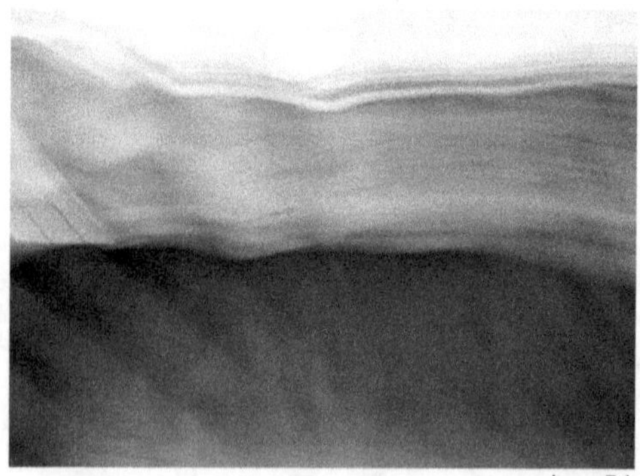

img.51

Blurred image with destruction of the subject

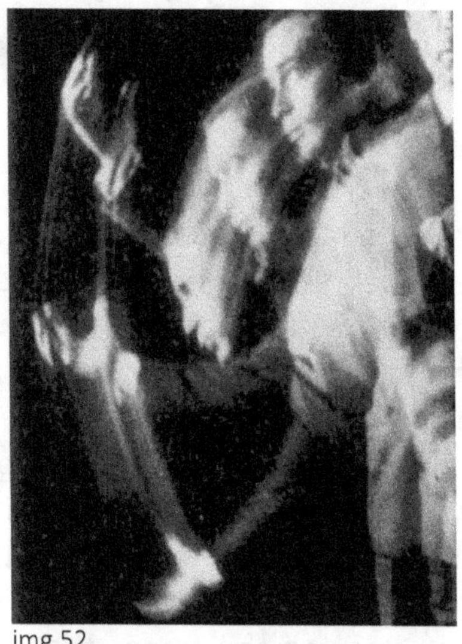

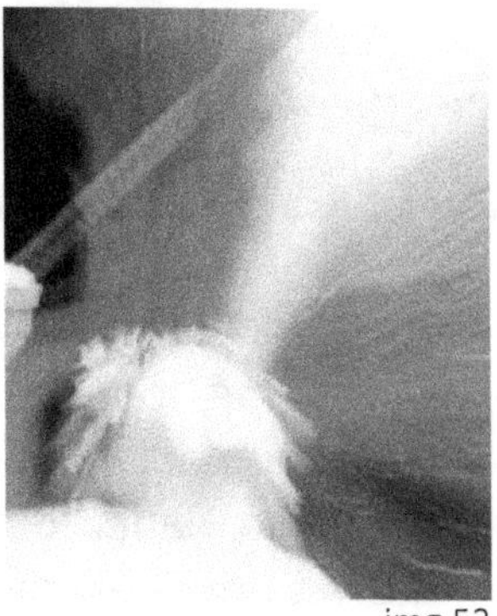

img.53

Image with micro-move-ment blur due to the cam-era or to the photographer

img.52

"...in the result of blurring, there is a short shift or a complete destruction of the bodies." (A.G. Bragaglia)

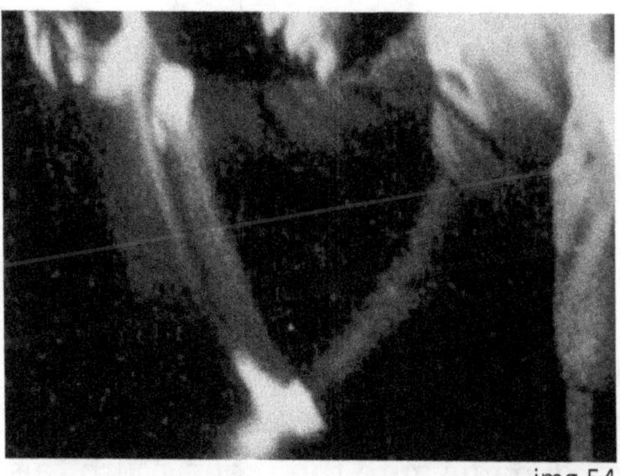

img.54

"...in the second (that is, in animated/blurred photography) exists only the dematerialization of these, with traces of movement."

the origins

The concept of movement is more complex; contrary to blurring, it must give evidence of motion. It can also be combined with the movement enacted by the author who wants to transmit their own participation in the action. The movement that appears in the animated representations must produce a dematerialization which then re-materializes, giving the idea of perceiving movement. So the movement can be produced by the representation of the subject moving, that comes or goes from destruction, leaving the traces that indicate its movement. Otherwise the movement can also be obtained from the action of the author who, by moving the camera, generates the destruction of the subject in order to make it re-materialize, thus generating relative movement. The combination of the two systems that produce the movement with dematerialization or re-materialization, can also produce highly expressive images. As previously explained, the movement can be created by the author by simply setting a relatively long shooting time compared to the movement of the subject. It is more engaging for the author to move the camera in order to impart his/her personal dynamism to the scene. With this we are still heading towards FoTotempismo.

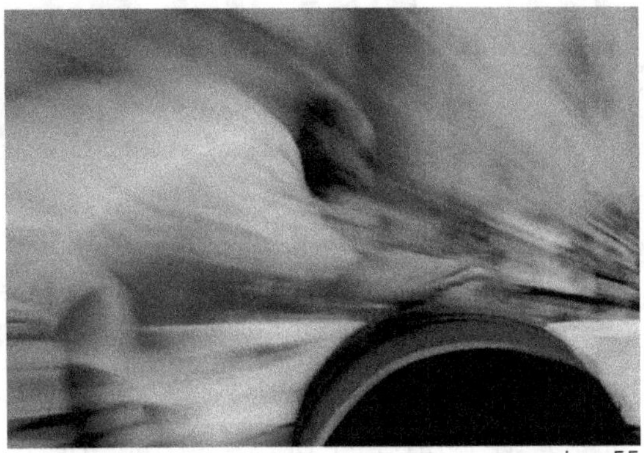

img.55

Popular games (animated image)

*Vincenzo Pacelli,
swordsmen (animated image)*

img.56

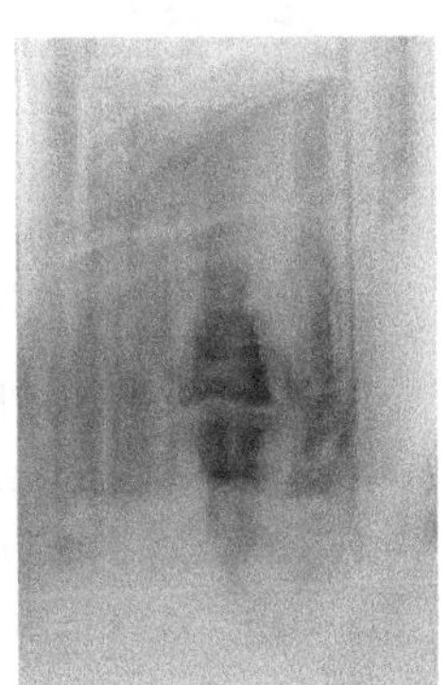

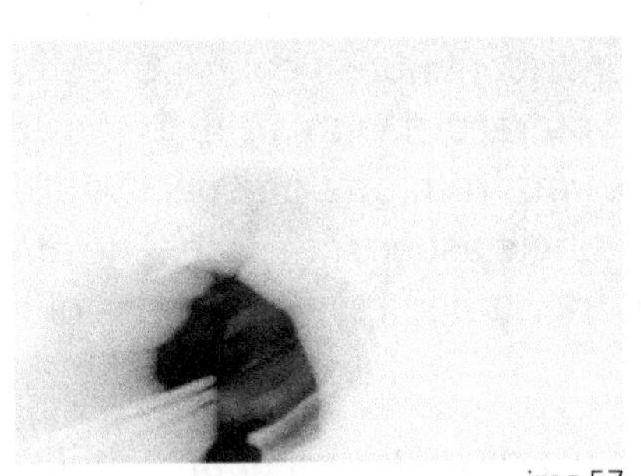

img.57

horse with jockey (animated image)

the origins
Photodynamism

In 1911 Anton Giulio Bragaglia wrote and published the essay Futurist Photodynamism, thus giving a specific name to his experiments and associating them with the Futurist Movement led by Filippo Tommaso Marinetti.

"If we reproduce only the trajectory of a movement, then our sensation of it will be still fuller and easier. Then we will have completely achieved our artistic goal, since a gesture for us is a pure dynamic sensation which, in turn, is nothing other than the effect produced on our sensibility by its trajectory, and hence we can re-experience the dynamic sensation of the gesture and achieve our goal."...

This, then is Photodynamism (img.58, img.59), with the camera still and the subject moving, leaving traces of its movement with dematerializations and re-materializations in relation to its discontinuous course of action. With Photodynamism you record with a single shot the exploration of time viewed from one perspective, thus shooting the view of a single aspect of space. The energies recorded with the trails traced are only those of the photographed subject.

..."We want to achieve a revolution in photography, for progress: in order to purify, ennoble, and truly

elevate photography to an art. 'Movement' and 'life' are the two watchwords; realising what is not seen superficially".

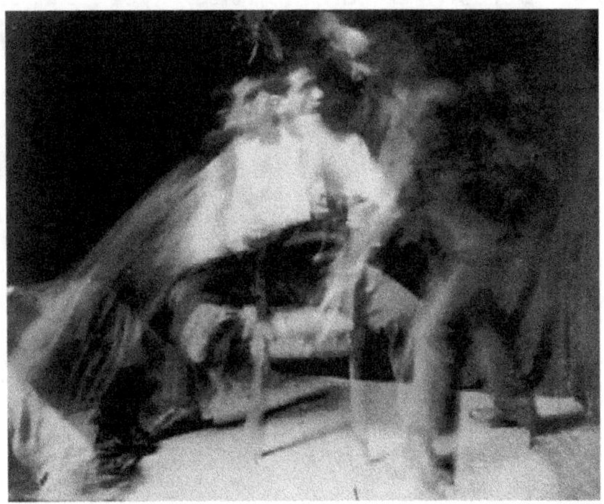

img.58

Bragaglia Brothers, The slap

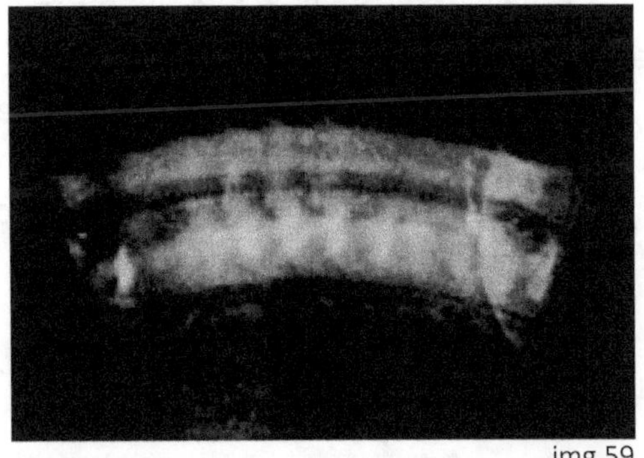

img.59

Bragaglia Brothers, Young person rocking

Photodynamism

"...Instead of a linear succession of moments, perceiving an infinite, yet dynamic, present forgetting the passage of time, absorbing me into the observed subject. That is, grasping that place where there are no time divisions, such as past, present and future; they are contracted into a single instant of the present in which life quivers in a real sense; and this present moment is not something that is at rest with all that it contains, but moves incessantly."

"... There, where photography appears so dynamic, and yet so immobile that there is nothing left on the plate, is where Photodynamism begins, having as its purpose the memory of the dynamic sensation of a movement with its shape scientifically faithful, even in its dematerialization." (img.60).

Anton Giulio Bragaglia (1911)

In 1910 the Bragaglia brothers (Anton Giulio, Arturo and Carlo Ludovico) theorized, and for the first time, justified conceptually an artistic use of the photographic medium. The brothers rejected the label of photographers, which was then identified with pictorialistic photography.

Photodynamics was thus to be distinguished from Chronophotography and from all those who had done only scientific research with photography.

For the Futurists the photographic image remains quite simply a direct competitor of painting, and the lens a sort of clumsy and limited brush.

img.60

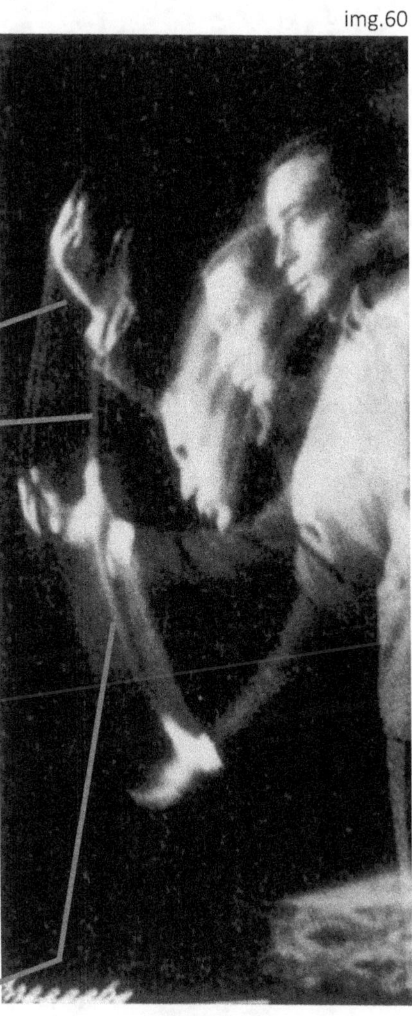

Panning originated in the 1950s from a need by Ernst Haas to photograph the subject in motion, immersed in environments not excessively illuminated, like at dusk, and also not having the sensitivity of the film so high as it is today in digital sensors, to allow him a good still photograph. Under such conditions, Ernst Haas decided to follow the subject in its movement, lengthening the exposure time. In doing so he attempted to have a still image of a subject, in this case a bull in a bullfight, and conversely he also achieved a blurring of the background; subsequently this shooting technique became known as Panning, and posthumously it was his definition related to time and all that that implied. Today, Panning is used to represent a subject which is moving in relation to the background, in particular in car racing, in cycling, in motion photographs in general, creating striking images.

Not all subjects are represented with the same effects: a train lends itself well to excellent results as its speed is constant and it is easy to represent it as 'still' while the background is blurred. A cyclist or marathon runner will result with legs or arms moving. To get interesting images and to obtain the desired result, the exposure speed with the speed of the subject have to be optimized.

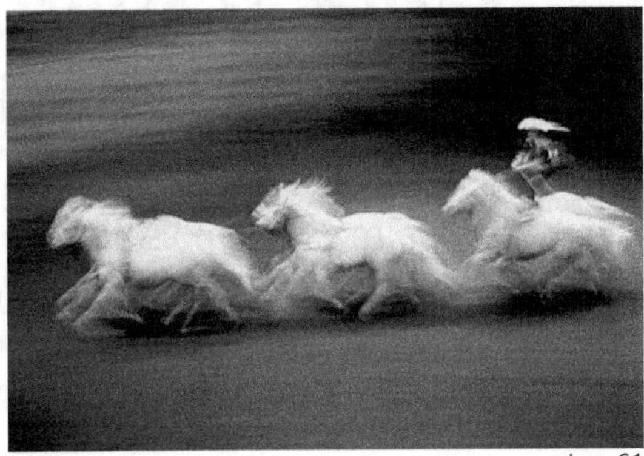

img.61

Ernst Hass, horses (Panning)

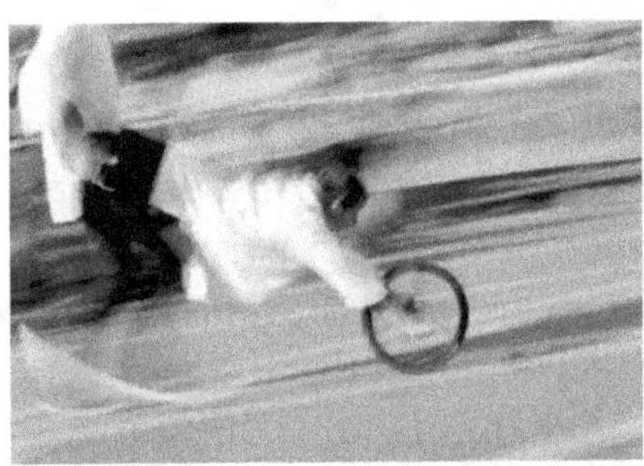

img.62

The wheelbarrow game (Panning)

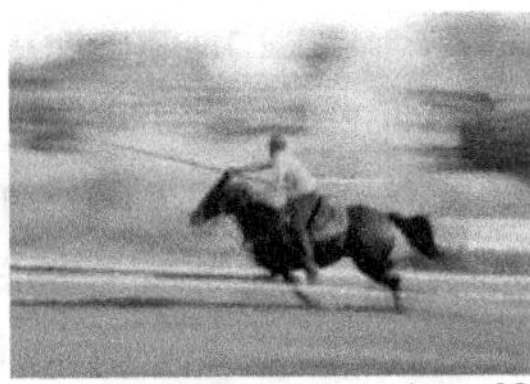

img.63

Horse with jockey (Panning)

FoTotempismo

introduction

Introduction to FoTotempismo

The need to express oneself unconventionally through photography arrives at exploring those dimensions that have always been in the desires of photographers forced to express themselves on a single surface in two dimensions; while the representation of movement has found an expression in Photodynamism, in Panning and in photos with controlled blurring.

These forms of representation express only the substance of the subject and sometimes, by using small movements of the camera, only on single spatial planes, they can give environmental dynamism. The origins in Photodynamism, however, are to represent the movement of the subject by highlighting the trajectory of its dematerialization and re-materialization. In its various reinterpretations it has also come to move the photographic medium slightly onto one or two of the axes of a spatial plane, while still maintaining the concept of energy and movement, and representing all the information only on one flat view of the subject. The search for the total transposition of the subject immersed in the space-time dimension is found and obtained in an ideological representation that I define as: 'FoTotempismo'. In addition to the unconventional representation of the energy released by the subject and the environment in which it

Logo of FoTotempismo

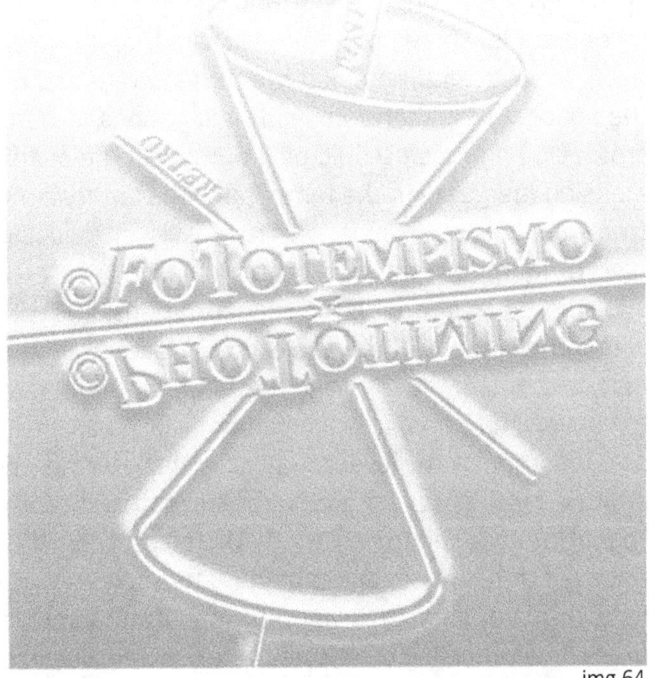

img.64

The hourglass logo represents time, that slow time compared to the speed of movement in space that we will have after (post) and ... behind (retro); this is the space-time that is explored with FoTotempismo.

is immersed, as an expression of light and vibrations, this concept endeavours, above all, to give a representation of three-dimensionality and of Space-Time, as well as the energy of the author who has taken the shot.

This study, which originated within research that had been carried out for some time, aimed at satisfying the desire to travel in space and time, led me to penetrate and merge the space-time dimensions with immersions in both microscopic and macroscopic environments. The spatial dimension merges with the temporal in the author's mental creativity, predetermining the final result, introducing the path of time from the infinitesimal minimum to 'eternal', and transporting us with the spatial 'dimensionality' from within the essence of the subject to 'sidereal spaces of infinity'. To obtain the message that the author endeavours to convey, the photographic medium is used as a witness and recorder of the event, highlighting both the energy emitted by the subject and what surrounds it, both the spatial location and the evidence of time passed. The clear traces of the dematerialization of matter and energy, lead to its re-materialization in another spatial and temporal dimension; immersing the viewer in this 'sidereal spiral' but with a soul, dependent on how the author manages the components that give substance to FoTotempismo.

In this context, the author joins in the scene also manifesting the release of his/her energy, giving the work uniqueness and rendering its message irreplicable.

In the creation of the photo/message everything is in motion, everything is active: space, time, movement of the subjects and the author, who drags the photographic medium with him/her, directing it where his/her thoughts go. With the mind rigidly anchored to the 'camera', the author moves skillfully to capture the subject in all its spatial forms, to then be able to reach other subjects, travelling once more through space and time. It is in this way that, in the photographic medium, not only the subjects are recorded, but the temporal and spatial history that the subjects themselves are experiencing, as desired by the artist. The relativity of space-time is recorded in this way and the spatiality and speed of movement of the author and photographic medium is palpable.

Examining the relationship between 'time' and 'space' with art, some considerations bring us closer to what photography can represent better than other disciplines. Let us see how the philosopher Pavel Aleksandrovič Florenskjǐ deals with space in art and the representation of all forces that give the perception of the world in which we live.

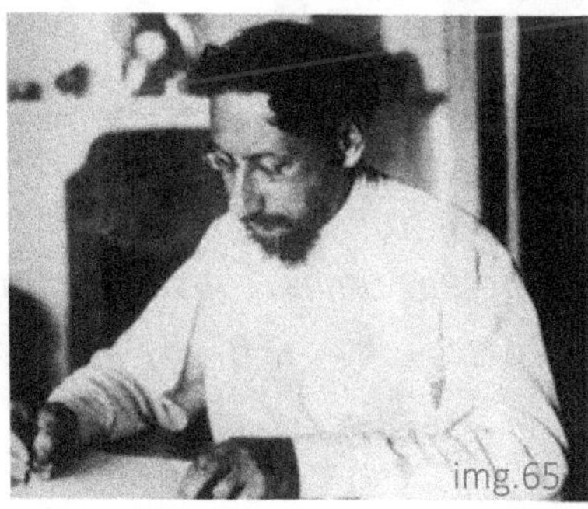

img.65

Pavel Aleksandrovič
Florenskjǐ

the visual essence of

perception of the world

Pavel Aleksandrovič Florenskjĭ (Leningrad 1892-1937)
Philosopher and mathematician, in a passage from the
VII university lecture of 1924 reads:

> *"All culture can be interpreted as the organization of space. In some cases, it is about the space of our vital relationships, and so the corresponding organization is called technical. In other cases it is the mental space of reality and the reality of its organization, which is called science or philosophy. Finally, the third class of cases is located between the first two. In them the space, or rather the spaces, are visible like the spaces of technique, but at the same time, they do not admit the interference of life, like the spaces of science and philosophy. The organization of these latter spaces is called art."*

Art is an 'organization' of culture that is found between
Technique and Science and Philosophy.
And again:

> *"It is entirely possible that physical time has certain characteristics and that the other time has others that we will rediscover in a work of art."*
>
> *"We must thus expect different times, constructed according to different typologies, like what happens for spaces in a work of art".*

Therefore according to Florenskjĭ we observe: spaces, times,

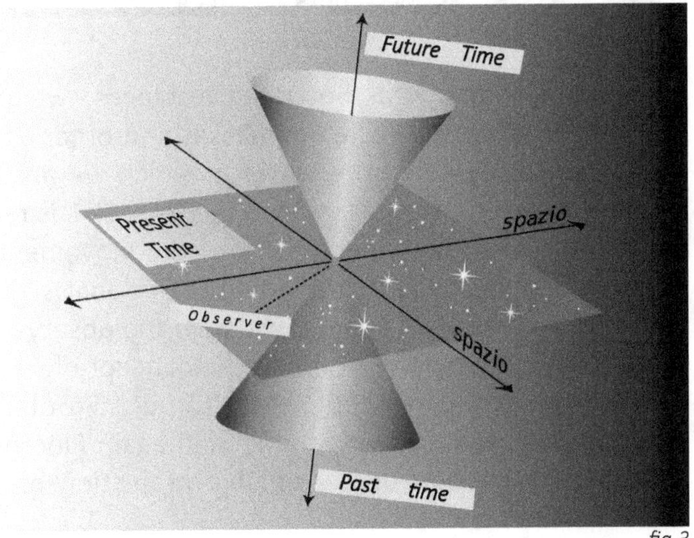

Space-Time Representation by Hermann Minkowski

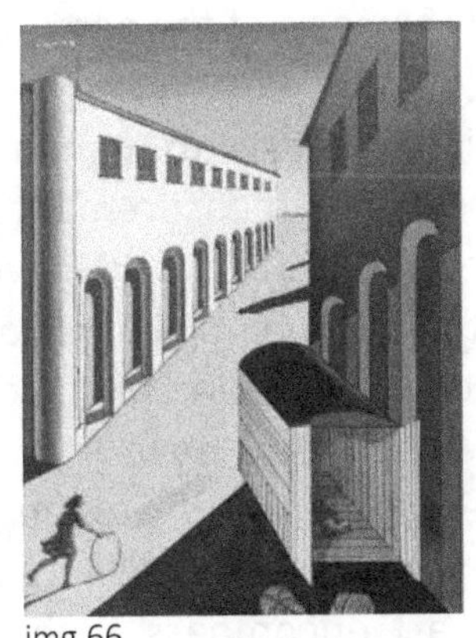

img.66

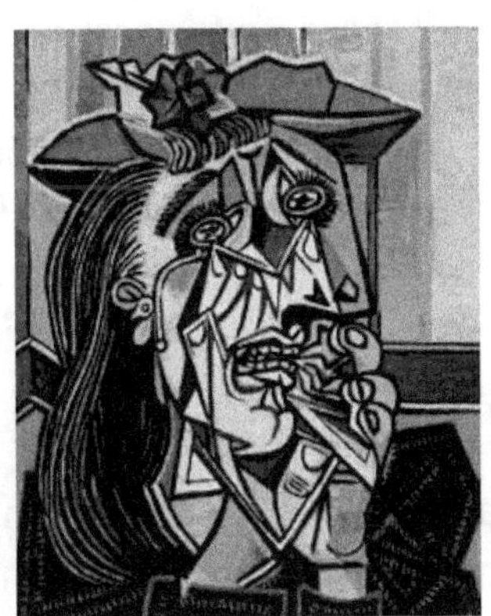

img.67

G. de Chirico, P. Picasso, Space-Time in art

spatial and temporal horizons, distances, weights, volumes, speeds, directions, masses and others, that allow us to perceive the world in which we are immersed. The concept expressed by Florenskjĭ, is related to the analysis of perception of the movement of the subject in space-time. Adding to this analysis also the consideration of space-time from the observation point, the perspective vision in the concept of space-time is complete, conceptualized through FoTotempismo for its artistic component. And again Florenskjĭ on the perception of perspective projection of the world asserts:

> *"The visual essence of movement consists precisely in the fact that not only one vantage point is observed, nor one horizon, nor one measurement scale, while all three units presuppose the basis of the perspective projection of the world".*

So the visual essence consists precisely in human binocular vision of all the forces and measurements involved which give the perception of the world in which we live, it is not hence the technical binocular vision of a machine, let alone the monocular vision of the cameras widely used today. Many authors have tried and as many will try again to represent creatively the perception of movement and the environment in which we live. All expressions of art encompass a physical and emotional aspect, and arouse more or less interest as a function of the emotion transmitted in that historical moment. Unfortunately in the current period it has been highly 'dissipated' and despite individual attempts to present innovations, no school of thought has been able to offer conceptual and representationally innovative and valid portrayals.

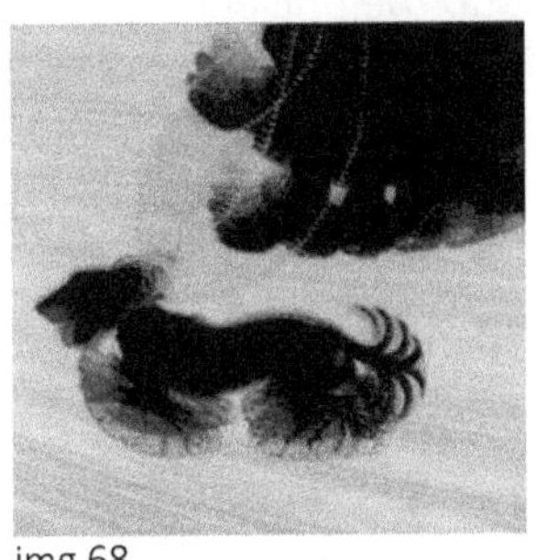

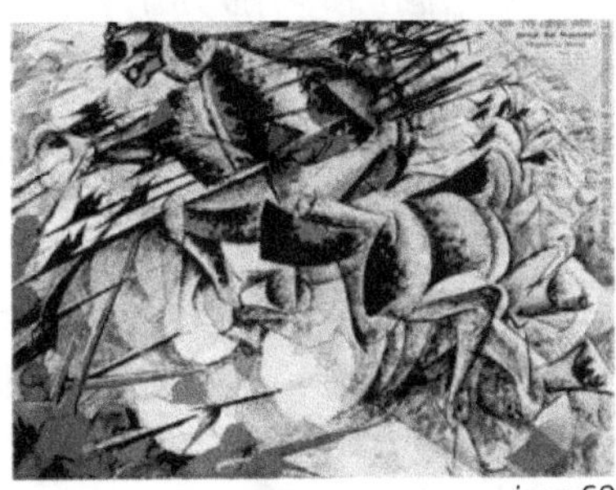

img.68

img.69

G. Balla, U. Boccioni, representation of Space-Time

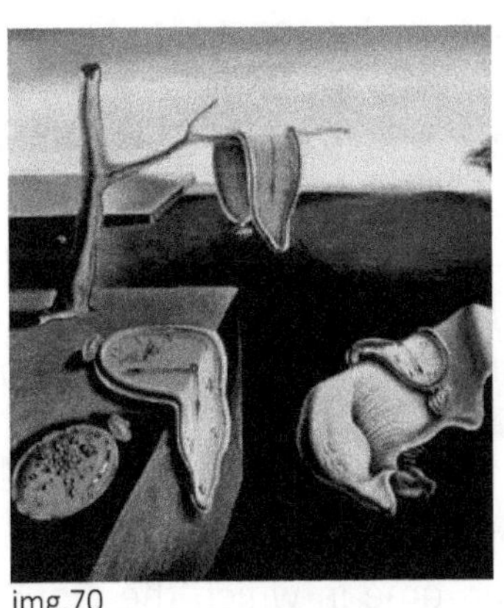

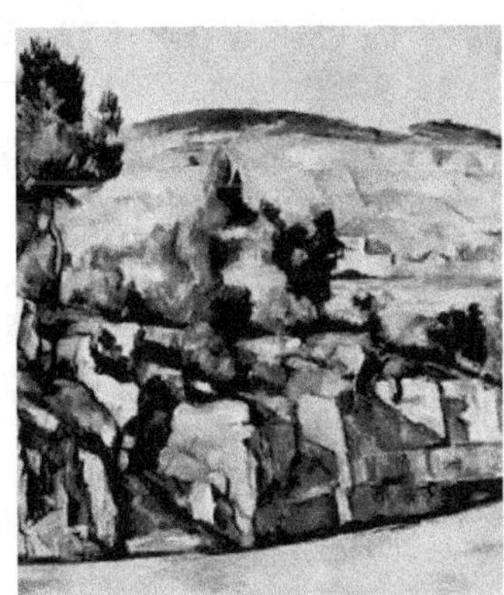

img.70

img.71

S. Dalì, P. Cezanne, Space and Time in art

in Space and Time
discontinuities and rhythms

"...continuity in space and time does not allow the shape of objects, nor their freedom and uniqueness to be grasped. So there are rhythms that make up the universe."

"If space really exists it doesn't necessarily have to be continuous."

Again on the subject of rhythms, P.A. Florenskjĭ wrote:
"Then man, like a thing in the midst of things of the world is carried along with the others on the surface of the river of time. ... "

The work of art is forced to arrange itself in perception along a path of successions that configures its internal scheme according to a specific dynamic and pre-set rhythm. A homogeneous time, that is, that flows continuously is not able to create a rhythm:

"The latter presupposes pulsations, concentration and dilation, slowing down and accelerating, steps forward and stops."

The time in which the work is found as a subject has nothing in common with the time in which the work is found as representation: the internal articulation that organizes the temporal structure of the work must be divided into moments of quiet and moments that leap. The elements of quiet are analytically indifferent to the duration and are fixed on a single unitary element for a moment in time. The leap elements are not perceptually assessable but they produce, together with the elements of stillness, a temporal rhythm. In the temporal structure therefore, a resolutive-analytical (observation) and a compositional-synthetic (demonstration) aspect of the work can be distinguished. Both are fundamental for the interpretation and enjoyment of the work.

Continuous elements that **lead, moments of quiet**

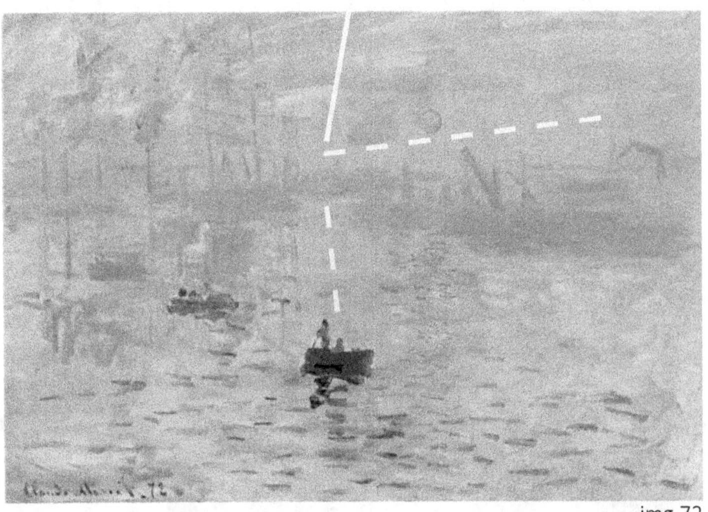

img.72

Claud Monet, Impression, Sunrise:
which, at 7.35 on the 13th November 1872, originated Impressionism

discontinuity and rhythms

In examining the images produced in FoTotempismo, all those characteristics explored by philosophers and mathematicians emerge with extraordinary value, compared to those images produced by different means, which now acquire less meaning. The characteristics that are present in non-fototempistic images, such as: rhythms, continuous elements that lead, focuses and others, are fundamental in compositions in general, but in comparison with those generated and present in the new images produced in FoTotempismo leave space for and are overwhelmed by the latter. So in this new concept, which enables both photographic images and those from other disciplines to be created, communicativeness acquires further expressive and emotional elements.

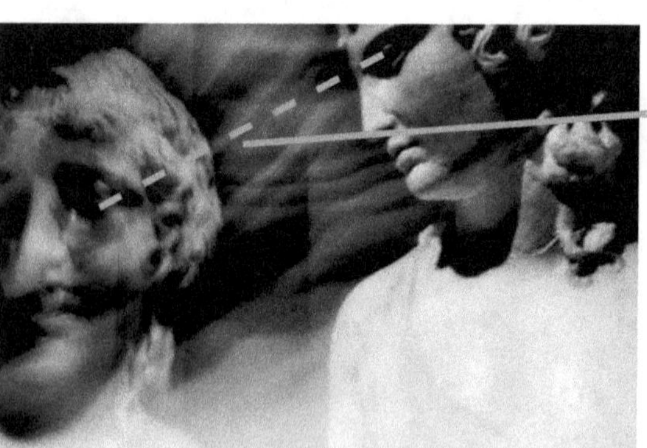

img.73

image in FoTotempismo

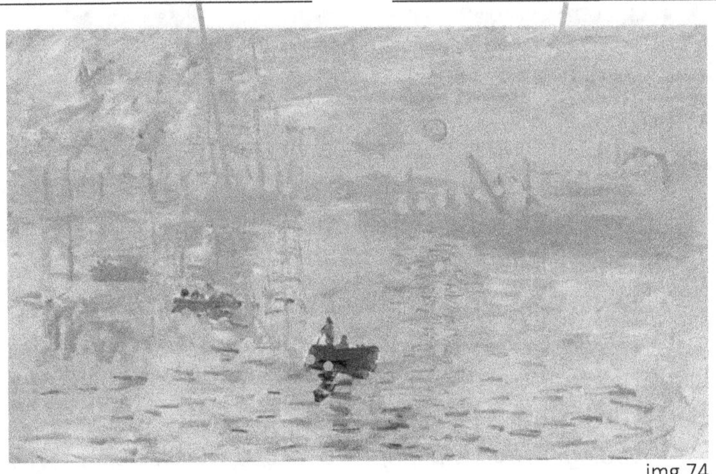

Moments of *leap*

Elements with *rhythms*

img.74

Continuous elements that *lead*

Rhythms and moments of *leap*
moments of *quiet*

img.75

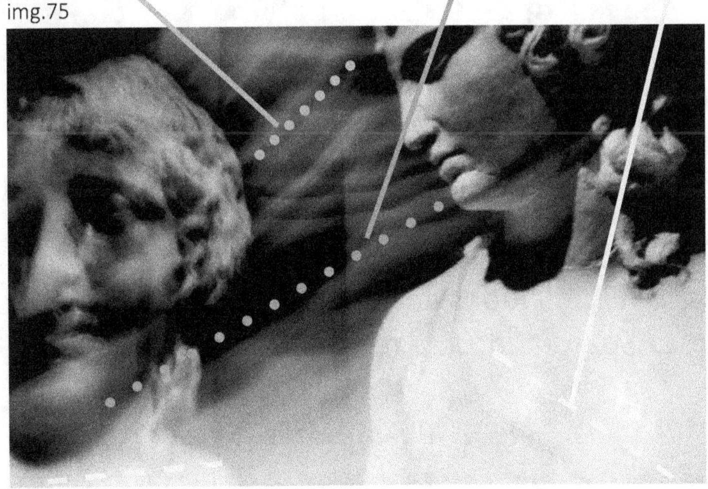

79

in Space and Time

'Space and Time'

The end of rigid separation, absolute space and absolute time, leads Florenskjĭ to support the qualitative difference between the time of the emotions and that of the physical:

"It is entirely possible that physical time has certain characteristics and that the other time has others that we will rediscover in a work of art. We must thus expect different times, constructed according to different typologies, like what happens for spaces in a work of art".

With FoTotempismo it is verified that times and spaces are different from the times and spaces of physics, satisfying the claims of Florenskjĭ.

SPACE AND TIME.
By moving the camera
roto-translationally with variable speed,
dilations and compressions of the
Space and Time represented are obtained;
this is
FoTotempismo

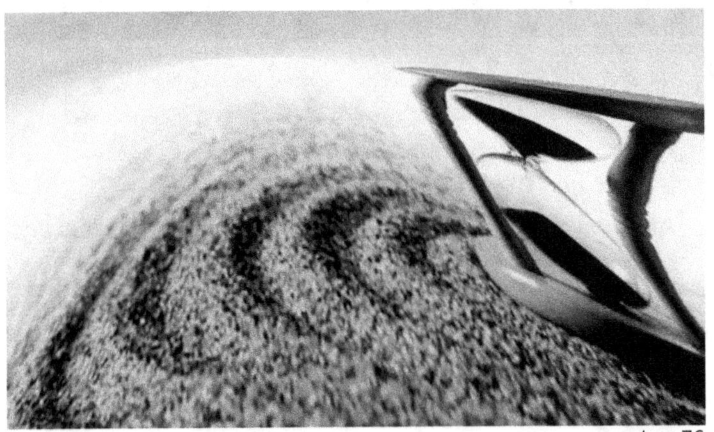

img.76

Distortion of time in FoTotempismo

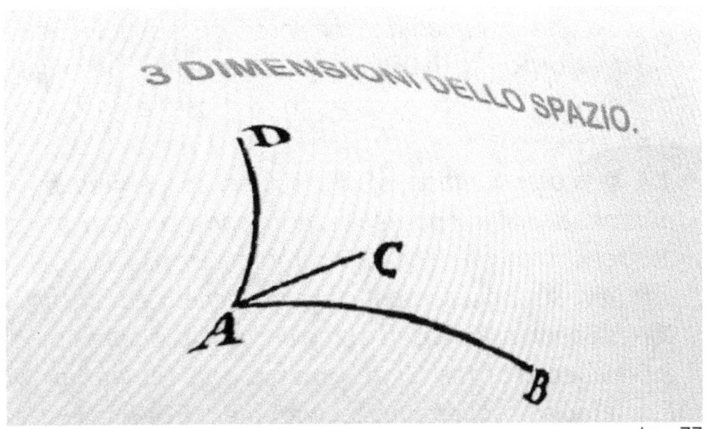

img.77

Distortion of space in FoTotempismo

What FoTotempismo comprises

After examining the thinking related to representations of images by philosophers, mathematicians, art critics, and communications experts; we now go on to analyze the innovative content that FoTotempismo generates in photographic images but also in representations of any other discipline that uses this principle.

The content in images in FoTotempismo:

1.0 multi-perspective three-dimensionality (img.79)

1.1 representation of the subject from an initial perspective (img.80)

1.2 dematerialization of the subject, generated by the action of the author as opposed to the unconscious optics (img.81)

1.3 destruction of the subject, generated by the action of the author in direct contrast to that of the unconscious optics (img.82)

1.4 re-materialization of the subject, generated by the author's action as opposed to the unconscious optics (img.83)

1.5 representation of the subject from other perspectives (img.84)

2.0 new strongly present tensions generated by the author's action as opposed to the unconscious optics (img.85)

3.0 evidence of the 'Sign' generated by the author with fototempistic action, that is, with their 'Gesture' (img.86).

All these points can be repeated several times in the same image according to the author's creativity.

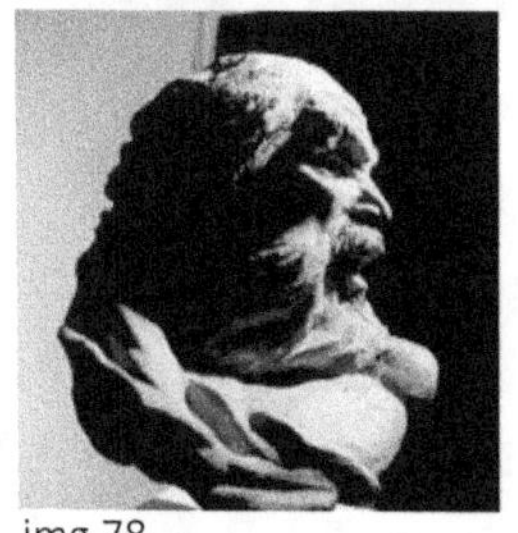

img.78

Subject

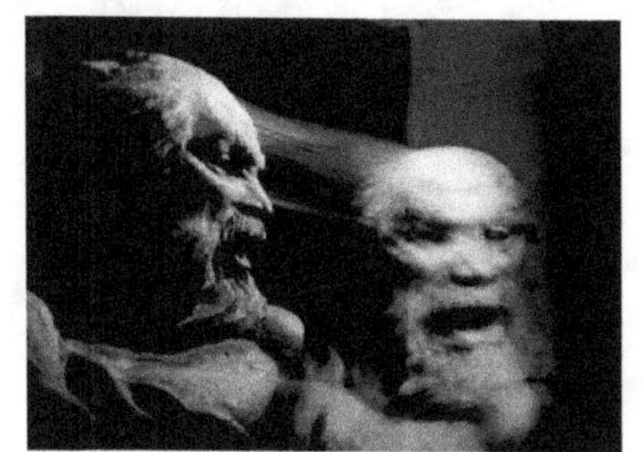

img.79

1.0) Multi-perspective

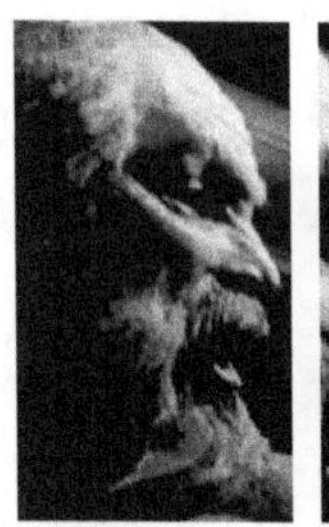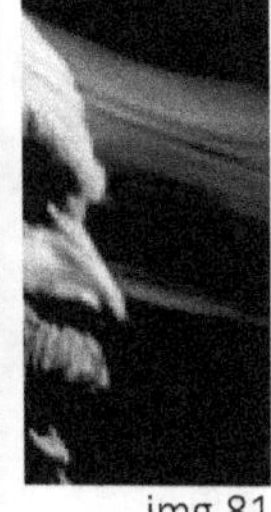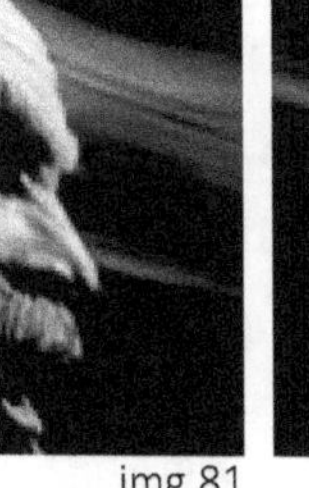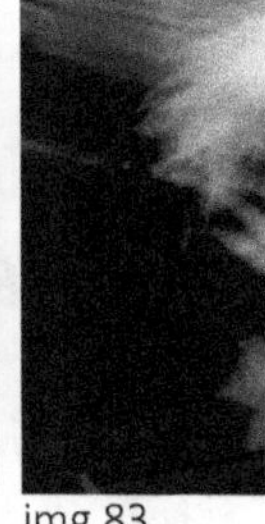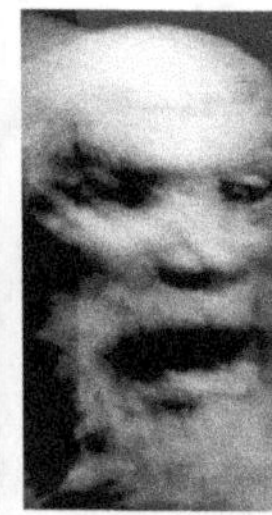

img.80   img.81   img.82   img.83   img.84

  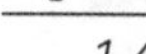

1.1   *1.2*   *1.3*   *1.4*   *1.5*

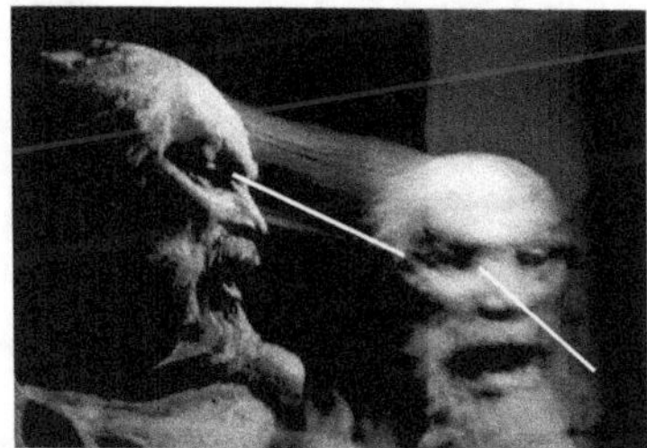

img.85

2) New Tensions

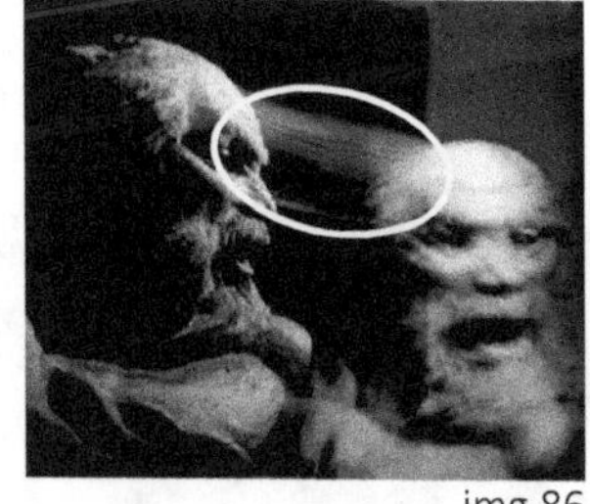

img.86

3) The 'Sign' of the 'Gesture'

The domain of the instrument

With the operator's total control over the camera reduced to an instrument subject to the intentions of the author, FoTotempismo conquers its dominion to generate an image that did not exist, which was only in the author's mind. This struggle, now to the advantage of the author, unleashes and represents new forces, energies and new 'dimensionality', which controlled and managed allow new representations and sensations to be expressed, where time and space belong to the emotions and not to physics.

The Focus of FoTotempismo:

- draws strength from the means by which the Gesture is carried out
- does not wish to imitate painting
- uses camera movement on multiple planes
- is the representation of the subject
- gives a new and absolute irreplicability of the image
- brings about the reduction and loss of indexical value
- brings about the reduction and loss of iconic value
- gives revelation and control of the unconscious optics
- allows for meaningful exploration and representation of space-time
- enables the representation of the multi-perspective
- the author generates the dematerialization of the subject
- the author generates the destruction of the subject
- the author generates the re-materialization of the subject
- generates new three-dimensionality of the image
- includes new subjects in the image during shooting
- generates new elements that 'lead'
- generates new 'rhythms'
- generates new 'tensions'
- multiple horizons are represented
- multiple points of view are represented
- several measurement scales are represented
- reveals that the space of physics is different from that of the emotions
- reveals that the time of physics is different from that of the emotions
- creates new dream visions
- fully introduces the 'Gesture' in photography
- fully introduces the 'Sign' in photography

Space-Time

If we understand photography as the transposition of a part of reality onto a flat surface; therefore with the representation of three-dimensionality through perspective and the fourth dimension, time, as a trace derivative of the passing of the same, FoTotempismo introduces a new concept of representation. In a natural way, the third dimension of the subject, that is the depth, is represented by the laws of perspective, where the *camera obscura,* now camera, has its innate property; and since ancient times the *camera obscura* was used by painters to facilitate execution of their paintings.

Different paths were taken in representing time in the various disciplines. The first cultural movements that had a significant impact on the representation of time were in the early years of the 20th century. In particular, the environment of the *Futurist Movement* gave strong impetus to photography, where, for the first time, the Bragaglia brothers represented the dynamism of the moving subject with their Photodynamism. In the photodynamic images are represented: the components of a moving body, the energy they release and the trajectories in the form of dematerialization trails up to the destruction of itself, to then re-materialize in another time and space.

*F*o*T*o*TEMPISTIC*

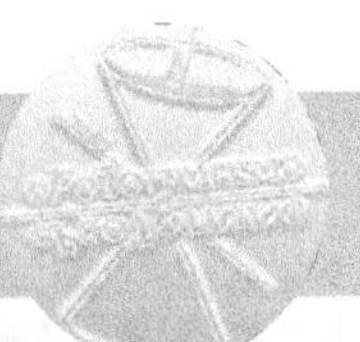

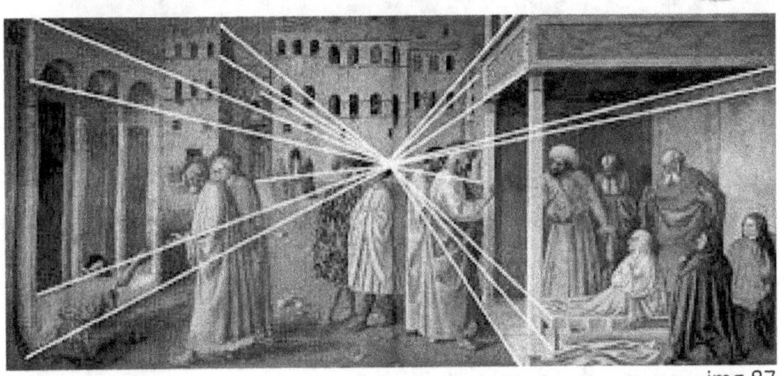

img.87

Masolino, Resurrection ... (Space from the Renaissance perspective)

Still Photography represents a state that is no longer modifiable by representing a past moment, which is no longer in existence. So 'time' can also mean: the greater the exposure time approaches zero, until reaching it, the less life there is, until it is completely annulled when the time equals zero. In the photograph that fixes the moment and immobilizes the subject, Barthes, sees an excessive static of the moment, and hence the feeling of macabre representation of the circumstance represented, which no longer exists, which is 'dead'.

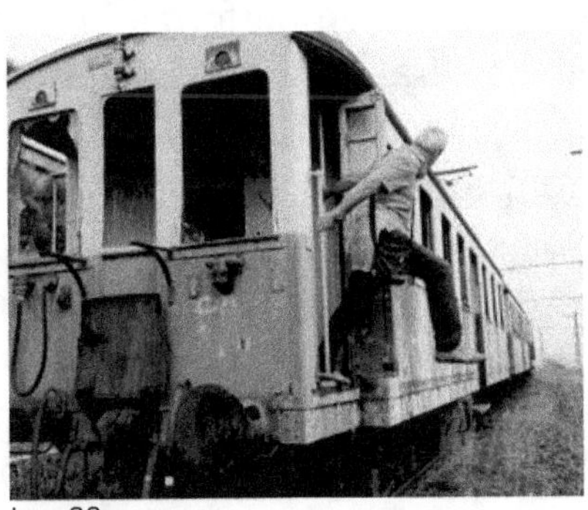

img.88

Still photograph. Time of a still photograph immortalized by a camera

Space-Time

The origins of Panning were different, which aimed to have a still image of the moving subject, using equipment that did not allow it, given the low film sensitivity.

A comparison between the origins of Panning and Photodynamism is important. The former takes the photograph and then formulates its definition, while the second formulates the concept beforehand, to then implement and materialize it with a photographic image. In addition to the concepts of Photodynamism and Panning, FoTotempismo formulates the desire to represent the space in time (Space/Time) with multi-perspectives beforehand, leading the author, no longer a photographer, to be the creator of the 'Gesture' that generates the 'Sign'.

The 'Gesture' consists of the action performed by the author in moving the camera in three-dimensional space, hence the spatial shift from the micro to the macrocosm, that is, from atomic to cosmic space, in function of the technologies currently available.

This 'Gesture' is similar to the gesture made by a painter with his brush, spatula or any means used in his/her discipline. It can also be compared to the action that the sculptor performs with the chisel, the hammer or tools to shape hard materials or plastic models. That same 'Gesture' traces a unique and irreplicable 'Sign', which

can create a 'work of art'.
Any author who uses techniques that produce photographic images in FoTotempismo, generates a different and unrepeatable 'Sign' by another author with their 'Gesture', thus determining the uniqueness of the work. So photography is no longer simply icon, index and communication, but is elevated even more to equal disciplines such as painting, sculpture, music and literature.

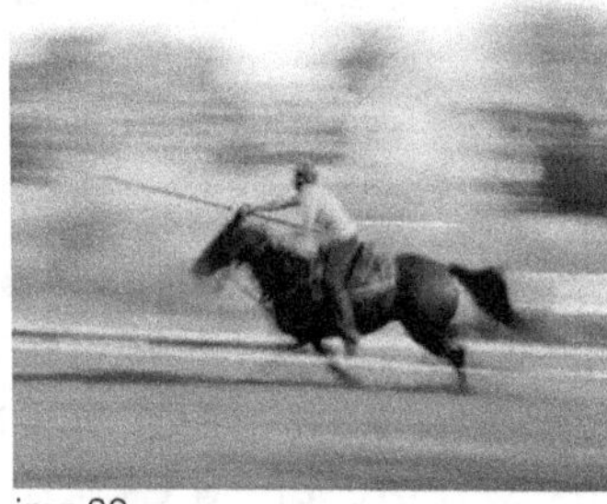

img.89

Panning (The Palio)

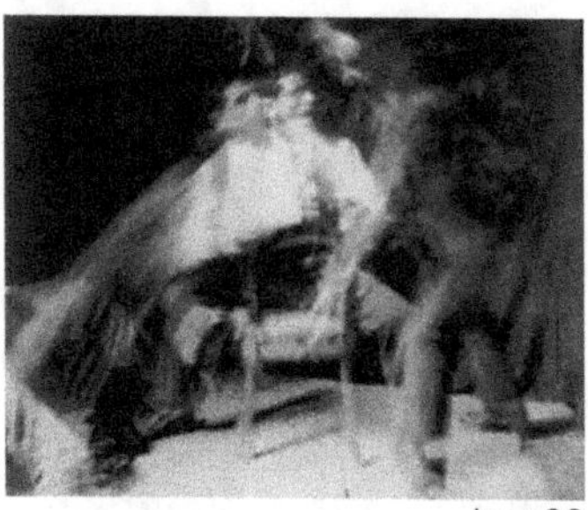

img.90

Photodynamism (The slap)

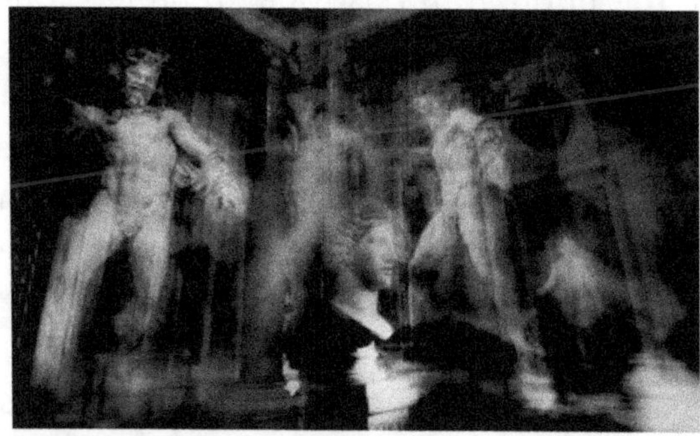

img.91

FoTotempismo (Dancing satyr)

With FoTotempismo, for the first time, the camera is moved significantly in space, with the aim of fixing onto the sensor multiple perspectives of the subject and environment to be represented. The author, moving the camera in the three spatial dimensions, engaging in a struggle with the mechanical unconscious, generates continuous micro-images giving life to traces of energy that testify to the resistance of the camera, with its mechanical unconscious, to energy expressed by the author. Subsequently, when the author decides to stop their movement, their action forces the mechanical means to represent the chosen perspective. The technical domain of the camera, with the programs that overwhelmingly determine the success of the photograph, is today redimensioned with FoTotempismo, attributing to the author all authorship of the result.

With FoTotempismo a new characteristic of photography is revealed that enables us to discover one that was pre-existing but not yet thoroughly examined; the *'technological subliminal'* concept present in all photographic systems is tackled.

The 'technological subliminal' concept consists in revealing all that the various components of the shooting system introduces into the 'management' of the subject,

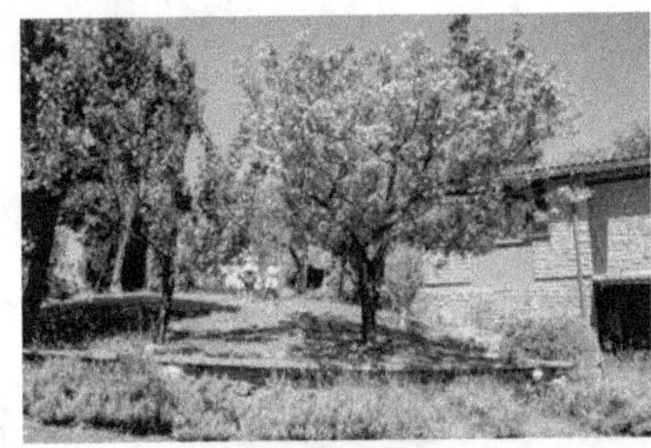

img.92

Scene represented with wide-angle lens

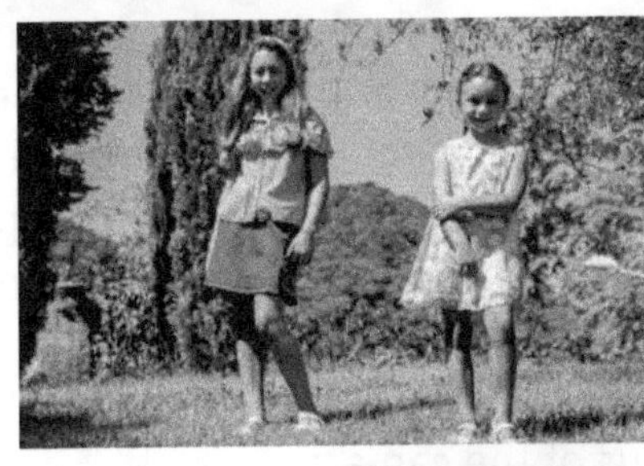

img.93

Scene represented with telephoto lens

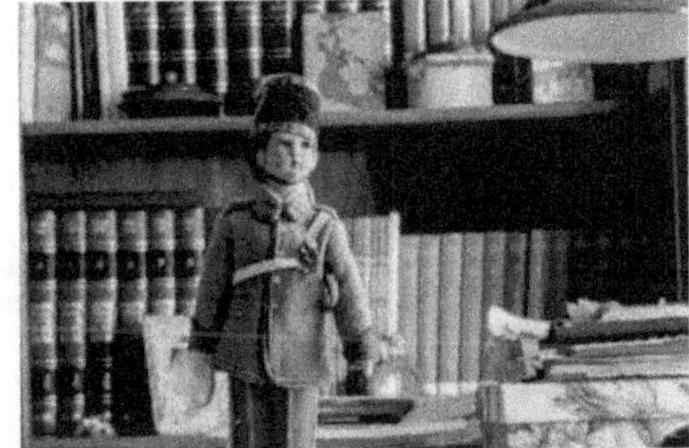

img.94

Subject taken with very small aperture

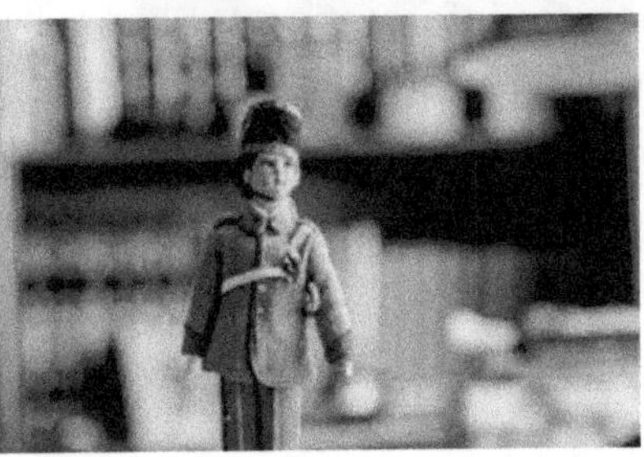

img.95

Subject taken with very wide aperture

during shooting the scene up to the final product, be it digital (e.g. JPG) or printed.

This means that subliminally the user of the photographs submits to everything that the lens proposes, such as: aberrations, geometric distortions, micro-blurring, micro-movements, focal lengths, blurring, lack of stereoscopy, lack of perception of the so-called 'corner of the eye' and last but not least, post-production and printing. All this is present in the photographic images which send us transformed messages compared to those of the real scene, leading the observer unknowingly to artificially obtain stimuli and sensations from the unconscious of the camera.

Now that the general concept of the *'technological subliminal'* has been clarified, we will examine the fototempistic concept, that intertwines with the technological but assumes its own valence in that component, which is the photosensitive sensor. So the *'fototempistic subliminal'*, which materializes to a decisive extent in the sensor and in a different way depending on the type, generates information subliminally during the 'struggle' between the author and the instrument, in a subliminal way, influencing the mood of the observer.

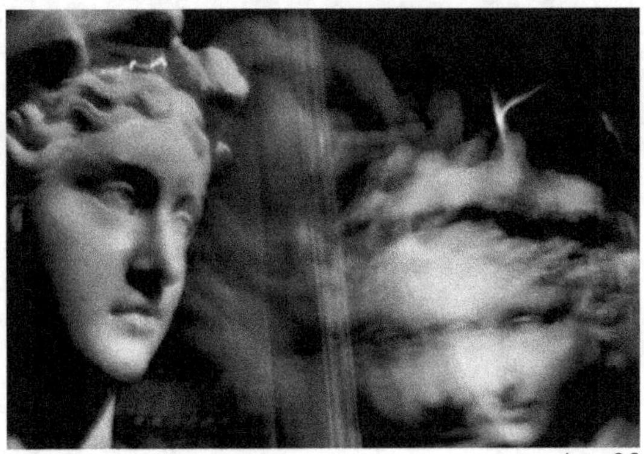

img.96

Subliminal with FoTotempismo (Ceres)

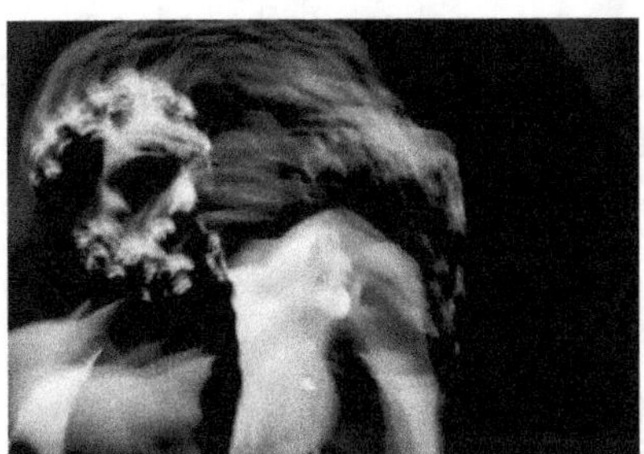

img.97

Subliminal with FoTotempismo (Hercules fighting)

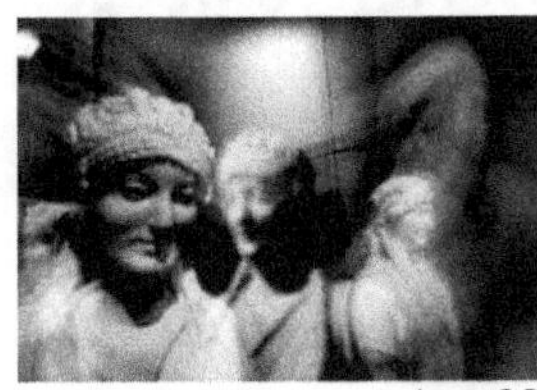

img.98

FoTotempismo (Hermae of Caryatid)

the concept

An important aspect of photography are the 'tensions' between scene-subject that are captured in the moment of shooting; these 'tensions' are already present in reality and the more sensitive the photographer is, the more they are expressed in the photograph. In addition to the 'tensions' implicit in the subject, with FoTotempismo the author introduces others according to the gesture that is carried out while shooting. In a portrait with a uniform background, which would not cause 'tensions', these result only from the face of the photographed subject and the light that highlights its features. Photographing the same subject with one of the techniques of FoTotempismo, the author's action introduces the energies that, opposing the staticity of the unconscious and mechanical optics of the camera, generate new images with strong, previously unknown 'tensions'.

In portraits you can compose images where the subject can dialogue with themself, turn around, move away, be positioned as if the soul were confronting the body. The sculptures, motionless and stationary over the centuries or millennia, 'move' in a surreal setting taking us back to the history of their origins.

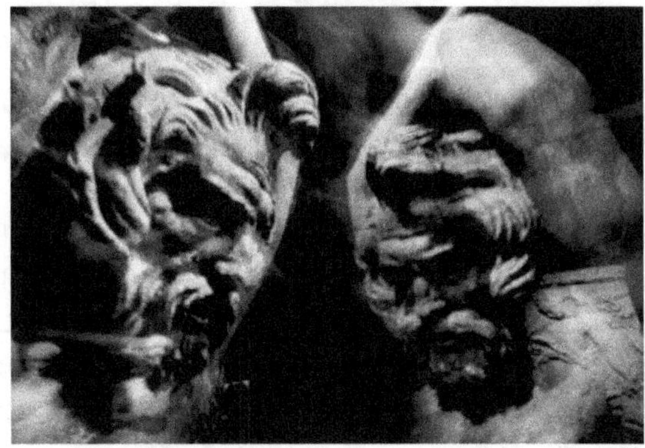

Tension in FoTotempismo (Marsia)

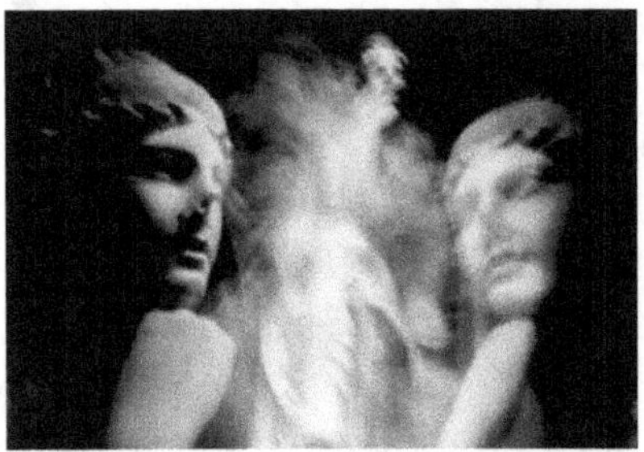

FoTotempismo (Thetis, female deity and Triton)

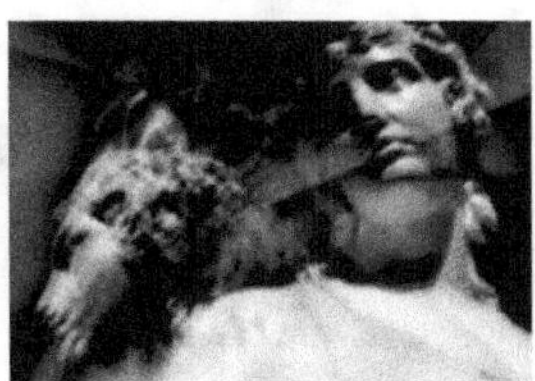

FoTotempismo (Eros and Thanatos)

reliving

In contrast to what Roland Barthes correctly claims on the concept of 'death' represented in photography, with FoTotempismo the subject appears to resume life, at least for the time of shooting and during the time it is observed. Below is what Barthes states:

"So here's where that particular sense of staticity comes from; that's what causes photography to resemble Death: the 'macabre' sense of a being without a future. The only thing available is a 'was', no longer modifiable."

In photography that fixes the moment and immobilizes the subject, Roland Barthes sees an excessive static nature of the moment, hence the feeling of macabre representation of the represented circumstance that no longer exists, now 'dead'. Indeed, photography represents one state that can no longer be edited, representing a moment past, no longer in existence.

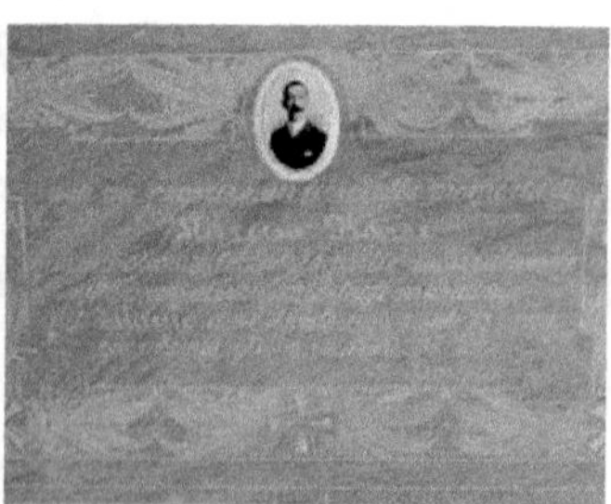

img.101

Still photo (an instant that is no longer; 'dead')

So here is what the 'Time' in FoTotempismo means: the greater the exposure time approaches zero, until reaching it, the less life there is, until it is completely annulled when the time equals zero. So, to have life in photographic representation, it is essential to move away from that unique static state, to move away from an exposure time approaching zero which 'freezes' the subject causing it 'to die' in that instant.

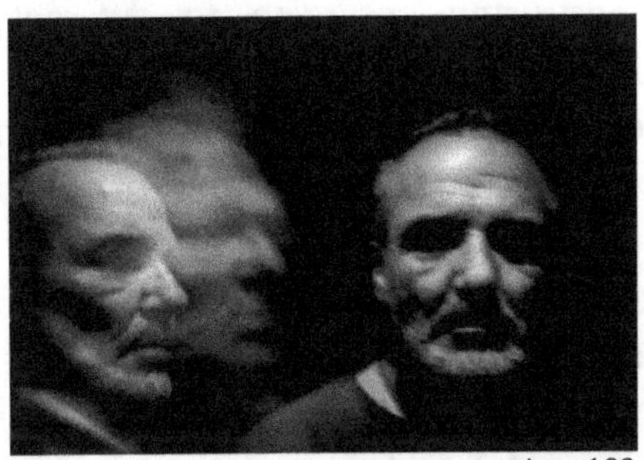

img.102

FoTotempismo (portrait that relives with every glance)

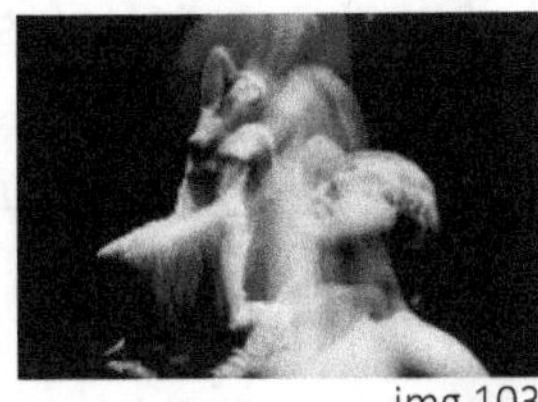

img.103

FoTotempismo (the statues come to life)

the 'Sign'

Already in the second decade of the twentieth century the Russian philosopher, mathematician, physicist and theologian *Pavel Aleksandrovič Florenskjĭ*, indicated the valence of time in figurative representations with the following:

> *"It is entirely possible that physical time has certain characteristics and that the other time has others that we will rediscover in a work of art. We must thus expect different times, constructed according to different typologies, like what happens for spaces in a work of art".*

The concept of time thus represented is separate from time of physical vision and reality compared to that which can be observed in a work of art, highlighting the expressive difference of the time of the emotions from that of the physical. In FoTotempismo the 'two Times' intertwine, merging with the 'two Spaces' involved, becoming indissolubly 'Space-Time'.

In contrast to all the theories that connect photography to the pictorial discipline is American, *Rosalind Epstein Krauss*, art critic, curator and professor of art history, who states:

> *"...but its worth, as *Walter Benjamin* wrote, is always given by the photographer's relationship with his/her own technique".*

FoTotempismo can only confirm this concept, "photography is not painting, but with the introduction of the essential components of the 'Gesture' and the 'Sign', it enters fully into artistic disciplines".

The 'Gesture' is the decisive physical action that traces the 'Sign' onto the sensor as if it were one flat surface or a volume to 'inscribe'.

Franco Vaccari's statement:

> *"Photography is really such if it helps us to discover what we do not know instead of confirming what we already know",*

thereby opening up new scenarios for the interpretation of innovations introduced by FoTotempismo.

So here are the innovations brought to photography from the concept of FoTotempismo: representation of perspective multidimensionality of space in time, introduction of the 'Gesture' of the author and representation of the 'Sign', bringing new revelations to light.

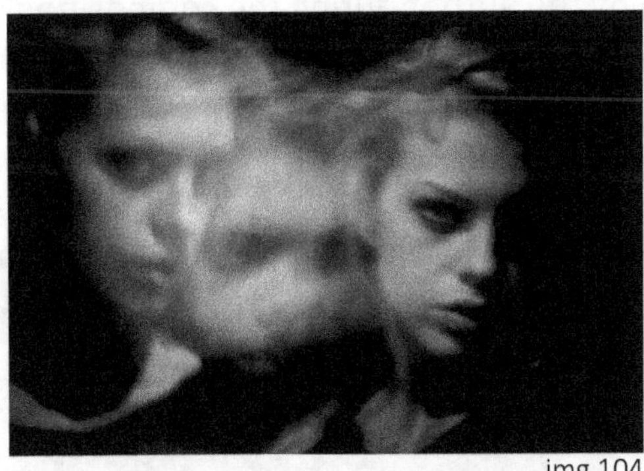

img.104

FoTotempismo, time and space not of physics (Portrait)

FoTotempismo
the 'Gesture'

Since the first formulation of FoTotempismo to represent non-perspective space photographically, precise characteristics emerged which presented themselves
in the image produced. The first characteristic, the one that inspired, was the representation of multiple perspectives with dematerialization, destruction and rematerialization of the photographed subject (img.106). This characteristic was obtained by moving in space with the camera shutter open *(fig.4)*.

The movement of the camera managed by the operator, according to his/her creativity, would become the gesture that took place during a single photographic act. Consequently, from the 'Gesture', the 'Sign' is generated, that is, that trace that derives from the physical action performed by the author during the composition of the work. Therefore, a 'Sign' of unique, personal nature of the author derived from an equally unique 'Gesture'. Hence the uniqueness of the almost irreplicable work.

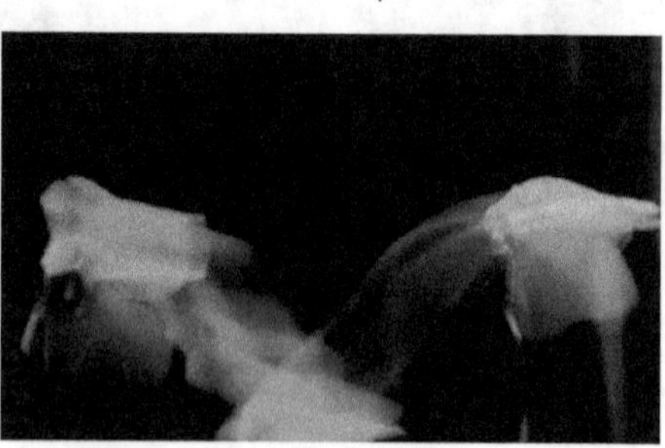

img.105

*Cyclamen
first image in
FoTotempismo
complete with all
the characteristics
of the concept*

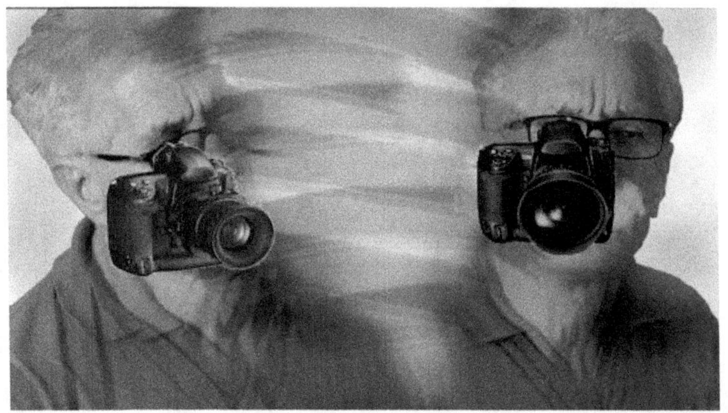

img.106

Simulation of shooting in FoTotempismo

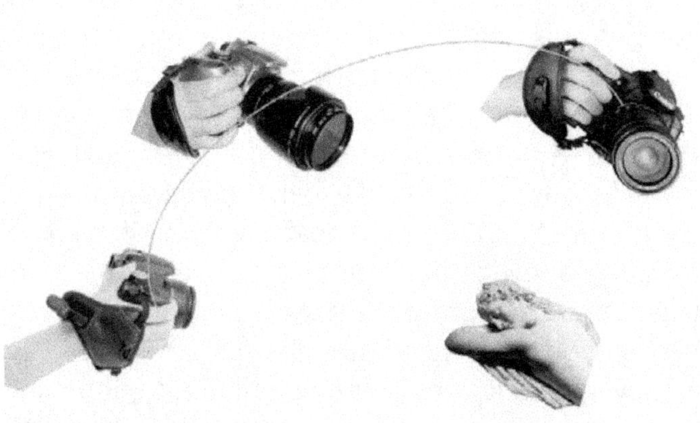

fig.4

Diagram of shooting in FoTotempismo

The elements characterizing FoTotempismo are shown in figure 5 (facing page). In this case the object was a cyclamen placed on my desk and illuminated by a table lamp. In the sections outlined in red, the subject is represented from its different perspectives, in the blue section its dematerialization can be seen, arriving at its destruction, represented in the purple rectangles, to then begin its re-materialization in the green area and finally the representation of its new perspective indicated by the red circle. In this image the 'Gesture' of the author produced these traces, packaged in a way to determine its 'Sign'. From the first image in FoTotempismo, new forms of tensions have emerged generated by the subject in new interrelationships with itself. In the image of the cyclamen, the background is dark but other backgrounds can be just as creative and interesting, depending on what the author wishes to express.

The first portrait of a human figure was carried out on a set with a black background and all the fototempistic characteristics were made explicit. However, it is action and gesture that determine that a work is fototempistic, revealing, above all, multiple perspectives. Some studies have started to represent architecture in broad daylight, moments of everyday life and street photography in daylight. Pictures require different approaches depending on the case and the type of lighting, thus making the challenge to achieve new communicative emotions so stimulating.

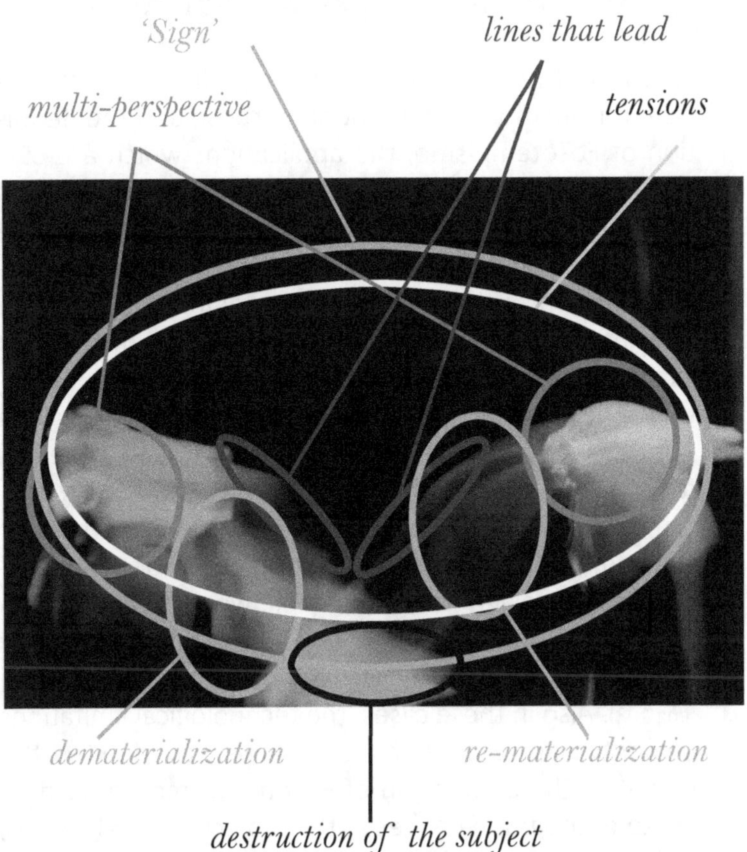

fig.5

Diagram of the components of FoTotempismo

FoTotempismo

developments

Following the initial discussion regarding the conception, formulation, the intended purpose and the definition of FoTotempismo, the applications which are currently feasible are analyzed below, with hypotheses for future developments. With the means currently available on the market the results achieved show great potential for this new way of photographing.

The images produced to date have been made with exposure times ranging from one second to four minutes. There are no difficulties in terms of increasing the duration of the exposure time, it is, however, different for a reduction of the minimum time; in this case special equipment is needed that allows the movement of the camera in space to be managed. As for the physical space involved in fototempistic work, distances of a few centimeters in the *still life* (img.107) and a few tens of meters in architectural photography have been explored (img.108). Also in these cases, the technological limitations of photographic equipment available have limited the extent of the application of FoTotempismo. In particular, to photograph images at the molecular level (img.109) extremely fast nano cameras and movements are required, which are not manageable manually, since they are all sized for microscopic environments. Similarly, to explore macroscopic environments, special means are needed to cover vast, even 'cosmic', spaces (img.111).

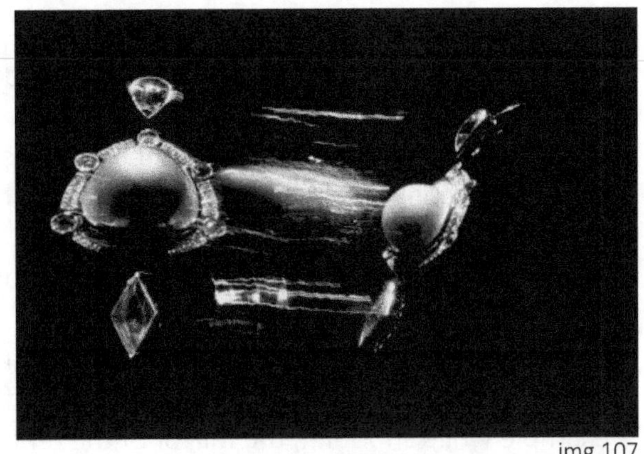

Jewellery by LoveLook (small spaces and short times)

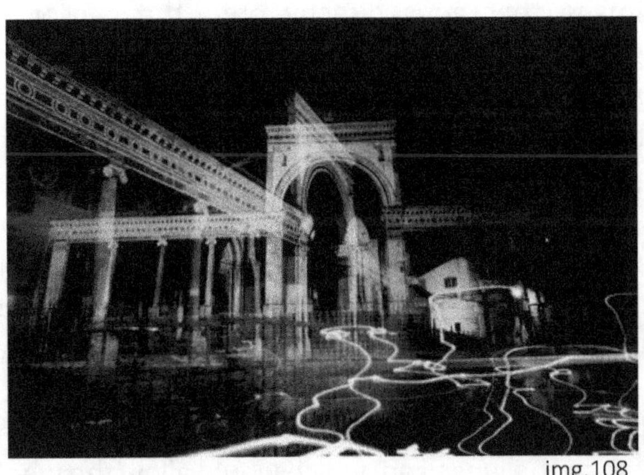

Architecture (large spaces and long times)

From these considerations it is possible to perceive the great extension of spaces, times, genres and styles in which FoTotempismo can be applied. This new way of photographing allows the author all the creative possibilities as in conventional photography, and allows others to emerge, all to be discovered. From the first experiences, the need to visually follow the whole scene during the shoot was evident, unfortunately most cameras don't permit this and create real difficulties; for example while shooting, the mirror of the reflex rises from its position obscuring vision, while in mirrorless cameras the image is visible in the optical viewfinder, if fitted, and not on the display.

To date, the scene to be photographed can only be followed where the view in the viewfinder is independent of the image that goes directly onto the sensor, as the images on the sensors are never displayed during shooting. This technical limitation greatly affects the possibility of facilitating the composition of the scene while shooting. In these cases, the application of a so-called 'sports viewfinder' on the flash holder shoe can help. It is safe to assume that in the near future some camera manufacturer will provide the ability to see the subject being shot throughout the duration of the exposure; but an ideal solution to all these needs that currently greatly hinder shooting, would be an ocular viewer with the same focal length as the lens used, which would allow the whole scene to be followed during the shot.

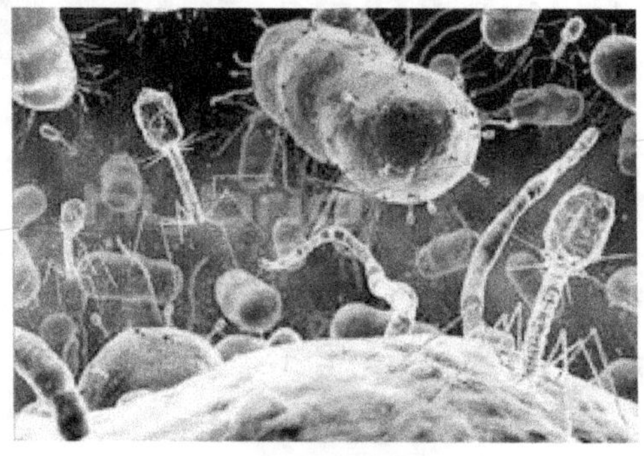

img.109

Microscopic objects in space

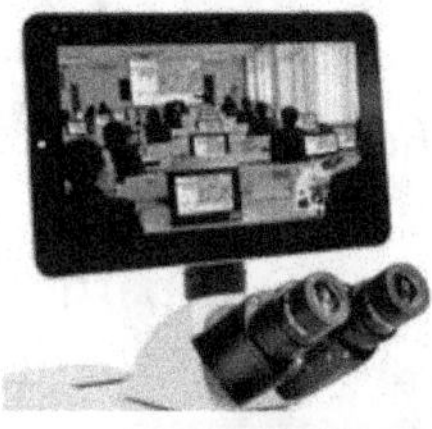

img.110

Sub-molecular camera

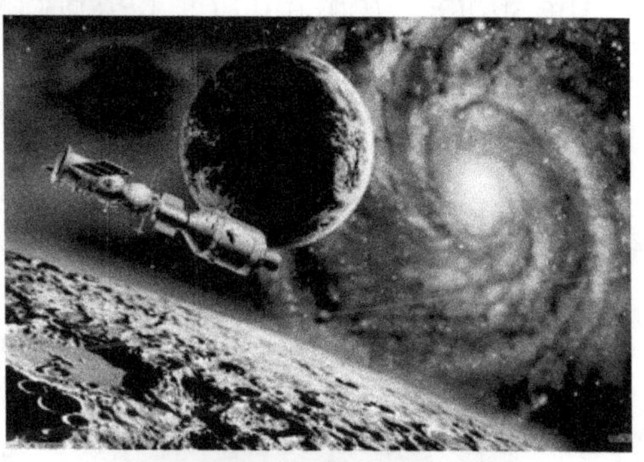

img.111

Macroscopic objects in space

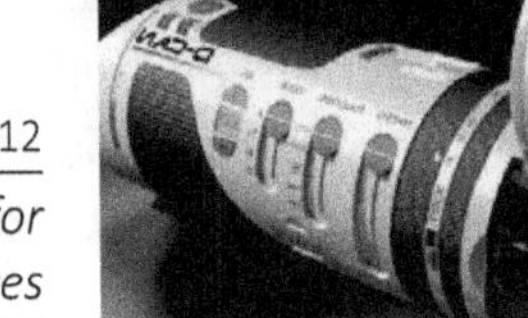

img.112

Camera for vast distances

FoTotempismo

dissimilarities

Before proceeding with how to shoot in FoTotempismo, some similarities that could emerge by observing the images created with this technique will be analyzed.

Among the first similarities, could be the concept of the *'Demolition of the Renaissance perspective'*. In fact in 1885 during full Impressionism, *Paul Cezanne* painted *Monte Sainte Victoire* where in particular the vertical overlapping planes are arranged to induce analysis of the subject from multiple perspectives, sometimes with minimal shifts, thus demolishing the representation of the subject from a single perspective.

FoTotempismo does not foresee demolition of the image as conceptualized by Paul Cézanne, but aims to make the representation 'Multi-perspective' with continuous space-time translation even where there are short shooting displacements.

Another element that could emerge as a similarity is the concept of Simultaneity by Umberto Boccioni, discussed in his book, *'Futurist Sculpture Painting'* 1914: *"the condition in which the various elements that make up dynamism appear".*

In the images in FoTotempismo the concept of Simultaneity is not present; what can look like the contemporary representation of multiple subject positions is actually the space-time representation of the displacement of the view of the subject generated by the author.

And again, Pablo Picasso's Cubism with its representations of multiple perspectives of the subject in the same image, could lead one to equate it with the continuous perspectives of FoTotempismo.
In Cubism, only fragments of reality of different perspectives are represented, which the observer reconstructs mentally.

In contrast, in FoTotempismo, reality is actually represented with continuity of space and time, even where there are dematerializations and re-materializations created by the speed of representation.

The introduction of this new space-time variable of FoTotempismo is a fact that does not concern only the construction of the image, but also its interpretation. These images cannot be read and understood with a quick glance, they must instead be perceived with a precise reading time, that required to analyze the individual parts, to arrive gradually at understanding every detail of the subject and its overall space-time meaning.

FoTotempismo

how to implement it

After the exploration of time
with Bragaglia's Photodynamics, arrives also
the exploration of space with FoTotempismo.

It was clear from first formulating FoTotempismo that to photograph the third dimension (three-dimensionality not just perspective) the camera had to be moved while shooting *(fig.6)*. The simplest and most readily available subjects to photograph were the objects on the desk in my studio or those in an everyday environment.

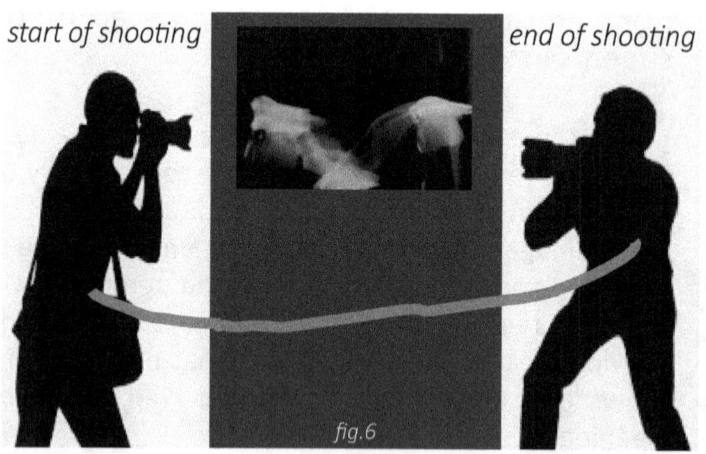

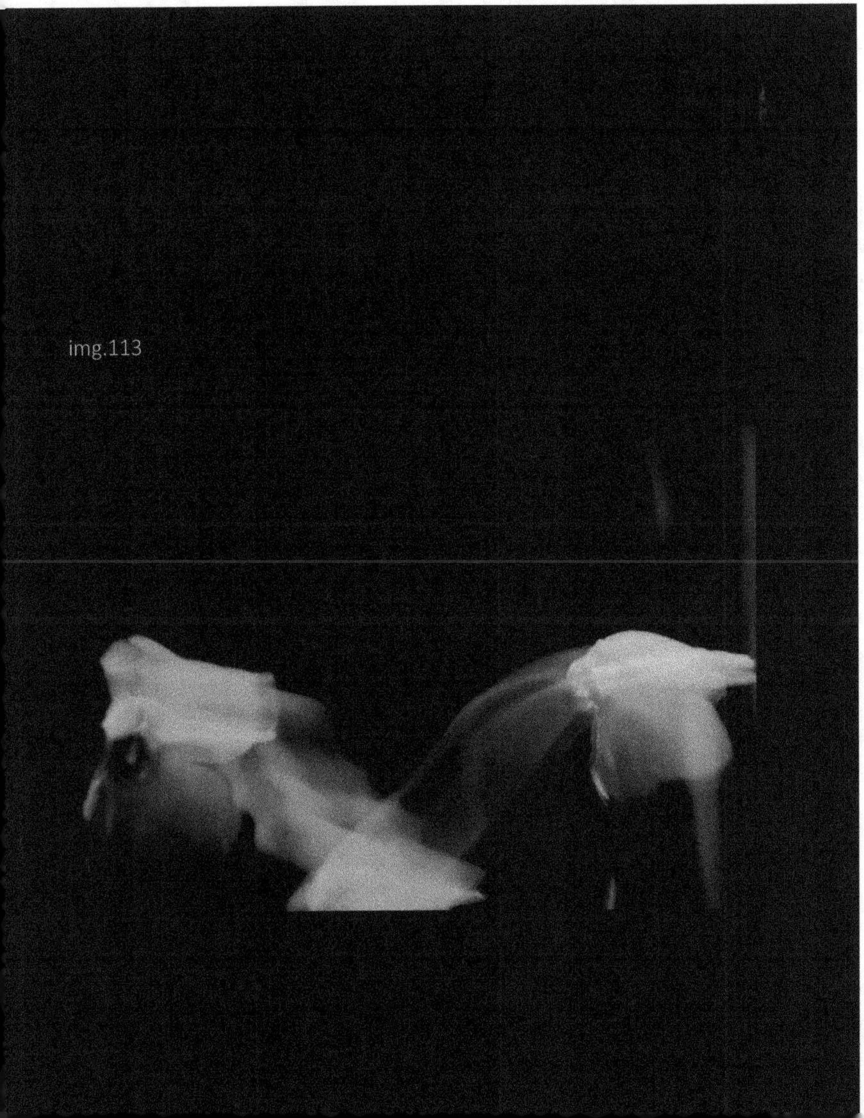

img.113

The first available subject for the first photograph were some flowers, more precisely, the one that was most successful in FoTotempismo was a cyclamen (img.113). The first image was produced freehand, holding my breath throughout the shoot.
Before you start shooting in FoTotempismo, you have to plan what to include in the image. In this case, the simplest representation of FoTotempismo was chosen, the basic. I wanted to represent this concept depicting only two different perspectives with the evidence of dematerialization, all with a single shot. So the duration of the photographic act would have to be divided into at least three stages. In the first stage of the action, lasting about a third of the total time, the subject from one perspective was framed; in the second stage the camera had to move in space to achieve the designated final perspective; in the final stage, relating to about the last third of the shot, I had to stop to frame the subject thus ending the shooting. The result was surprising as can be seen on the previous page. The two perspectives can be seen clearly as well as dematerialization. The scene appears against a dark background, while the cyclamen was illuminated by a table lamp.
After taking the first photograph in FoTotempismo, others were then carried out, always on small objects. At this point repeatability of the technique could be considered to photograph all genres, even

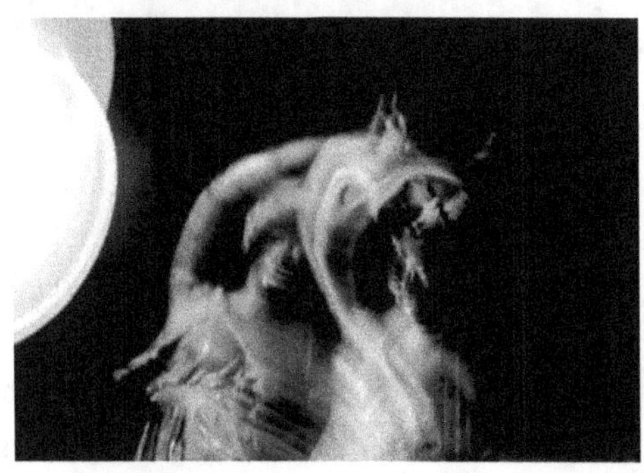

img.114

Glare, lights and festivities

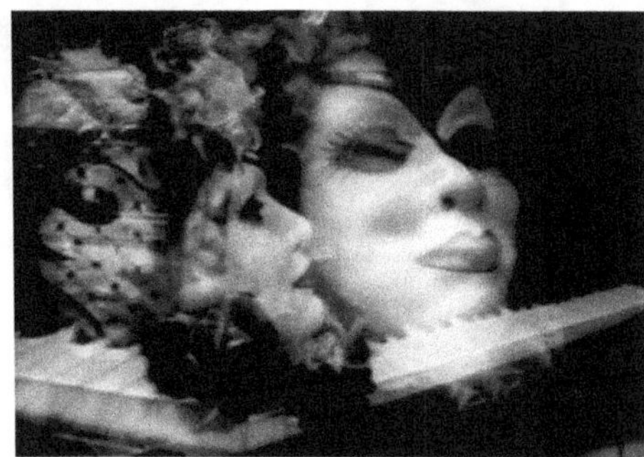

img.115

Fascinating falsehood

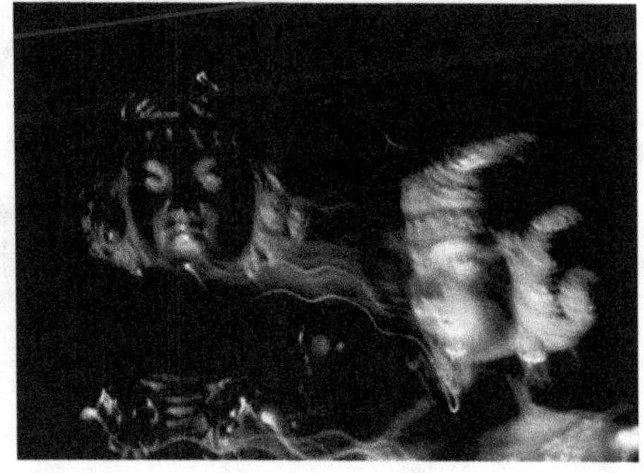

img.116

We grow, we understand

portraits (img.117, 118, 119).

The only thing that changed was the subject and its dimensions that forced me to travel over more space during shooting. This circumstance called for greater stability during initial and final shooting, which, however, left me various possibilities to impress the 'Gesture' by moving the camera freely in space. In carrying out the action you could make use of a monopod or tripod to aid stability of the camera during shooting stops; but in the photographs of people or objects of these dimensions, I preferred to shoot freehand. In this way I felt I was totally shaping the 'Sign' obtained with my gesture guiding the camera into the composition of the image, without however detracting anything from it compared to the use of stabilizing aids.

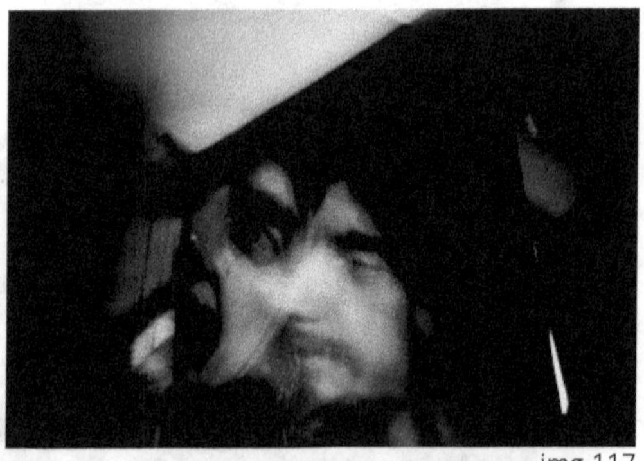

img.117

Portrait with light and dark background

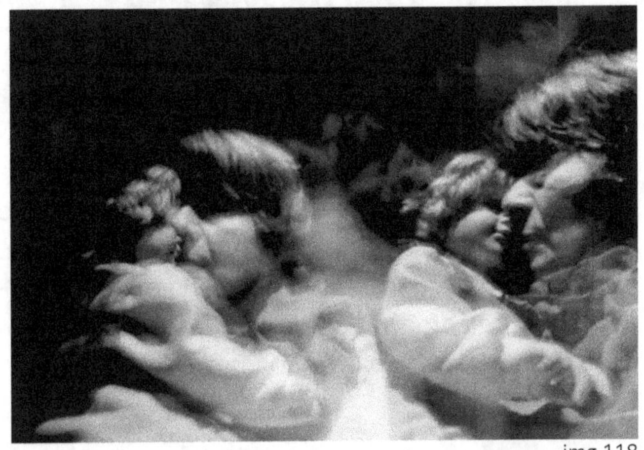

img.118

Portrait with doll

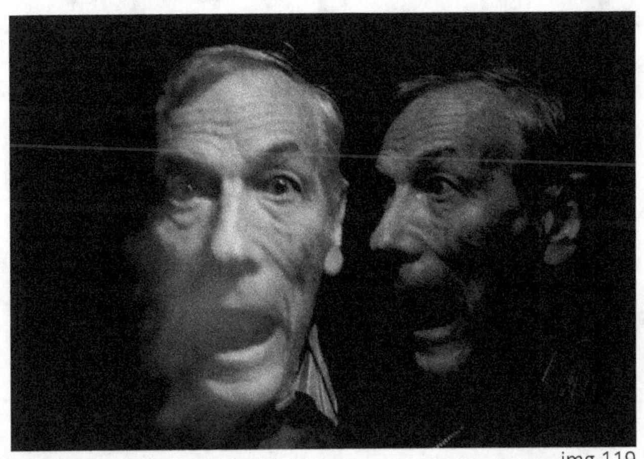

img.119

Portrait of Gianpiero Ascoli, expert in photography and in FoTotempismo

Figure 7 shows the basic technical diagram of a typical shot, in this case it is applied to taking a portrait. The angle traveled by the camera represented in the diagram is indicative and is at the discretion of the author according to personal creativity. The composition of the image, both at the beginning, during and at the end of the path (img.121), is part of the composition desired by the author in function of the message to convey. (img.122-123).

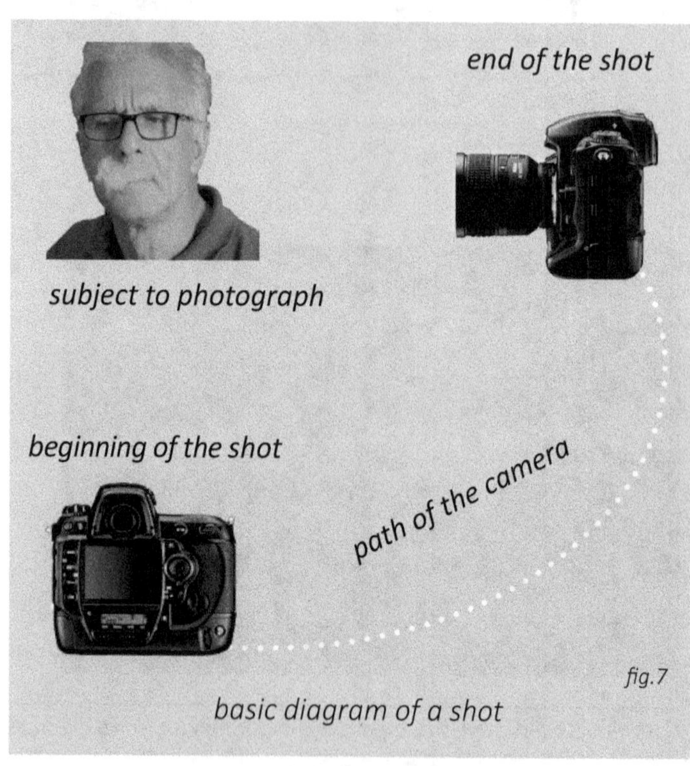

basic diagram of a shot

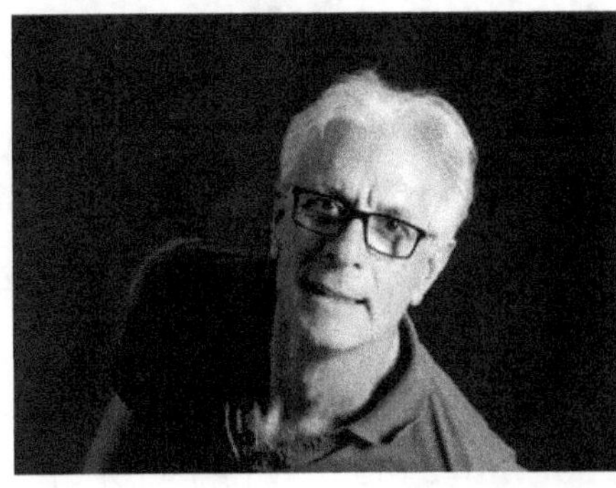

img.120

Subject to be portrayed in FoTotempismo

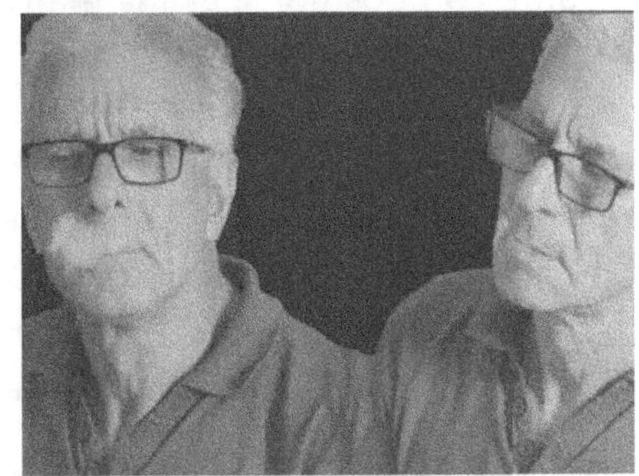

img.121

Expected image at the start and end of shooting

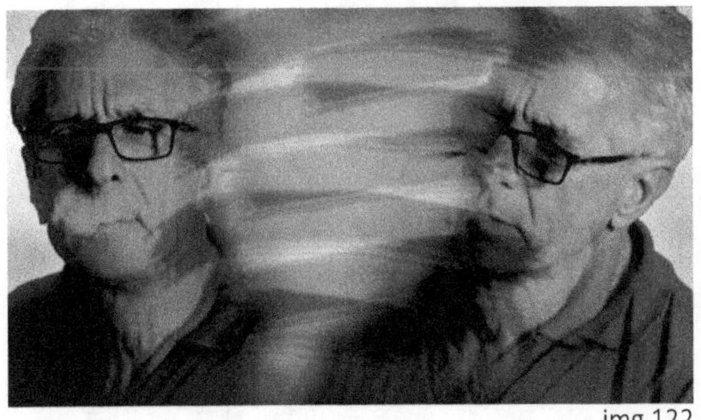

img.122

The expected 'Sign' left by the 'Gesture'

In the following lines I will do everything possible to explain my experiences so that these can form the basis on which to continue to explore all the possibilities of FoTotempismo.

'Composition' in FoTotempismo is similar to composition in conventional photography applied to all the desired stops of the camera, but with a multiplying factor of the same compositions, giving many more opportunities to pack the message than with a single photo taken in a single shot. In addition to the images captured from the stops there is the sign that enriches the message, with that charisma that each author leaves in their work.

So, the composition, according to the diagram in figure 7, could be done with a 20-50 watt halogen lamp on a dark background, following this procedure:

• frontal shot for about a second,
• move the camera about 90° following a path over one second (with or without micro-stop and dictated by the author's inspiration),
• arrive with the camera in the space where the shot will end,
• frame and pause for about a second, or better until the end of the pre-set opening time of the shutter.

In this case the camera was set to manual, f / 16, t / 3'', ISO at a minimum, focal length 36mm.

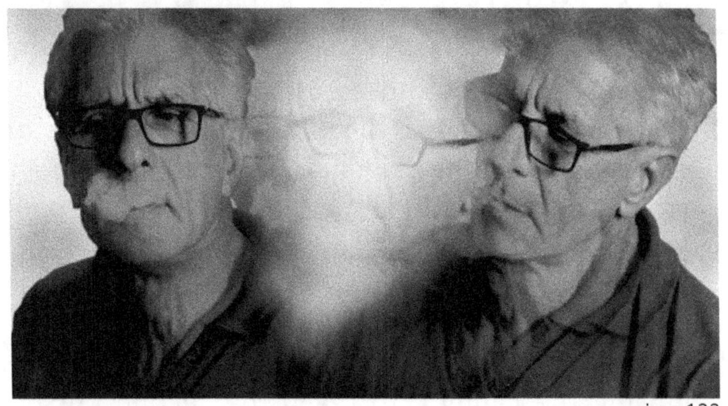

img.123

Expected image of start and end of shooting with intermediate stop

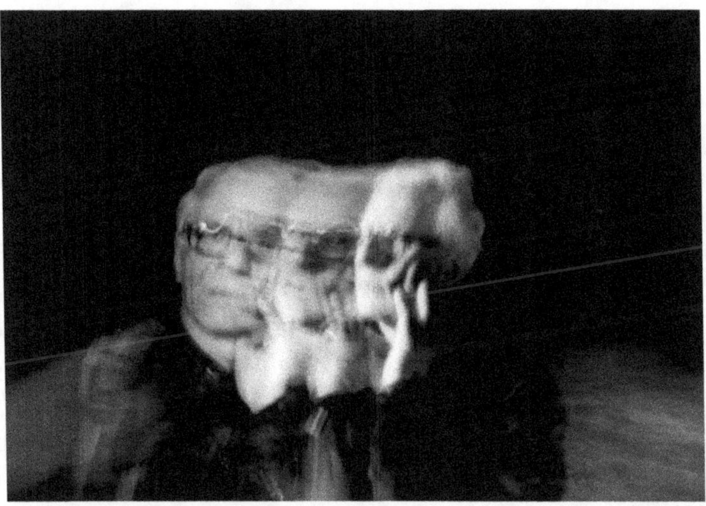

img.124

Freehand portrait in FoTotempismo by a student during the first workshop

Knowing how to compose a frame according to the rules of photography, such as: the rule of thirds, the golden section, the diagonals, the masses, space not space and others; the same rules can also be applied when photographing in FoTotempismo.

Taking into consideration the representation of image 125, in the first stop the subject was placed in the first third to the left of the sensor, then while moving the camera, to reach the second perspective, the camera was rotated on itself in order to represent all the dematerialization and re-materialization of the subject and finally placing it to the right of the sensor.

This description of the shot is just one way to clarify how to obtain a photograph that can represent all the features of the fototempistic concept. As in all disciplines, both creative and artistic, it is then up to the author how to express a message and information, using: blurring, backlight, various compositions and others.

The technique described above was also used to represent the jewels in image 126. In this circumstance a support was used for the object and an arm to anchor the camera, to have more stable stops than freehand. In image 126b, the so-called 'masking' technique, denominated '*MCMS*', was also implemented during the move start action of the camera, which will be discussed later.

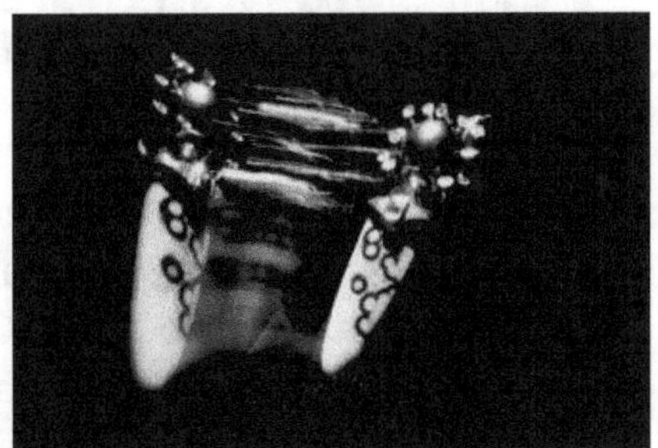

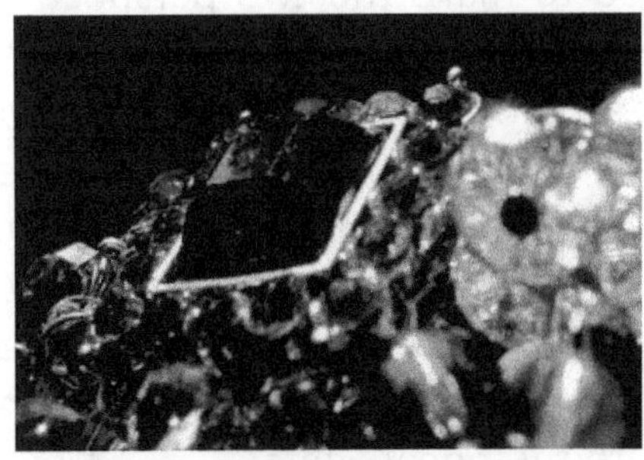

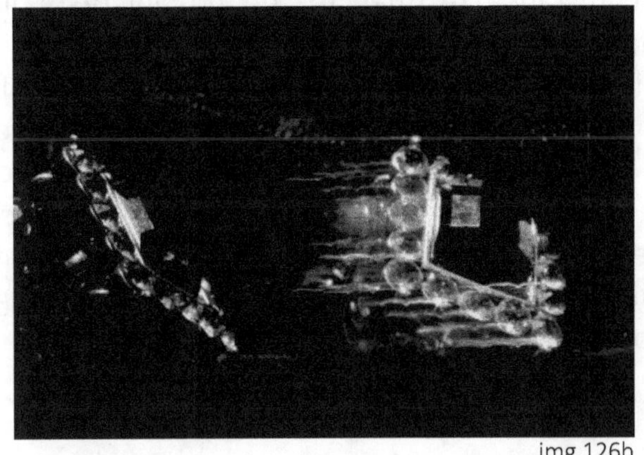

Still life (shooting in small spaces and short times)

In representing architectural structures as a subject in FoTotempismo, the same technique was used, but I allowed myself to be inspired by the subject.

The arch of the portico of the Cathedral of Santa Maria Maggiore, Duomo dei Cosmati, in Civita Castellana (img.127), was the inspiration for the composition, and so the author wanted to make the two perspectives intersect, by making them coincide precisely in the arc. The resulting representation (img.128) is suggestive, with a valid aesthetic expression and with all those composition values which are contained in various photographic types. The light trails increase the evocativeness, which in addition to being generated by the action of moving the camera, are also due to the movement of cars with their headlights.

This circumstance testifies to the possibility of introducing subjects in motion into the images in FoTotempismo, giving completeness to the concept. In these photographs the non-perspective representation of space and time that the author experiences integrate with other expressive forms of time, such as movement of the subject, blurring and movement, confirming itself as the most complete form of photography to date.

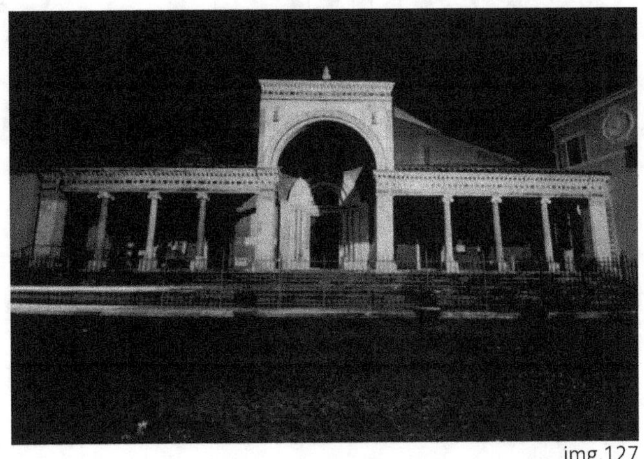

img.127

still photo, Duomo dei Cosmati, Civita Castellana (VT)

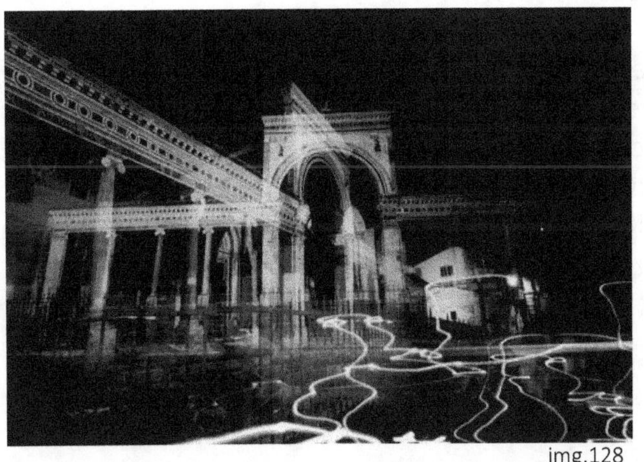

img.128

FoTotempismo, Architecture, large spaces with long exposure times

The exploration of space with FoTotempismo; the *Gesture* that generates the *Sign*

To represent any concept you need a technique, therefore more ways have been devised and developed to operate and manage the camera to represent FoTotempismo, by simply moving it in Space-Time. In the description of the various techniques developed to date, I also wanted to specify the manoeuvres carried out with the camera which do not, however, represent FoTotempismo.

The technique in handling the camera is not intended as a camera setting technique, or that of the lenses, sensors, software or technology exposure and shooting in conventional photography, but all this technical knowledge consolidated up to now, is necessary and applicable to implement the fototempistic concept and technique.

To clarify, the differences between the techniques and concepts of creative blurring that are not FoTotempismo will be considered.

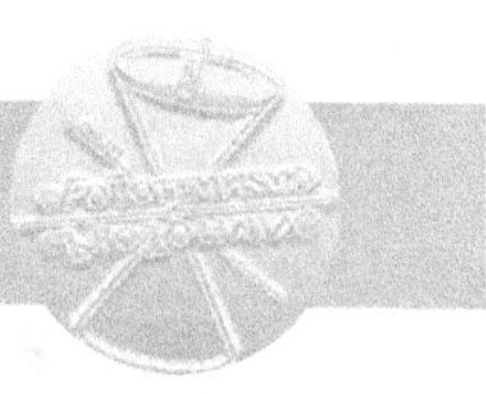

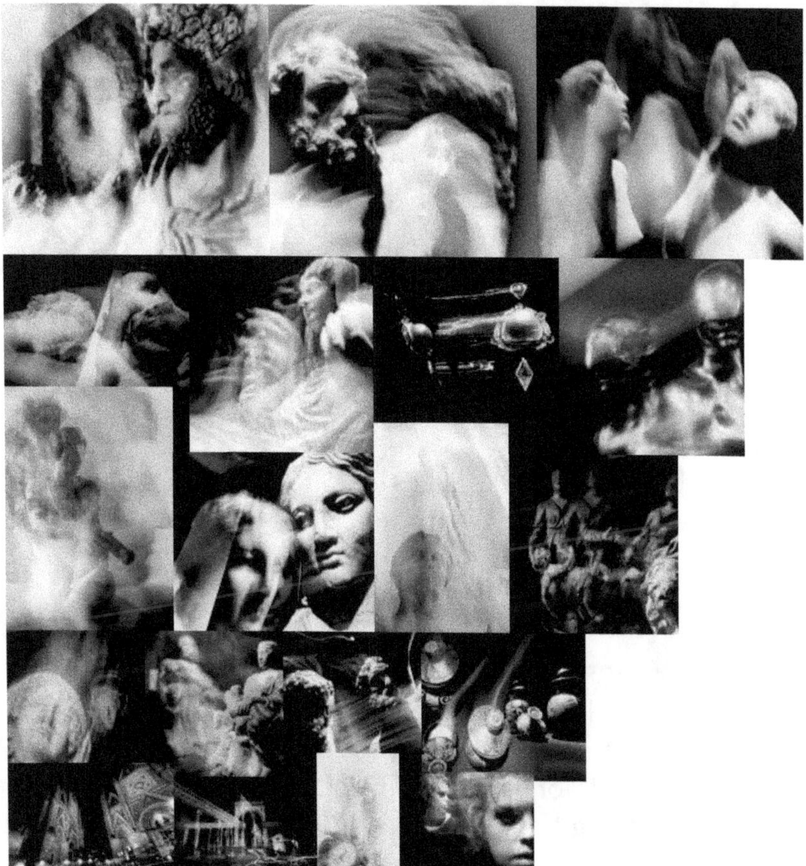

simply tilting the camera is NOT FoTotempismo

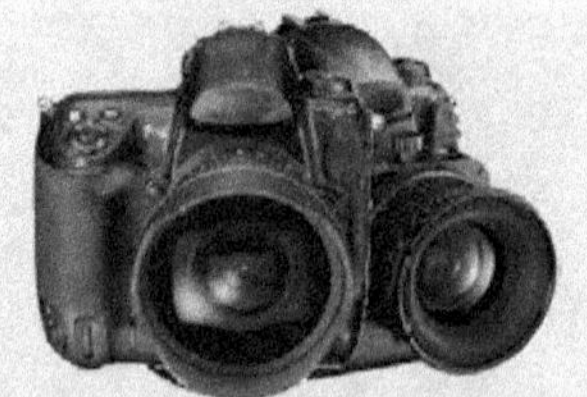

horizontal tilt of the camera

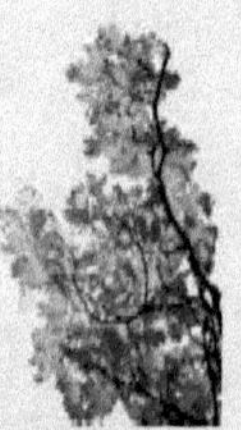

fig.8

subject to be photographed still or in motion

The diagram in figure 8 represents the movement of tilting the camera horizontally during shooting of the still or moving subject, shot with a slow shutter opening time. In image 129 beautiful oaks in autumn are suggestively represented.

The shot was carried out in broad daylight with an aperture of f/13 and an exposure time t1/8''. The operator tilted the camera from left to right. The graphic effect obtained is the enlargement of the bodies horizontally giving the impression of movement. In this case there is no change of perspective, or it is so minimal that its value is inconsistent, indeed zero. The principle is the same as how the background of Panning is represented, where time should be even slower to detach the moving subject which would be represented as still. This kind of shooting generates fascinating images; it is the first approach to enter the world of photography with a slow shooting time. This and other camera movements, which while being exploratory of the image, and that the eye does not see, will lead to FoTotempismo;

but the images generated with these techniques do not depict the concept of FoTotempismo.

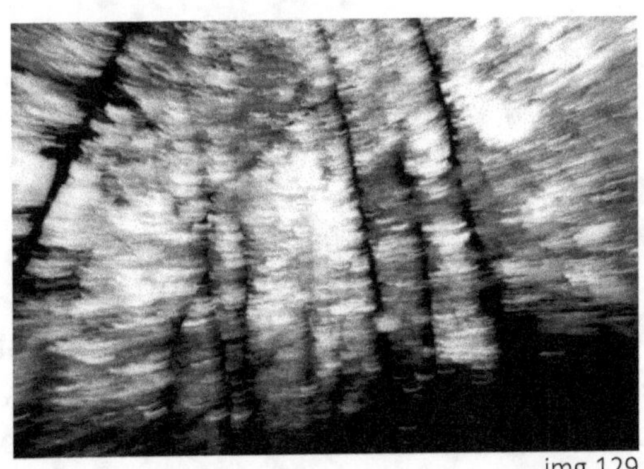

img.129

'Oaks' horizontal tilt of the camera

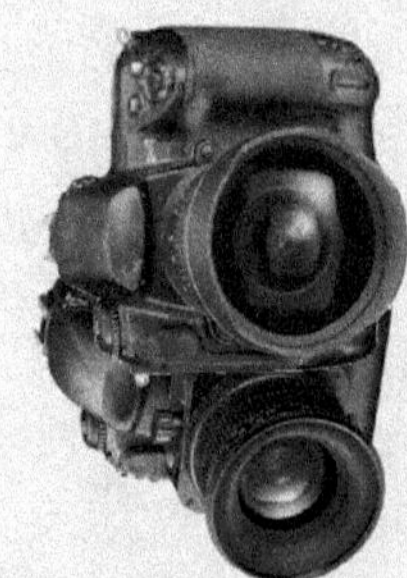

vertical tilt of the camera

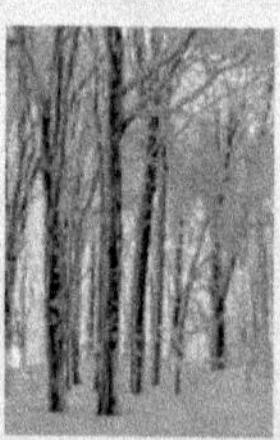

fig.9

subject to be photographed still or in motion

By tilting the camera vertically, interesting and suggestive photographs can be obtained, as in the previous case. In this circumstance the images lengthen if their shape is vertical and widen if they are horizontal (img.130).

Tilting can also be carried out by moving the camera diagonally, obtaining a representation which is the combination of the two orthogonal tilts (img.131). In figure 9 the pattern of vertical tilting during shooting is represented. The images below are an example of the results that can be obtained.

Also in this case, shooting generates a blurred image whether the subject is stationary or in motion; so the camera does not significantly travel through space during the shooting time, which despite being slow **does not generate an image in FoTotempismo, but in ICM.**

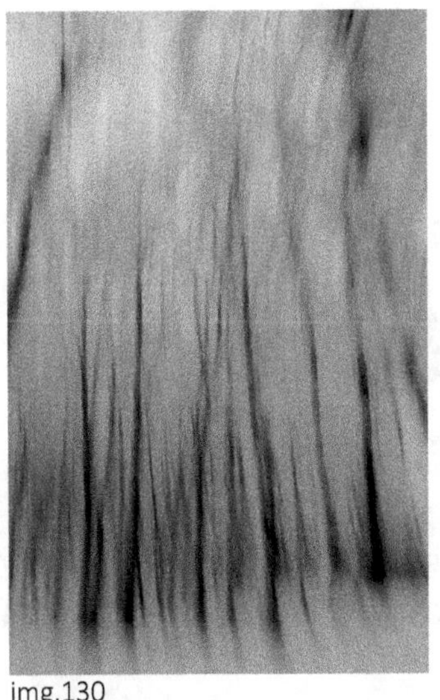

img.130

img.131

'Beeches' and 'portrait', vertical and oblique tilting of the camera

FoTotempismo is not

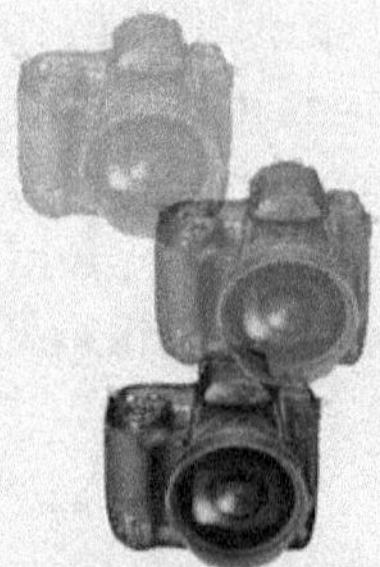

circular movement of the camera

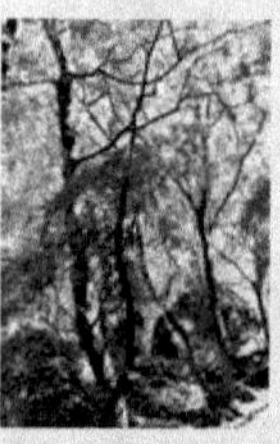

fig.10

subject to be photographed still or moving

Figure 10 shows the diagram in which the camera makes a circular movement perpendicular, or almost, to its axis of shooting. As in previous shots, the shutter speed is slow relative to the speed of rotation of the camera.

Subjects can be stationary, but if they are moving this is integrated with the movement of the camera and the images thus produced take on a circular dynamicity. In the case of circular motion a nice effect is achieved, which generates small circles for each point of the subject whose width is determined by the movement of the camera. By properly calculating times, speeds and the amplitude of movement, suggestive representations are generated, as in images 132 and 133, **but they are not FoTotempismo**.

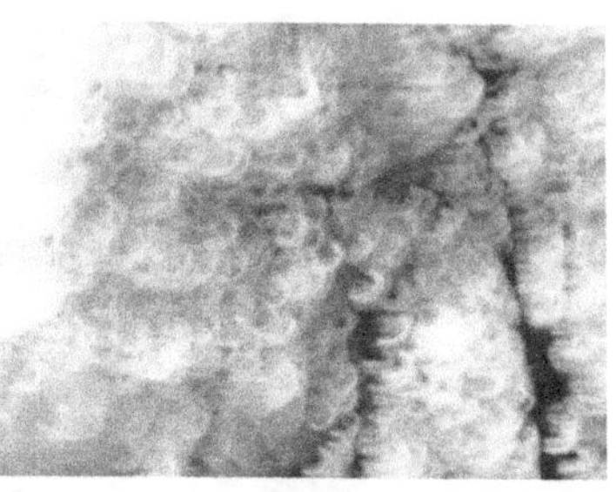

img.132

'Trees' circular camera movement

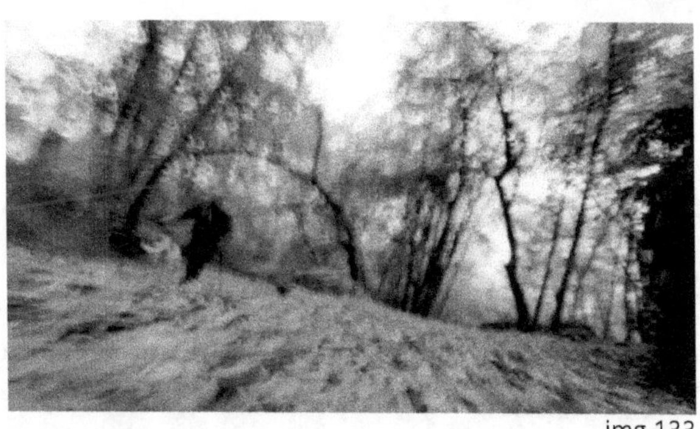

img.133

'Trees' circular camera movement

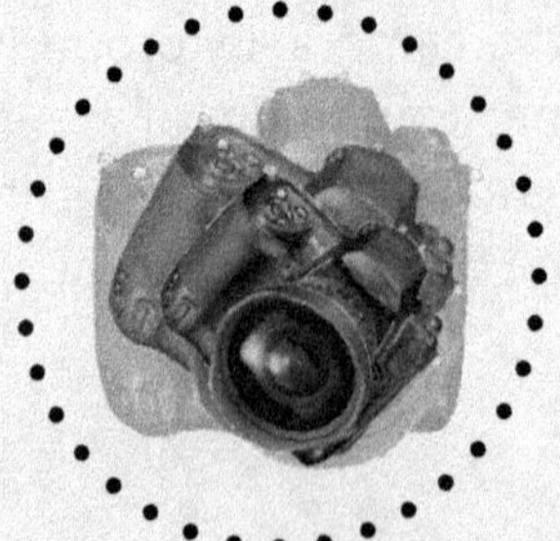

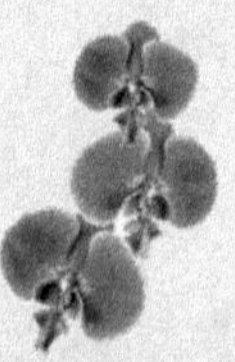

fig.11

Figure 11 shows the diagram in which the camera makes a perpendicular rotation movement to its axis of shooting. As in previous shots, the shutter speed is slow in relation to the camera rotation speed. Subjects can be stationary, but if they are in motion this is additional to camera rotation. Pictures produced in this way assume a rotatory dynamism; with this type of shooting, i.e. turning the camera perpendicularly to the central axis of the lens, the images produced will be represented as in images 134 and 135.

Also in this case, the appropriate movement-time combination determines an image which can be more or less interesting.

But even this type of shooting is not FoTotempismo.

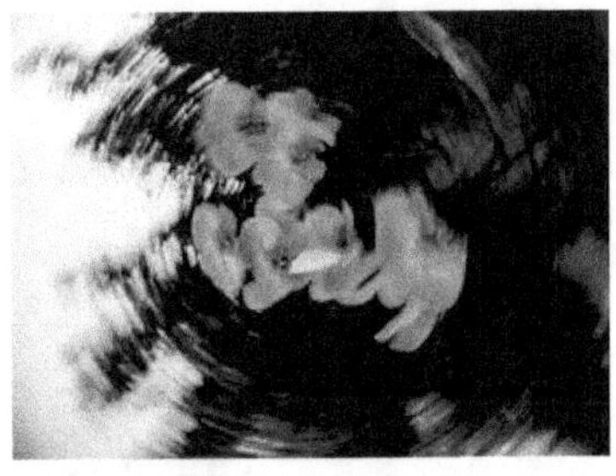

img.134

'Orchid'
rotating camera movement

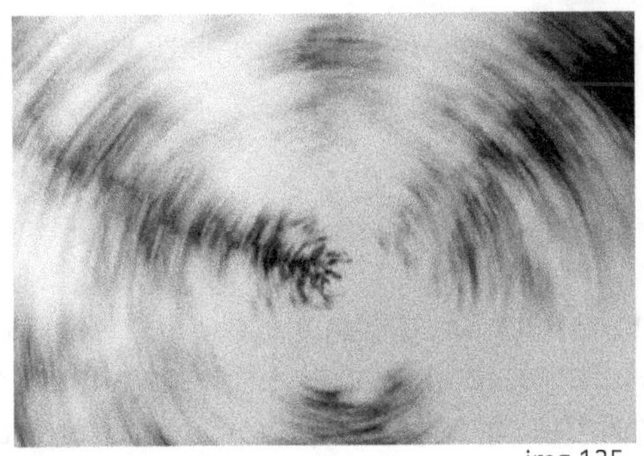

img.135

'Trees' rotating camera movement

FoTotempismo is not *Photodynamism*

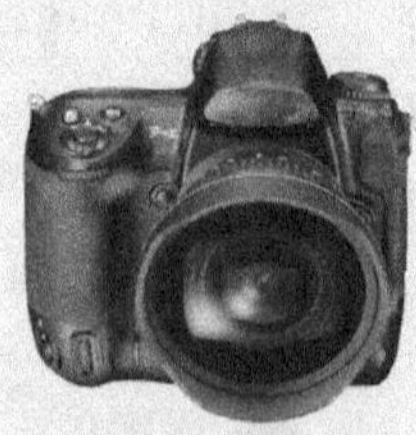

still camera during slow shooting

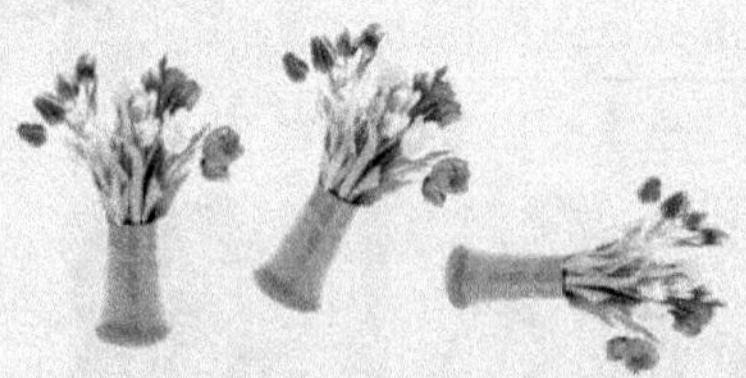

fig.12

subject to be photographed in motion during shooting

Capturing the movement of the subject (*fig.12*) and its energy was a great achievement of the photographers of over a century ago. The successful exploration of time was carried out by the Bragaglia brothers (img.136) in the context of the Futurist arts movement. The exploration of time allowed Photodynamism to represent trajectories of the displacement of a body, thus generating in the observer the sensation of movement but in a different way from Chronophotography (see Muybridge p.24 img.13) which was extended to represent the subsequent occupation of the sequential stages of the moving subject. Thus, Photodynamism takes photography away from that state of a moment that is no longer there, that has an air of 'death', as indeed Roland Barthes says; that sense of death that is not present in pictorial art.

Anton Giulio Bragaglia on the subject of art in photography states: (...for I am convinced that we can achieve art with the mechanical means of photography only if we overcome the pedestrian photographic reproduction of the real as some-thing static or caught in a pose in a snapshot. In so doing, the resulting photograph, achieved by experimental and other means, would succeed in registering the expression and the vibration of actual life, and in distancing itself from obscene, brutal, and static realism, and it would no longer be the usu-al photography, but something much more elevated...).

With Photodynamism the 'time' component in photography is explored, leaving the representation of space as the only perspective, and so delegating FoTotempismo to the exploration of Space-Time.

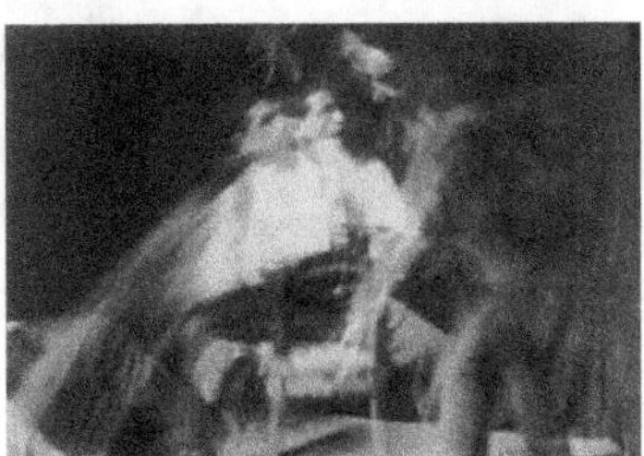

img.136

Photodynamism
'The slap' Bragaglia Brothers

CMS *Camera Move Space*

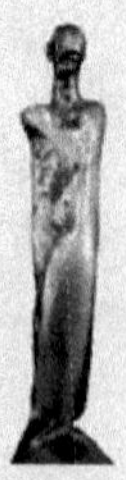

fig.14

The basic technique for taking photographs in FoTotempismo is represented in figure 14, which shows the essential movement of the camera in three-dimensional space for the first time.

In the action of the physical movement of the

camera carried out by the author, space-time is also covered, that is, the fourth dimension, which is added to the other three; height, width and depth, generating infinite visual combinations available to the author.

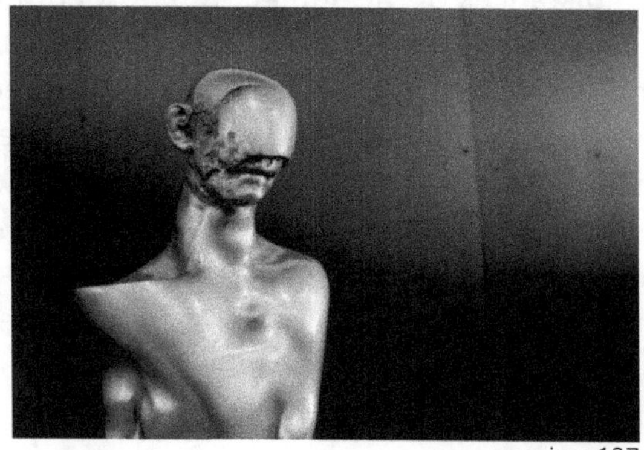

img.137

Perspective 1

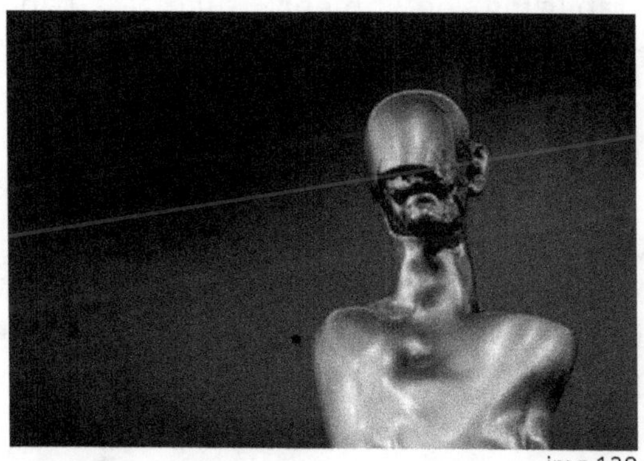

img.138

Perspective 2

So, the camera is moved, rotated and stopped in space at will, in order to compose the desired image (img.141). Then the various perspectives (img.139, 140) and distances of the subject to photograph, the travel speeds, slowdowns and accelerations that you want to give to the camera are chosen. The speed changes and stops during shooting generate dematerializations and re-materializations, which can be more or less evident, until the subject stabilizes in the pause. In the case of a moving subject, the combination of the photographer's action and the subject are combined to create images that are representative of the strength of both protagonists that generate the work. The movements and stops given by the author to the camera, can be carried out both freehand and with support equipment.

Some stabilizing equipment, such as tripods or supports, is necessary during stops with long shutter speeds to obtain clear images. Other equipment is useful for carrying out the movements of the camera such as: sliding guides, tilt arms, servo-assisted supports, up to the use of drones and fibre optics.

All these aids help the author to manage and control the movements of the camera according to personal creativity and the desired message, without being overwhelmed by the equipment.

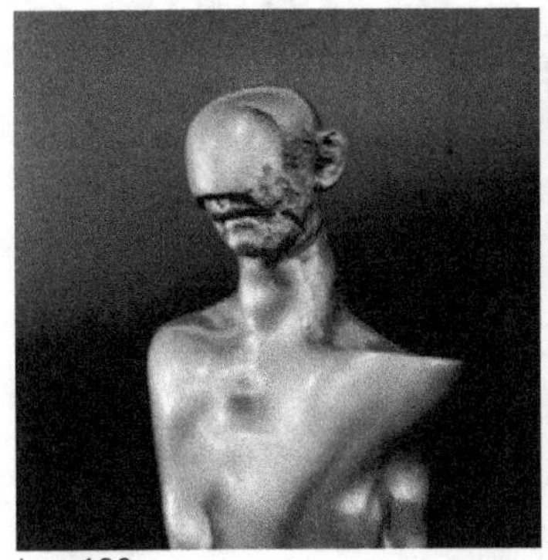 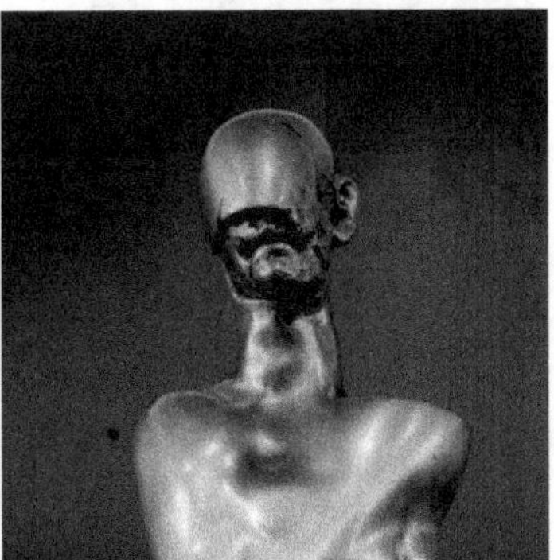

img.139   img.140

Preliminary study from two perspectives

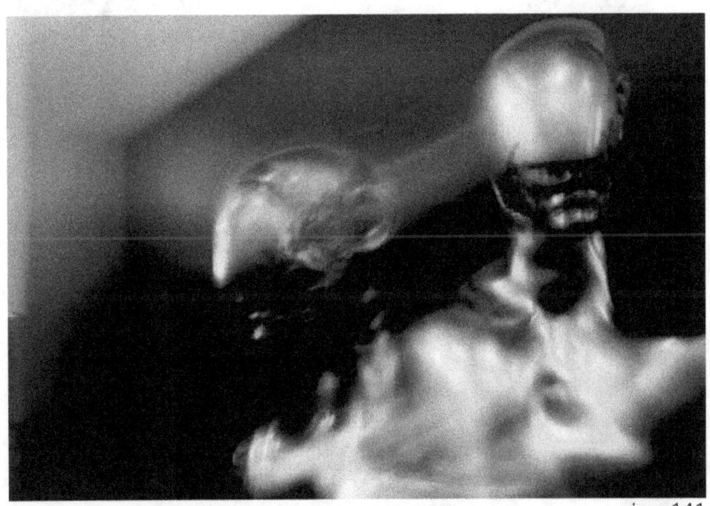

img.141

Image produced with the CMS fototempistic concept

CMSIS
Camera Move Space Intermediate Stop

movement of the camera in space, during shooting, with intermediate stops

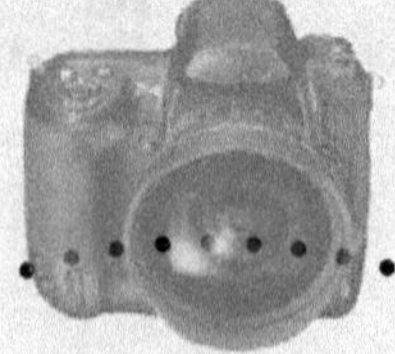

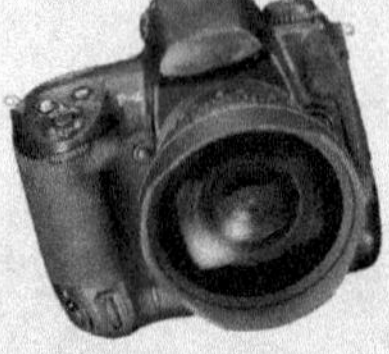

intermediate stops

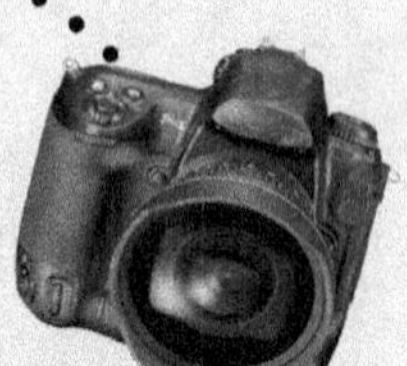

start of shooting

end of shooting

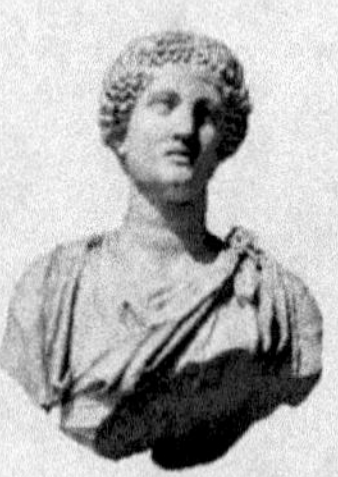

fig.15

subject to be photographed still or in motion

With the *CMSIS* technique, which consists of taking intermediate breaks when moving the camera in space, further materializations and new dematerializations are generated (img.142). In this case the composition of the image is enriched compared to shooting with only two perspectives (stops), as in the basic '*CMS*' technique. The basic diagram of shooting using this technique is represented in figure 15 and was created with a single intermediate stop; also in this case, higher or lower incisiveness is obtained, depending on the length of each stop, therefore giving a predominance to that part of the image itself.

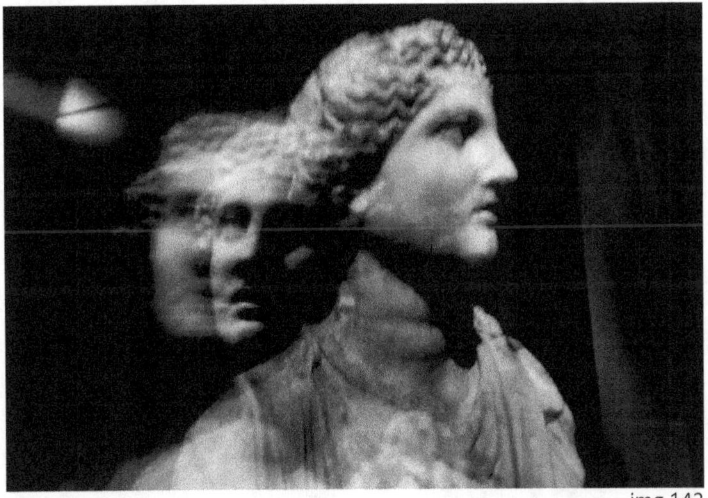

img.142

Image produced with the fototempistic concept CMSIS

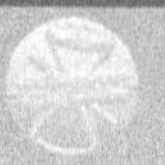

Since the image is complex, derived from the representation of various perspective materializations, planning of the composition before shooting must be very thorough. During these shots, as well as the movement through space of the camera to obtain the desired perspectives, camera rotation is important in order to frame the various perspectives that derive from it during the stops. As can be seen, this technique enables a great deal of creativity, but at the same time it is quite complex and requires experience in managing all the photographic techniques.

To this complexity, another is added which consists of a shift in space not exclusively in the same direction (img.143). Indeed, while taking the photograph, once an appropriate perspective is obtained, you can change direction of movement, even going backwards through space, but into another time and with any subject who may also move, alter or even change. So given the infinite possibilities of composing the image, it can be affirmed that the 'Gesture' of the author is decisive and leaves an exclusive and unrepeatable 'Sign'.

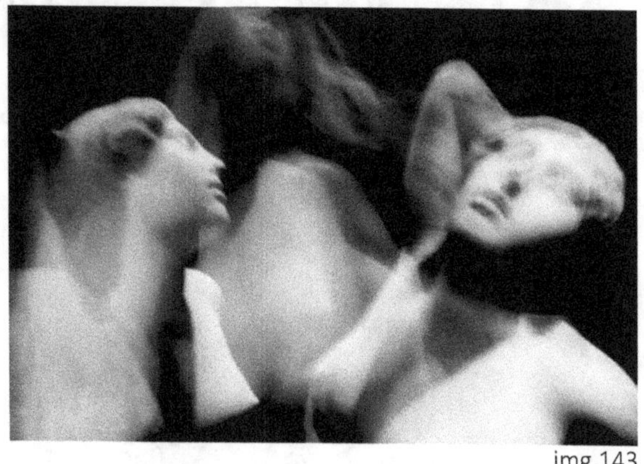

img.143

'Niobe' FoTotempismo with CMSIS intermediate stop

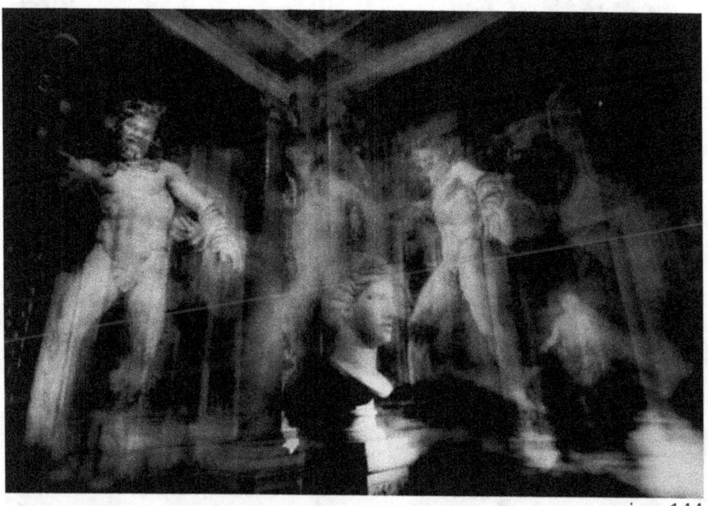

img.144

'Dancing Satyr' FoTotempismo with CMSIS intermediate stop

ZCMS *Zoom Camera Move Space*

moving the camera in space, with zoom during the resumption with possible intermediate stops

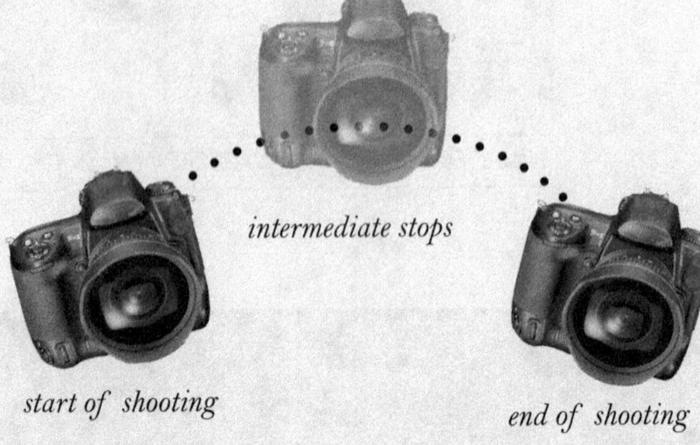

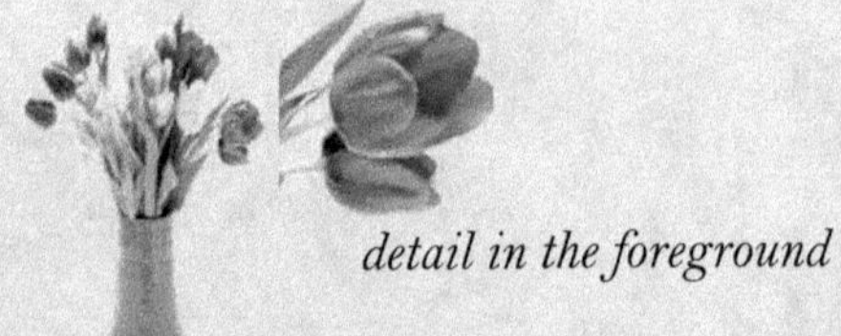

fig.16

subject to be photographed still or in motion

Using a zoom lens, the technique *ZCMS Zoom Camera Move Space* can be applied, shown in the diagram in figure 16. Considering that the movement through space that the author imprints on the camera is basic to the fototempistic concept, variation of the focal length during shooting can also be used (img.145). The photographic action can begin with either a short focal lens, such as a wide angle and then at the author's discretion switch to a longer one, like that of a telephoto lens. The use of different optics may also differ from that described above according to the creativity of the author, also in this case other subjects can be included in the composition.

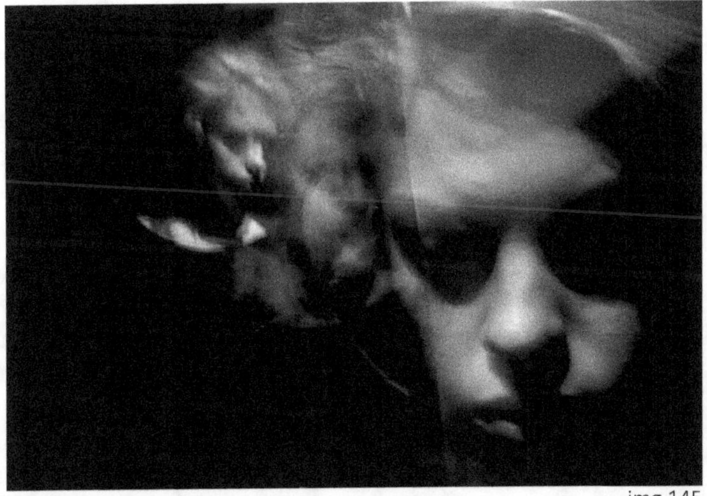

img.145

Portrait in FoTotempismo with ZCMS technique

Shooting with a zoom lens is quite easy, but with the right shutter speeds and lighting you can even think of changing to a fixed focal length lens. From experience, you can obtain good results by starting shooting with a long focal length lens and then moving through space and composing the final image with a shorter focal length lens (img.147).

You can create other compositions with mini intermediate stops by composing the image in the first and second stop using a long focal length, with the subject taken at different points of the image, and then finish the shot with a wide angle lens, shooting the whole subject appropriately placed. However, there are many variables and it is the author's imagination that generates the message in the work with his/her 'Gesture'.

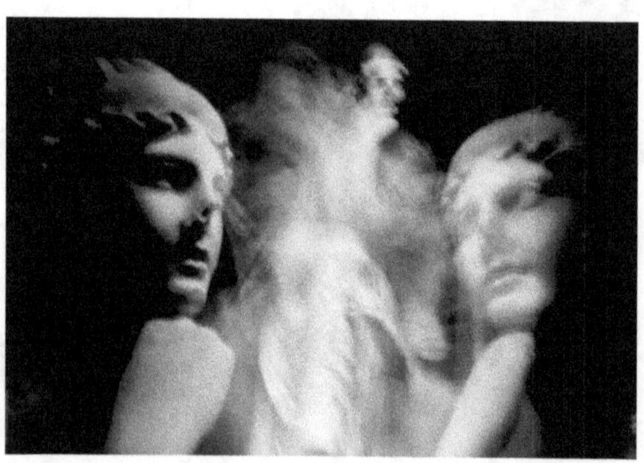

img.146

FoTotempismo with ZCMS technique with intermediate stop

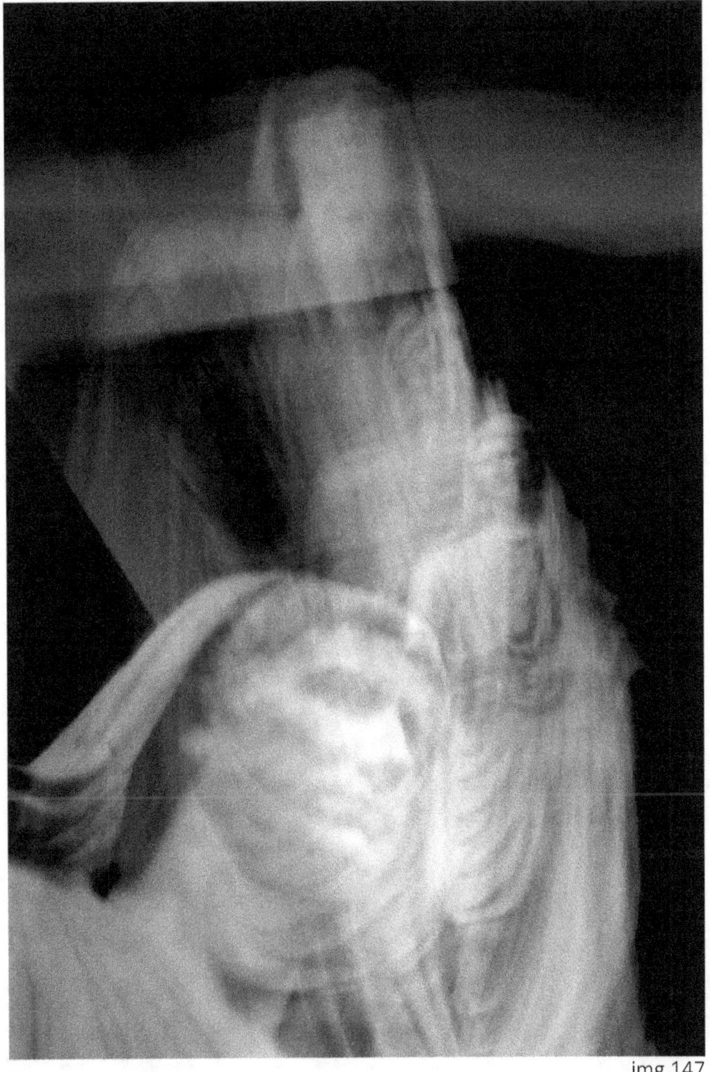

img.147

Image obtained with the ZCMS technique with several stops

PCMS *Plus Camera Move Space* 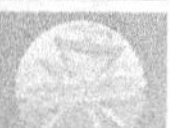

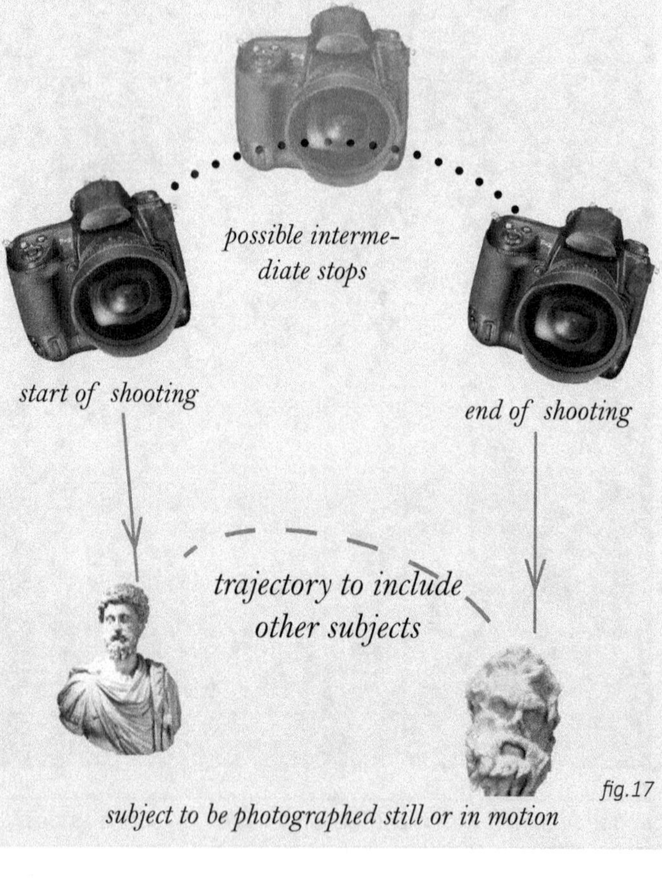

fig.17

FoTotempismo is traveling through space with the camera, and it is precisely this condition that allows us to create what the academic system of photography 'does not allow'. Among the different perspectives that the fototempistic action allows there is also that of reaching other subjects while shooting, which were not included in the initial frame (img.148). The fototempistic technique that enables these shots is called *PCMS Plus Camera Move Space* (*fig.17*). As already mentioned for the other techniques, this can also be used in addition to one or more techniques, generating an infinity of varied image combinations and creations. Subjects not included in the first perspective can be reached later, both singly and in the same initial field of vision, seen from another angle.

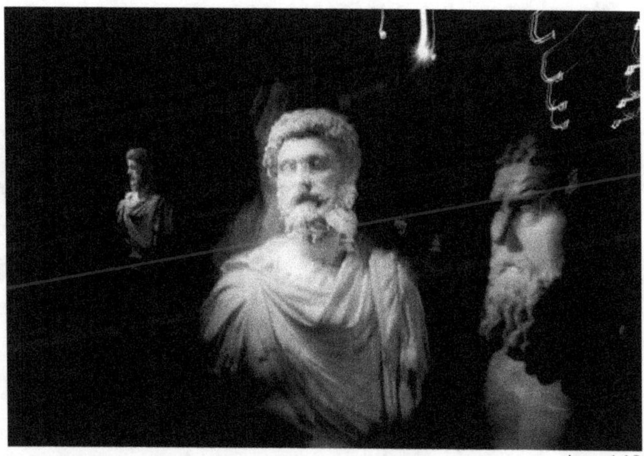

img.148

Shot in FoTotempismo with PCMS technique

The new subjects thus reached can be located in or out of the field of vision of the first frame, and so be very distant if not hidden from other elements.

In images 149, 150, and 151 the subject in the middle ground was achieved with the second framing of the subject in the foreground; therefore one could hypothesize about creating a photo where the first stop starts at the Colosseum in Rome and then by air transport with the shutter always open 'record' the journey until you reach and end the shot at Milan Cathedral.

By fantasizing, one could think of creating a work which would have the Tower of Pisa as its subject and then arrive on another planet by spaceship, to finish the shot with a subject in space.

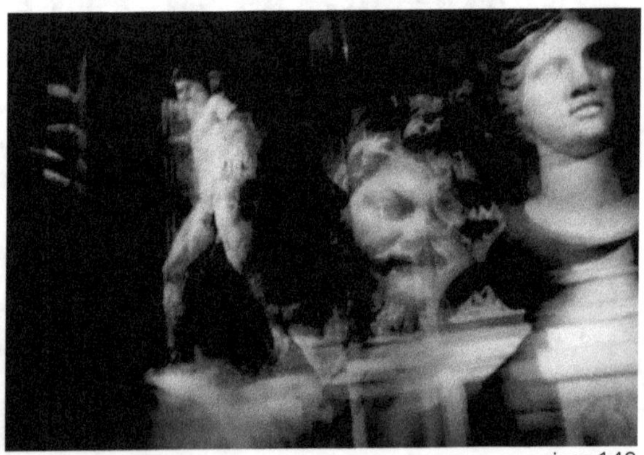

img.149

Shot in FoTotempismo with PCMS and ZCMS techniques

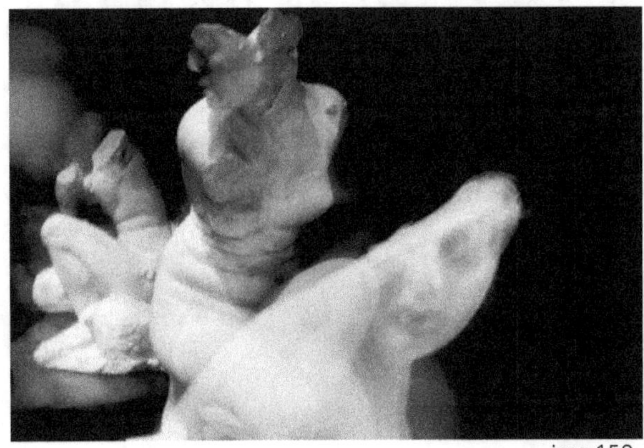

img.150

Shot in FoTotempismo with PCMS technique

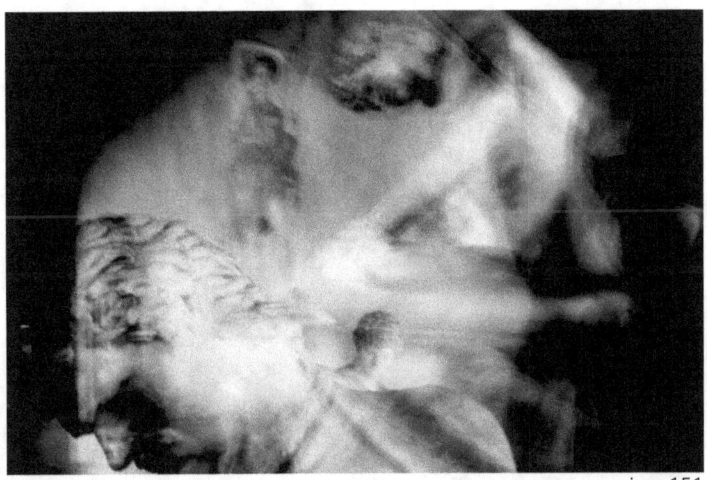

img.151

Dying Gaul FoTotempismo with PCMS and ZCMS techniques

LrCMS *Light regulation Camera Move Space*

*lighting modulation while moving the camera in space,
during shooting, with possible stops*

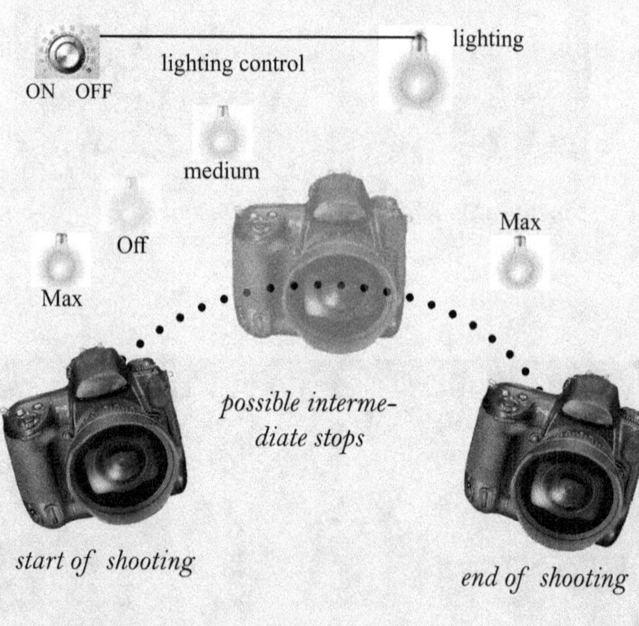

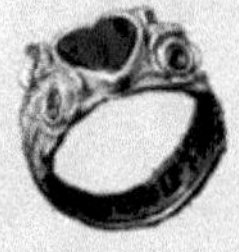

subject to be photographed still or in motion

fig.18

While shooting and moving the camera through space and over time, lighting changes can be made according to the creativity of the author (*fig.18*). The technique called *LRCMS Light Regulation Camera Move Space* uses lighting variation, modulating its intensity at any time during shooting (img.155).

The possibility to vary the chromaticity of the light source, as well as its geometric shape, by passing from diffused light to direct sources, both fall under the acronym *LRCMS*. In accordance with personal photographic ethics, I don't believe the use of flash lighting is appropriate, as the spirit of FoTotempismo is not to *'freeze'* the moment but to represent the passage of time that the subject and the author are experiencing.

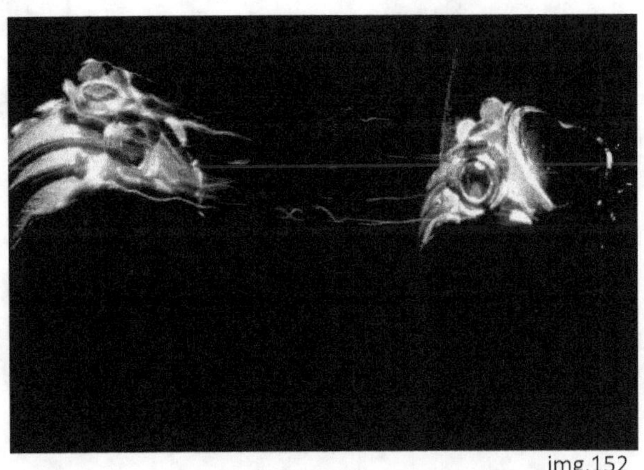

img.152

Shot in FoTotempismo with LrCMS technique

LdCMS — *Light distance Camera Move Space*

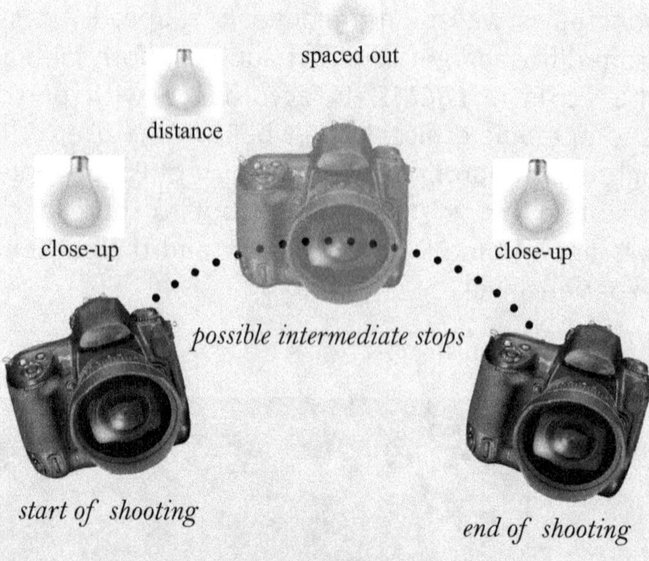

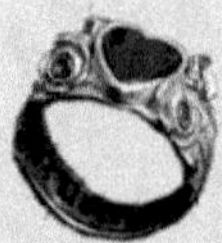

fig.19

Light is always the protagonist with which to impress the camera sensor, and in the technique described in figure 19, the light that reaches the sensor is modulated, moving the light source away and closer to the subject. The moving away and closer of the light source occurs during shooting, that is, during camera stops and movement through space. The resulting effect is similar to that of the *LrCMS Light regulation Camera Move Space* but with a different impact due to the cone of light with which the scene is illuminated.

In the scene illuminated with a variable intensity light source, but always in the same place, the shadows always remain located in the same position; while walking away or approaching the light source they change shape and intensity.

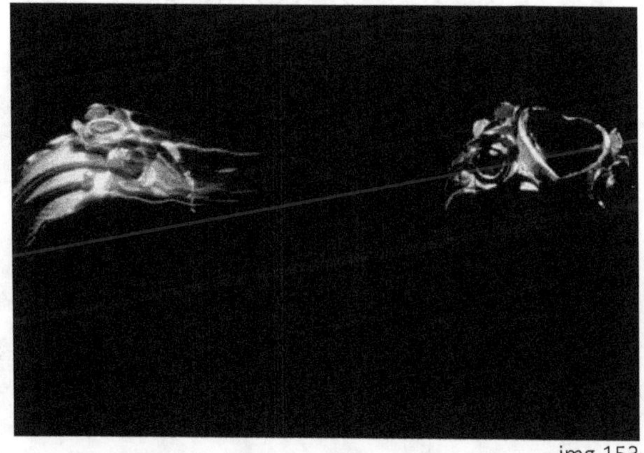

img.153

Shot in FoTotempismo with LdCMS technique

Furthermore, where the light source moves, also sideways, the shadows and lighting change position, giving different atmospheres to the image and the subject during the various dematerializations, re-materializations and changes of perspective. In image 153 you can see the effect of this technique, where the subject in the centre of the image appears less illuminated than the initial and final shot. This is due to the removal of the lamp in the intermediate stage of shooting, to the point of not illuminating the subject at all.

Another detail emerges from examination of the lighting of image 153, at the beginning of shooting the ring was lit mainly on the left, while at the end of the shot it was lit from above and perpendicular to it, but always at the same distance.

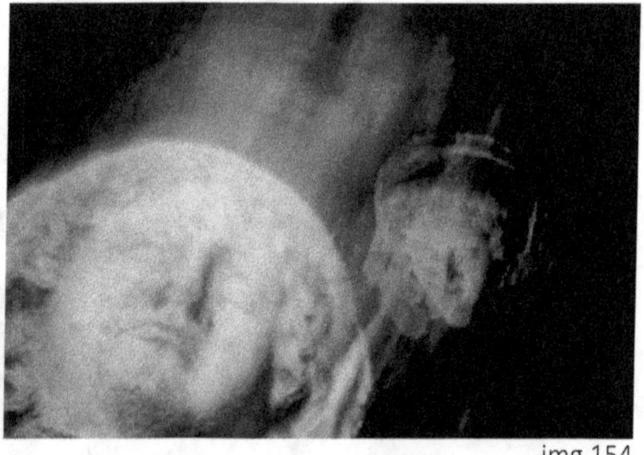

img.154

Shot in FoTotempismo with LdCMS technique

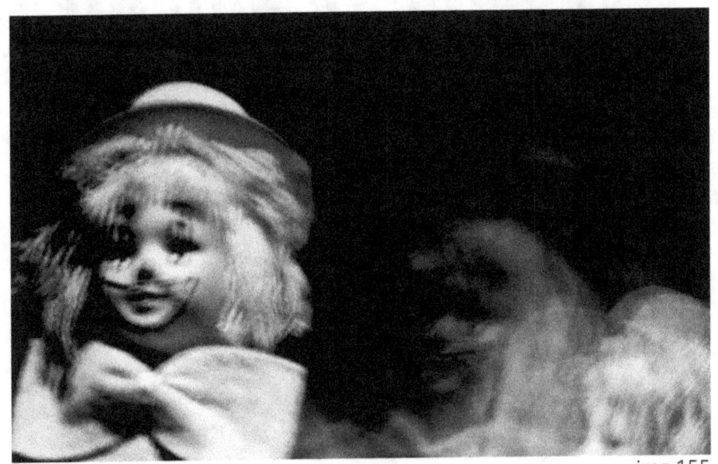

img.155

Shot in FoTotempismo with LdCMS technique

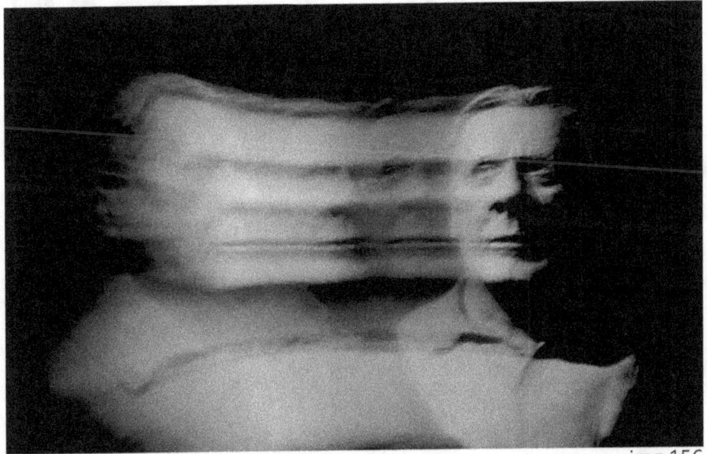

img.156

Shot in FoTotempismo with LdCMS technique

DCMS Diaphragm Camera Move Space 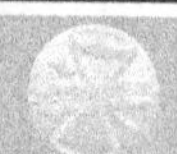

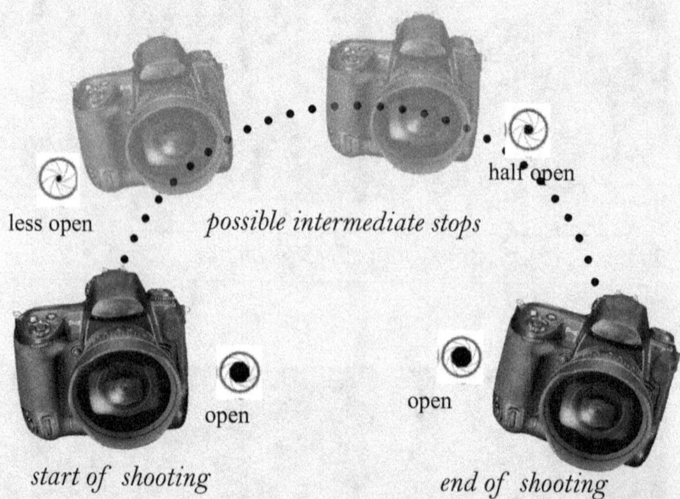

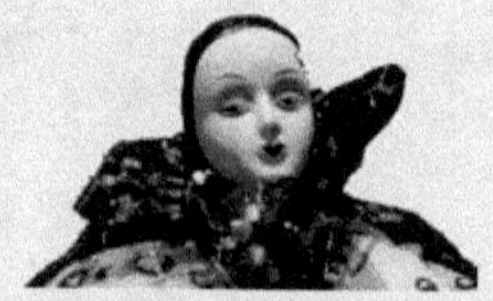

subject to be photographed still or in motion

fig.20

The *DCMS Diaphragm Camera Move Space* technique allows you to create photos in FoTotempismo by varying the aperture during shooting (fig.20). In certain aspects, the results obtained with this technique can resemble some previously described, but with the addition and elimination of certain characteristics. In particular, compared to the *LrCMS* technique, the effect of the shadows and their movements is lost, but depth of field variations are added, with blur on different planes given by the variations of the aperture of the diaphragm. In image 157 you can identify the two additional effects this shooting technique offers. In this image, in addition to having a modulation of brightness during dematerialization and re-materialization of the subject, the effect is also visible in the pause with the subject on the left. It is exposed correctly and with a depth of field appropriate given a suitable aperture of the diaphragm; while in the representation of the subject on the right of the image, the subject is brighter and with more blur due to less depth of field.

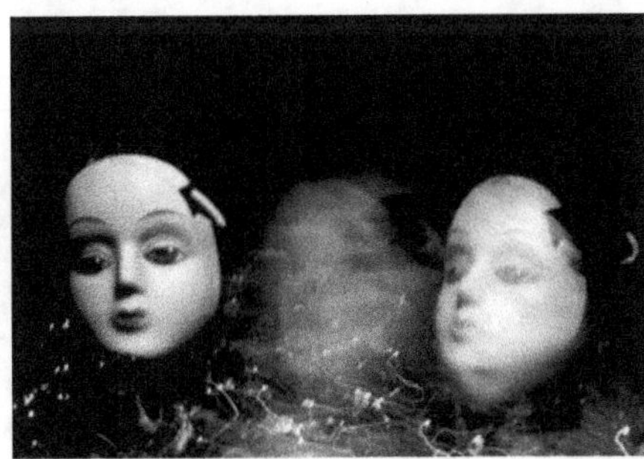

img.157

'Pierrot'
in FoTotempismo

MCMS Mask Camera Move Space

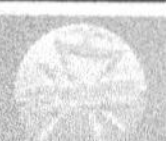

masking of the diaphragm when moving the camera,
with possible stops, during shooting

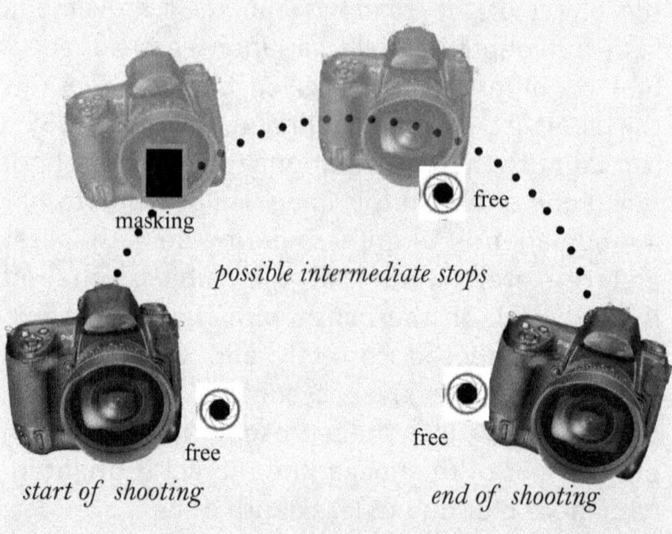

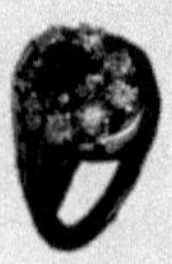

subject to be photographed still or in motion

fig.21

The masking of the scene while shooting is a valid means to obtaining creative images, which are, at the same time, very 'descriptive' of the photographed subject. In particular this technique called *MCMS Mask Camera Move Space* (*fig.21*) was used to obtain the photographs in images 158, 159, 160, 161. In the case of image 158, the client requested that the piece of jewellery be clearly visible since the image had to be published in a commercial catalogue. The shooting technique represented in the diagram (*fig.21*), entails that while moving the camera there is a darkening of the sensor; to obtain the required result the lens is masked the moment the camera movement begins. The expected result was to stop the dematerialization from the beginning of the

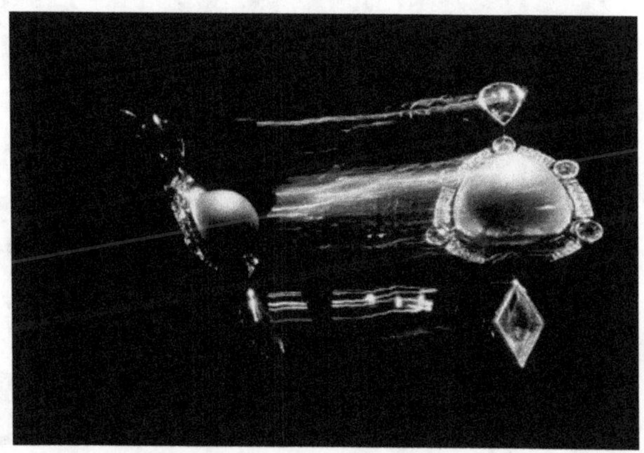

img.158

(MCMS) masking at the start of the move

move to continue it just outside the field of view of the subject itself. Therefore, the subject was represented clearly in its entirety, depicted in the 'conventional' way, to be then represented in its entirety in a creative version. With masking during shooting, or in all its possible phases, FoTotempismo unveils new compositions never before explored by revealing unpublished aspects of the subjects represented (img.158-161). Masking can be done and synchronized manually when time and space allow it, but automatic and synchronized systems can also be used.

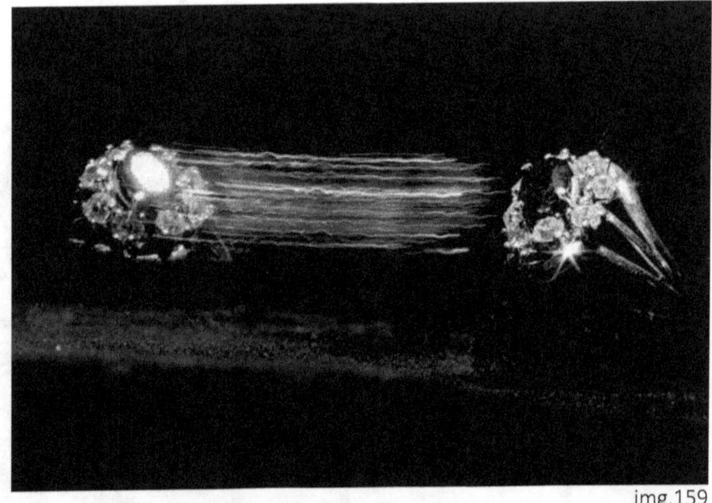

img.159

Shooting in MCMS with masking at the end of the movement

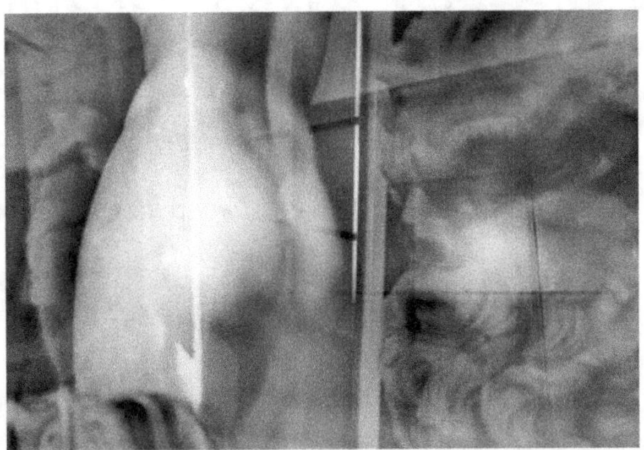

img.160

Shooting in MCMS with masking from start to end of movement

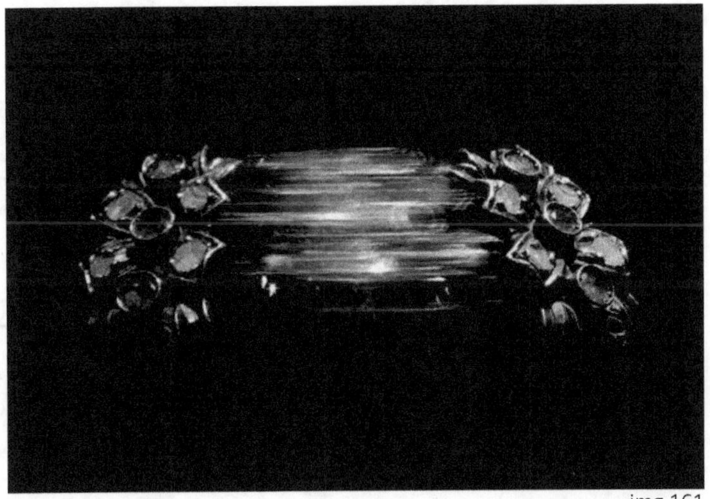

img.161

Shooting in MCMS with masking at the start and end of the movement

CMmS *Camera Move micro Space* 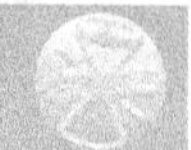

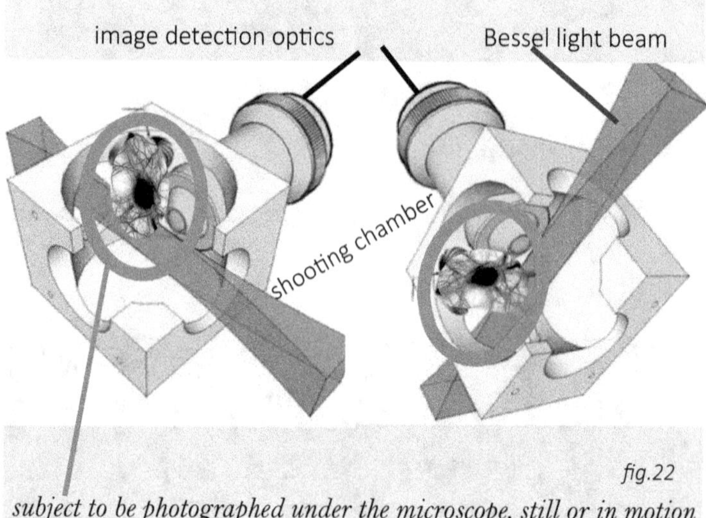

fig.22

subject to be photographed under the microscope, still or in motion

In cellular microphotography the camera is positioned on the ocular lobe of the microscope, then the fototempistic action is carried out, moving the whole microscope-camera in space to capture other perspectives of the cell (img.162) as in the previously described procedure. Shooting in FoTotempismo can also be implemented with new techniques that go beyond direct optical vision, as in Fluorescent

Microscopy or in the newest technique called *Lattice Light Sheet Microscope*; figure 22 shows the diagram of an Environmental Scanning Electron Microscope 'ESEM', in a possible shoot in FoTotempismo. These techniques illuminate the subject with a beam of light, called Bessel beam (driving beam), which scans it. The diagram in figure 22 shows a hypothesis of shooting in FoTotempismo with subject illuminated with Bessel light.

So even in this case, by moving the lighting and shooting point, it is possible have an image in FoTotempismo, thus confirming the extension of its application also to photography of microscopic elements.

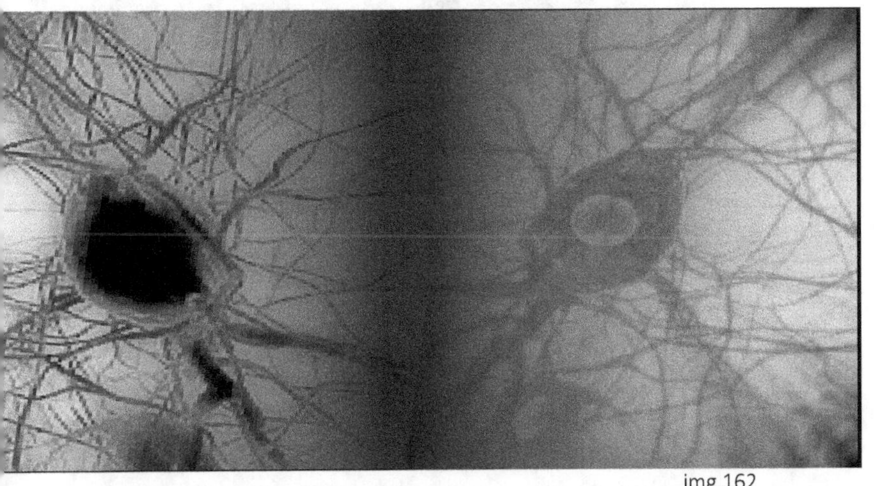

img.162

Possible FoTotempismo image of cells shot in the microscope with CMmS technique.

CMMS *Camera Move Macro Space*

*shooting system for long distances and spaces
with possible stops, during shooting*

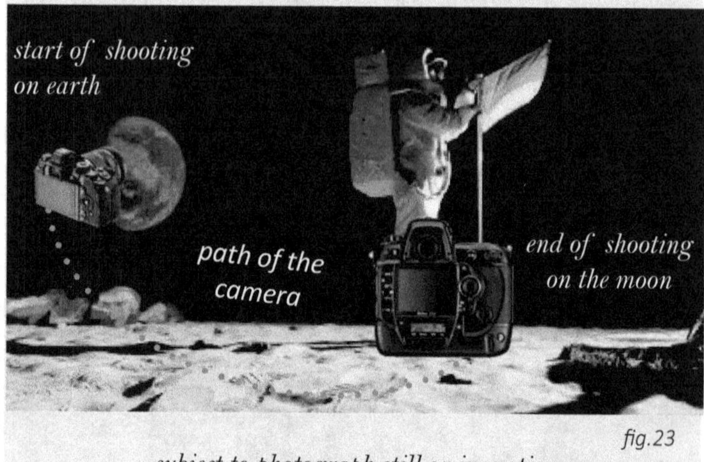

subject to photograph still or in motion

Using fast moving systems and for long distances, the technique *CMMS Camera Move Macro Space* can be applied.

As shown in the diagram (*fig.23*), one can hypothesize a photograph in FoTotempismo as a journey, with the shutter open, which starts from the Imperial Forums of Rome, for the time needed, until reaching another celestial body (img.163) composing the image according to the creativity of the author. Clearly, all the precautions and techniques to obtain the predetermined result would have to be used, but this assumption of extension into macro-space is used to demonstrate the character of universality intrinsic to FoTotempismo as a concept.

The applications presented so far are not exhaustive of all the possibilities that FoTotempismo offers, but are only indications to be expanded upon by authors who use this technique.

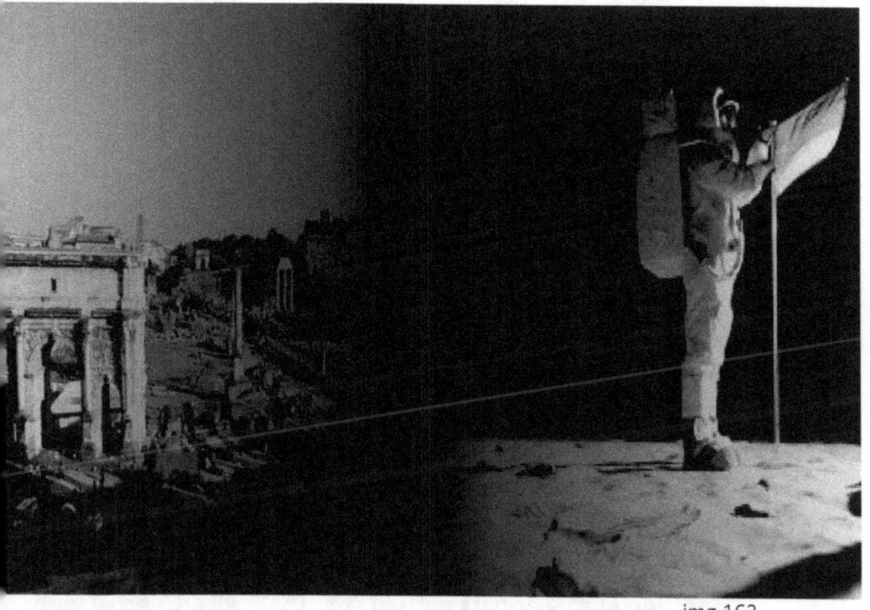

img.163

Possible image in FoTotempismo from the earth to space using CMMS technique.

Space-Time

- Documentary photography
- Reportage
- Portrait
- Sculpture
- Sports
- Architecture
- Street Photography
- Fashion photography
- Glamour photography
- Naturalistic photography
- Landscape photography
- Macro photography
- Still Life Photography

and many other photographic genres extend the list, which have been used for experimental work carried out in FoTotempismo. The history of photography is full of events and in its two hundred years of life it has been enriched with excellence, genres and expressions. Photography is now a fully qualified member of the art world, like other disciplines, making use of its means and its characteristics without ever emulating other artistic disciplines.

Now with FoTotempismo photographic research has added another step along its path, a step that will also grow with other authors who will expand its application into various genres and improve those already explored.

FoTotempismo

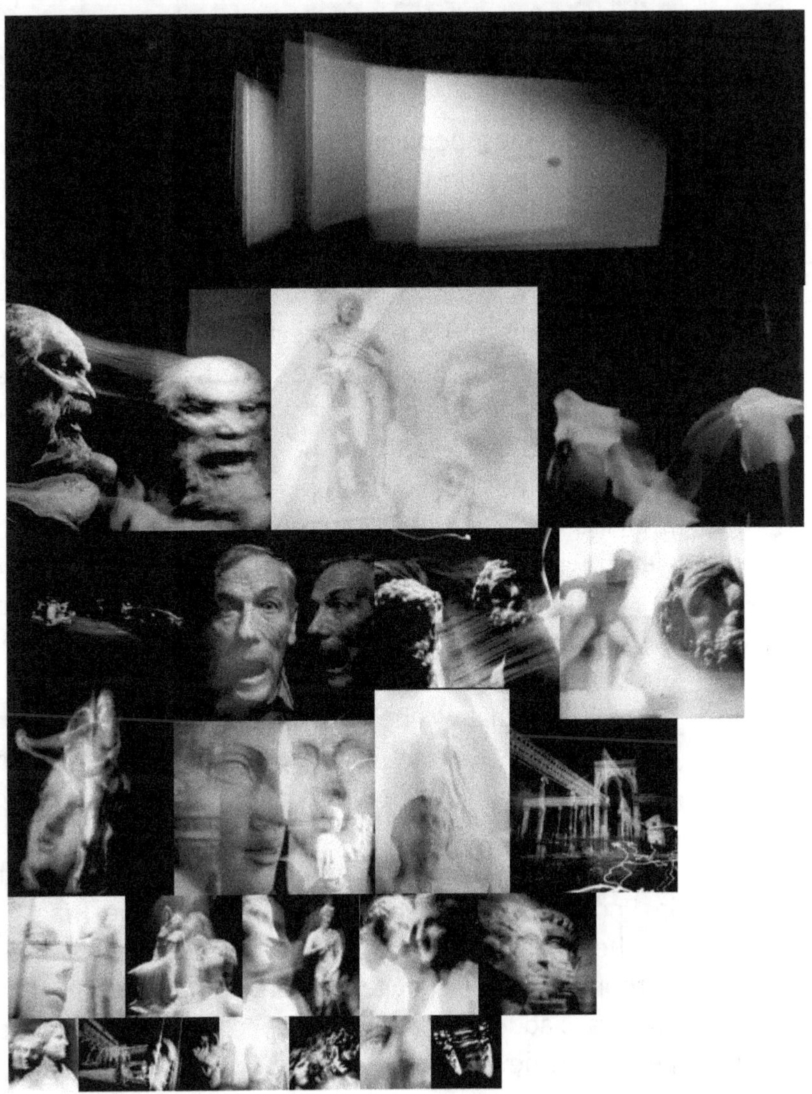

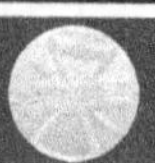

Among the most popular genres in the photographic field is certainly the portrait. Therefore, after experimenting with objects, representing a person in FoTotempismo with their own infinite expressions had a strong appeal for me. The literature in this category, with still photography, with Photodynamism and other creative means, has already been widely explored. All the known techniques used to create a photographic portrait according to academic dictates and not, can also be adopted in shooting in FoTotempismo, both with the subject stationary (img.164 ,166) and in motion (img.165). In examining image 165, the viewer will be able to ascertain a possible combination of movements, of both the author and the photographed subject, by examining the shadows due to the lighting. Shooting in FoTotempismo with a stationary subject, the perspectives that will be fixed on the sensor will have the illuminated areas always on the side where the light come from, and shadows on the opposite side. This circumstance helps us to understand that the author has moved and not the person to be photographed, in contrast to a photo in Photodynamism (specifically, those of the Bragaglia brothers). In the event that both the subject and the author move, the change in shooting perspective of the camera is added to the change of position of the subject, generating new dynamic variables with new emotions.

In particular, with FoTotempismo new tensions and new 'dialogues' with the subject are generated, which were previously unthinkable.

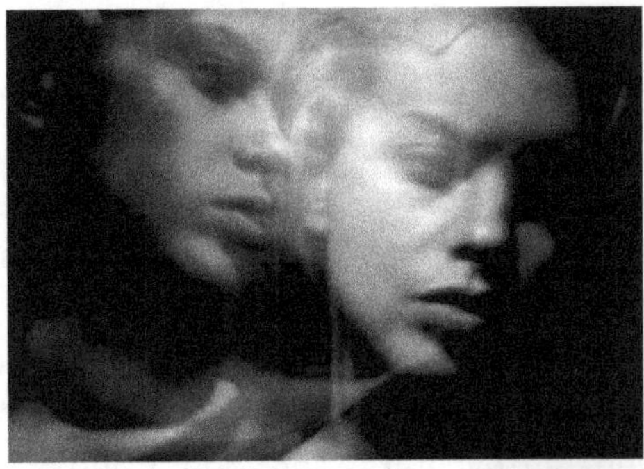

img.164

Portrait with stationary subject

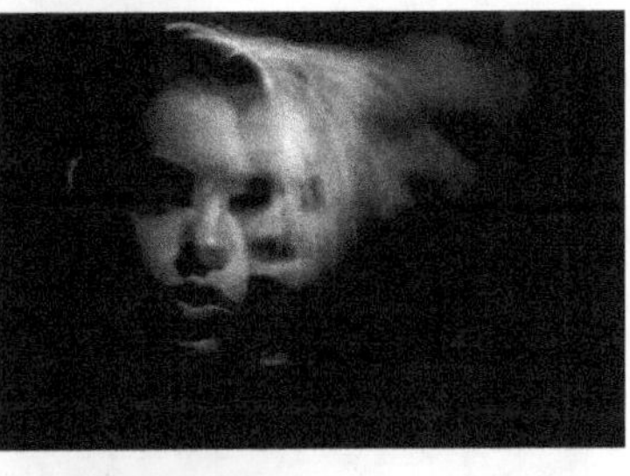

img.165

Portrait with subject in motion

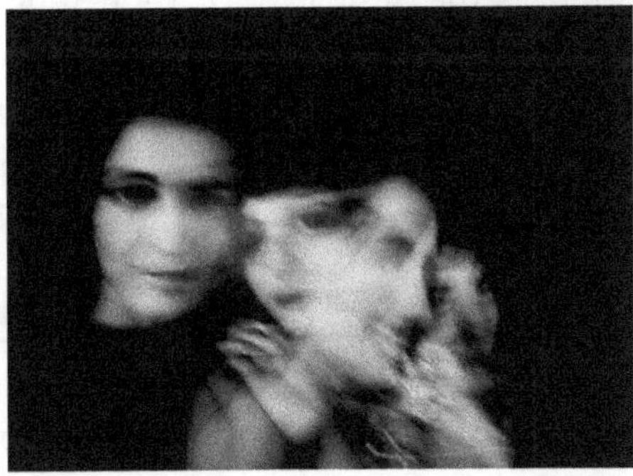

img.166

Portrait with various subjects

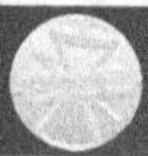

By exploring the applications of FoTotempismo among the vast array of photographic genres, architecture also offers a great deal of expressive value. The compositions that can be generated go beyond the imaginable, compared to those obtained with photographs: still photos, double shots, overlays and other techniques. This happens because FoTotempismo is a photographic concept with long shutter times, therefore, movement of the subjects in addition to that of the author generate dynamism and added value to the given multi-perspective continuity from the fototempistic action. To simplify the approach with the technique it was decided to examine images taken at night, like those on the facing page. Image 167 represents the Palazzo dei Papi in Viterbo taken with two perspectives that are orthogonal to each other, following certain rules of composition.

In image 168 the subject is the Cathedral of Orvieto and in this case, even in the simplicity of representation of the two perspectives, the movement of the camera and the movement of car headlights generate an intricate dynamism. Finally, the composition of image 169, in which the Cathedral dei Cosmati in Civita Castellana, with its front portico dominated by the arch that intersects with it in the orthogonal perspective, emphasizes its architecture. Other types of architecture and lighting can be explored and they will always give innovative results with new emotions.

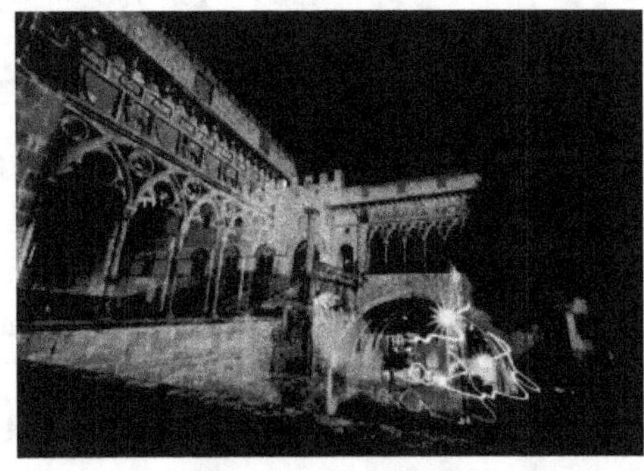

img.167

*Palazzo dei Papi
in Viterbo*

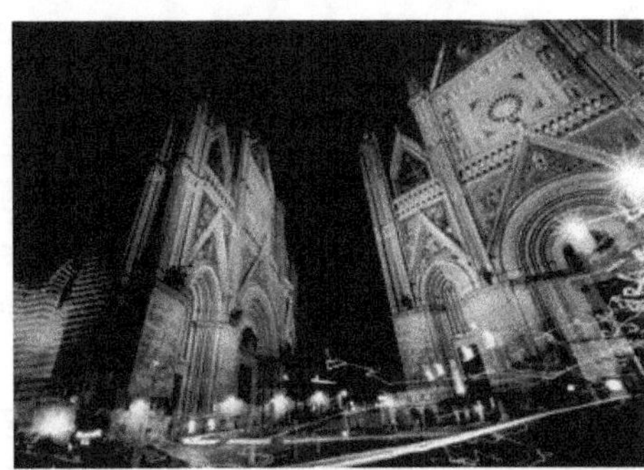

img.168

*Cathedral of
Orvieto*

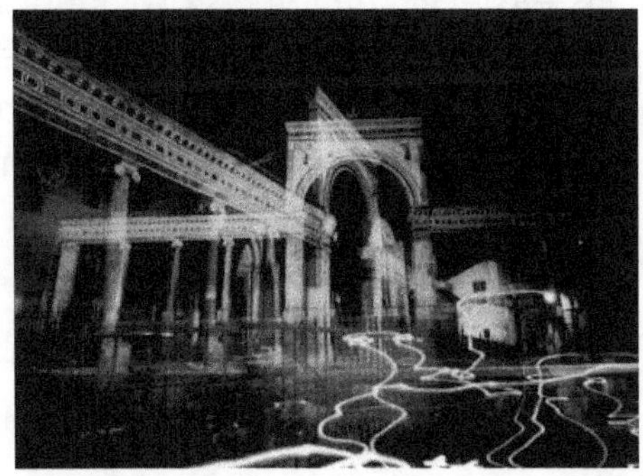

img.169

*Cathedral dei Cosmati
of Civita Castellana*

still life

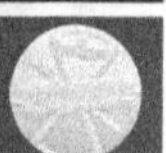

In photography, the classification 'still life' indicates a particular genre that describes the representation of inanimate objects, as in painting (img.170). With the techniques of FoTotempismo it is possible to give life to those objects that would otherwise give the impression of being static, or 'dead'. Using FoTotempismo in this photographic genre it is possible to give vitality with dematerializations and re-materializations to inert objects, even if of high artistic value. FoTotempismo is applicable to any object: flowers, leaves, fruit, jewellery (img.171- 172- 173), coins, vases, archaeological finds and whatever else must come to life to be placed in a new light for the attention of the user.

Technically it is advisable to use wide-angle focal lengths to better manage the subject and movement with the camera. Shooting with the 'macro' function is easier if the lens is provided with one, but in some cases, the use of extension tubes may be useful. The exposure times used for these photos fluctuate from 1.5'' to 4'' for full exposure, but may vary a great deal, depending on requirements. In some circumstances a support system or camera stabilizer can be used, leaving the author free to use movement in space, which, with their 'Gesture' will impress the 'Sign' in the image created.

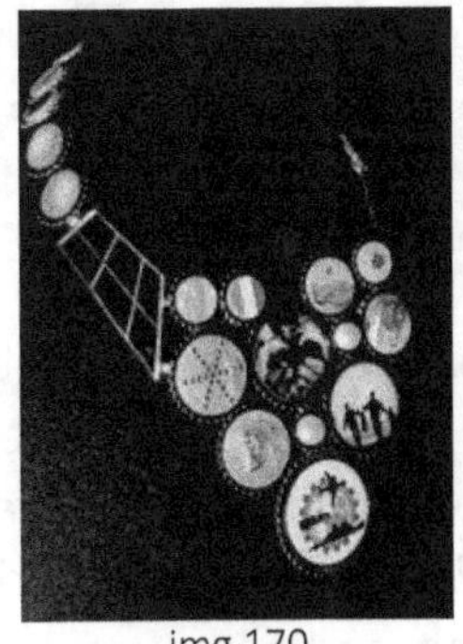

img.170

Still photo

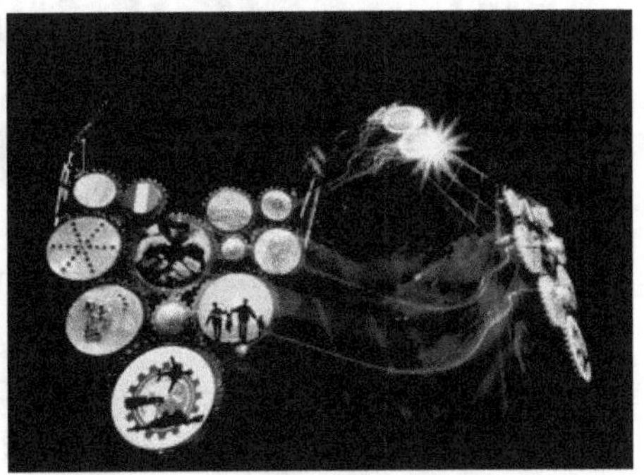

img.171

'Jewellery by Lovelook' in FoTotempismo

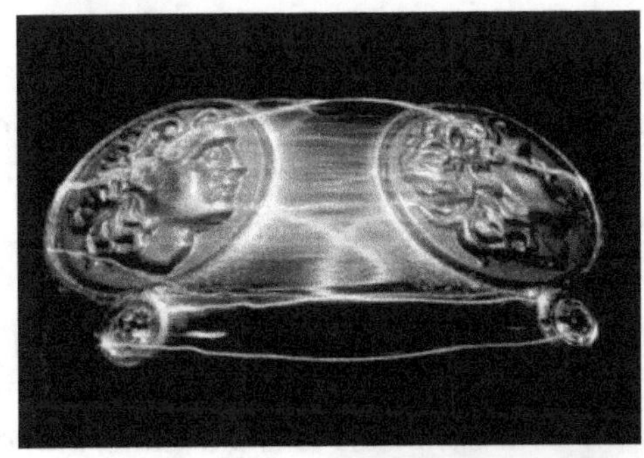

img.172

*'Medallion' in
FoTotempismo*

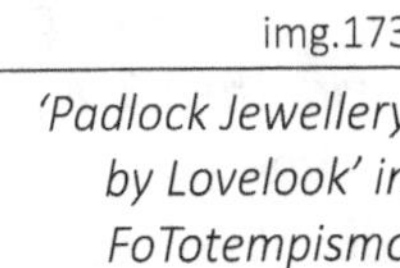

img.173

*'Padlock Jewellery
by Lovelook' in
FoTotempismo*

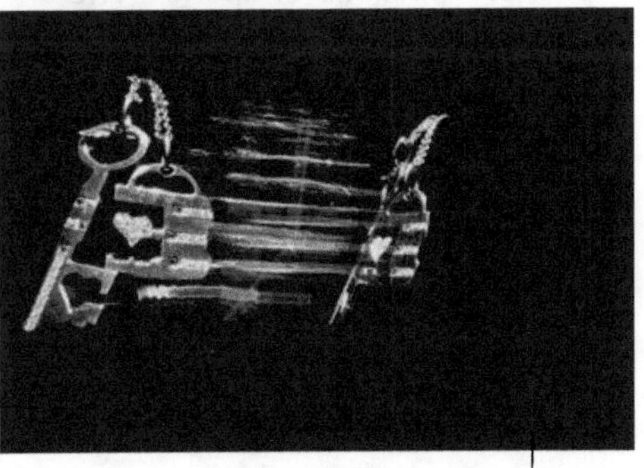

sculpture 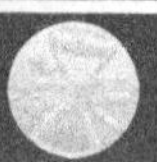

To date, sculpture has been the most photographed subject in FoTotempismo. Four books have been published that tell stories and reveal places populated by sculptures that in their stillness lend themselves to being 'revived'; the statues seem to move, talk, escape, and meet, creating new emotions and tensions between themselves and with themselves. In their manifold perspectives, representations, dematerializations, destruction, vanishing and then reappearing with that '*breath*' that they carry with them, these images represent even more a new artistic discipline, '*a contemporary classic*'. Most of the sculptures used in the photos of this book have been photographed in museums, as an ordinary tourist could, with all the limitations and difficulties that it involves. This circumstance confirms the applicability of FoTotempismo across the board and in all circumstances, although it certainly isn't as simple as taking a static, immobile, or 'macabre' snapshot. The difficulties of the 'Gesture' that generates the 'Sign' are significant, and it is precisely in overcoming this challenge that you get exceptional results. I remember an anecdote: I was photographing a statue that was surrounded by others, and in moving repeatedly to optimize the 'Gesture', a person observing what I was doing said to me: "*It looks like you're dancing with them, with the statues*"; in fact, looking back on it, I realized that you engage in a dialogue that is not only thought but also corporal.

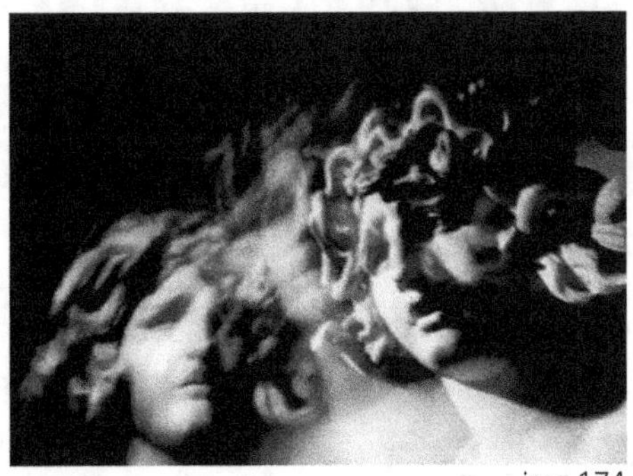

img.174

'Medusa'

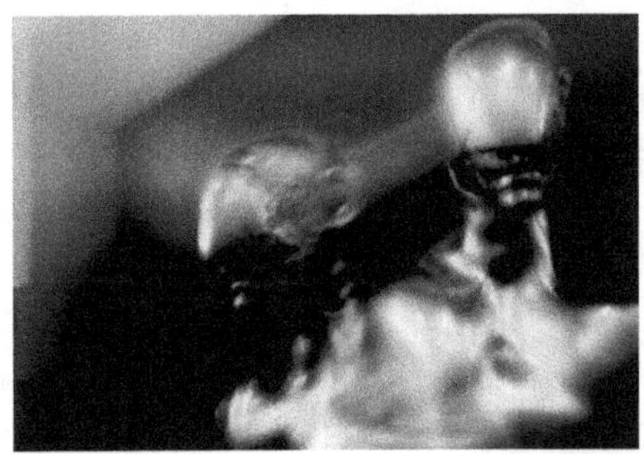

img.175

Contemporary work

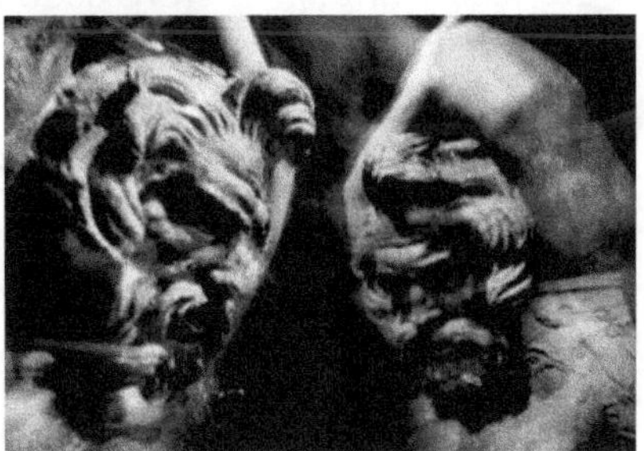

img.176

'Marsyas'

photographic genres
fashion, objects, perfumes 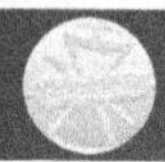

Among the first applications of FoTotempismo within a commercial context was the realization of some photographs of jewellery (img.171) required by a goldsmith on the occasion of the World Trade Exhibition 'EXPO MILANO 2015'. Other categories in the 'Beauty' area were explored, including: footwear (img.178), perfumery (img.179), cosmetics, watches (img.180) and others, which always achieved astounding results, and which significantly affected the means of advertising communication. In some cases, the *MCMS* technique was used to highlight the object photographed and then animate with its dynamism in the de-materialization and re-materialization, transporting the potential user into dreams of desire. In other cases, the technique used was the basic *MCS*, using soft lighting in order not to highlight the light trails, and in other circumstances point lights were used to make the reflections and the brilliance of the object more evident. The use of FoTotempismo photography has enjoyed a great deal of attention in the field of fashion, which has found an exploratory affinity in this new concept, given that it is constantly on the lookout for innovation. On the following page a few of the objects photographed are shown and some of these images were used in urban and extra-urban billboard campaigns. In conclusion, it is a *still life* that gives life to everything that up to now was still, immobile, blocked.

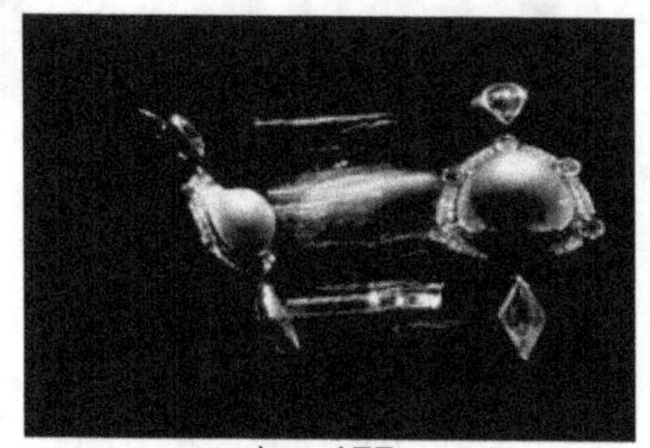

img.177

Jewellery

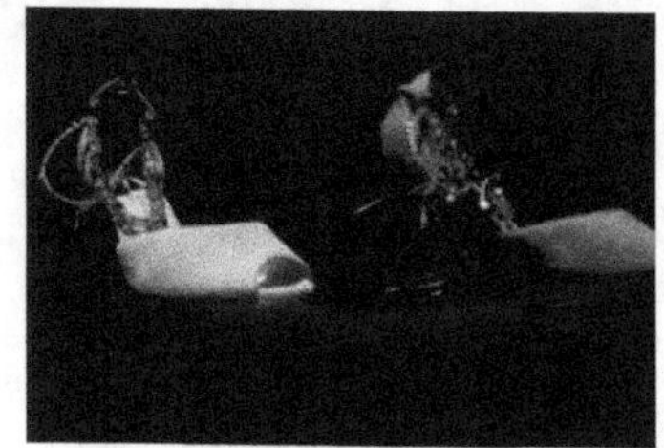

img.178

Fashion

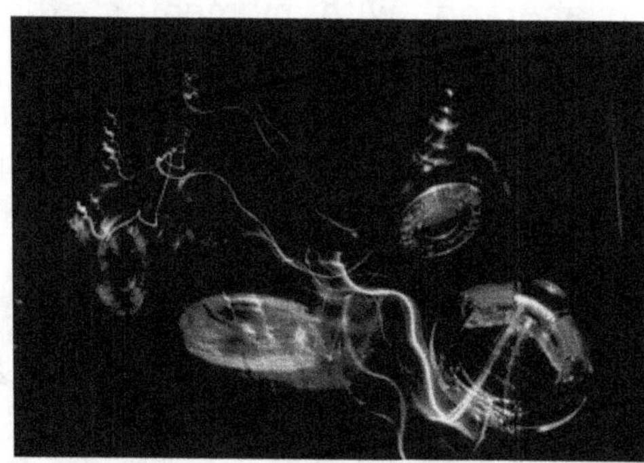

img.179

Perfumes

img.180

Watches

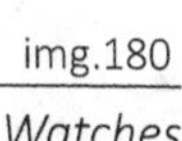

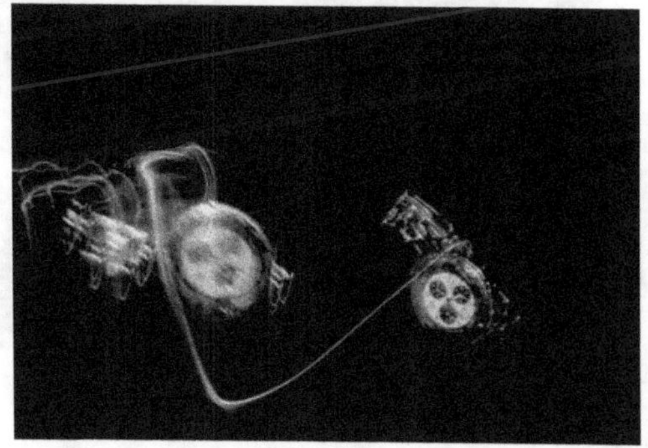

Composition
in Space-Time

In the image below (img.181) the exploration in space of a blank sheet with a red dot in the centere is represented, taken in FoTotempismo; in the final part of the shoot a person who was observing the sheet frontally was included in the scene. This image was studied in collaboration with my mentor, expert photographer and great friend, *Gianpiero Ascoli*, currently the greatest connoisseur of the entire history of FoTotempismo and its contextualization in the various disciplines.

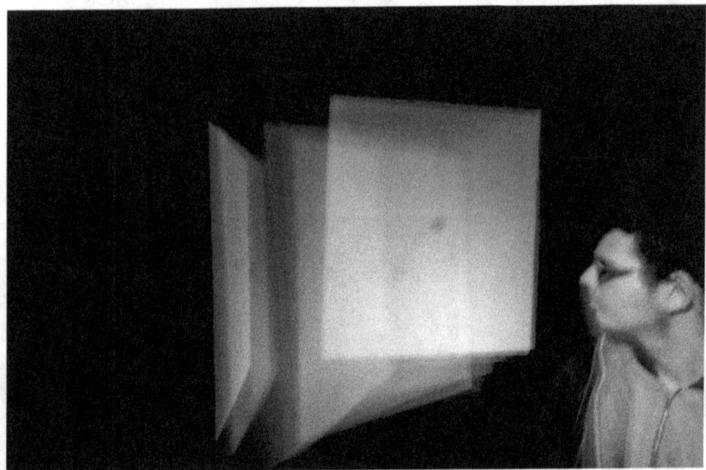

img.181

A sheet of paper and an observer seen by the author in Space-Time

FoTotempismo

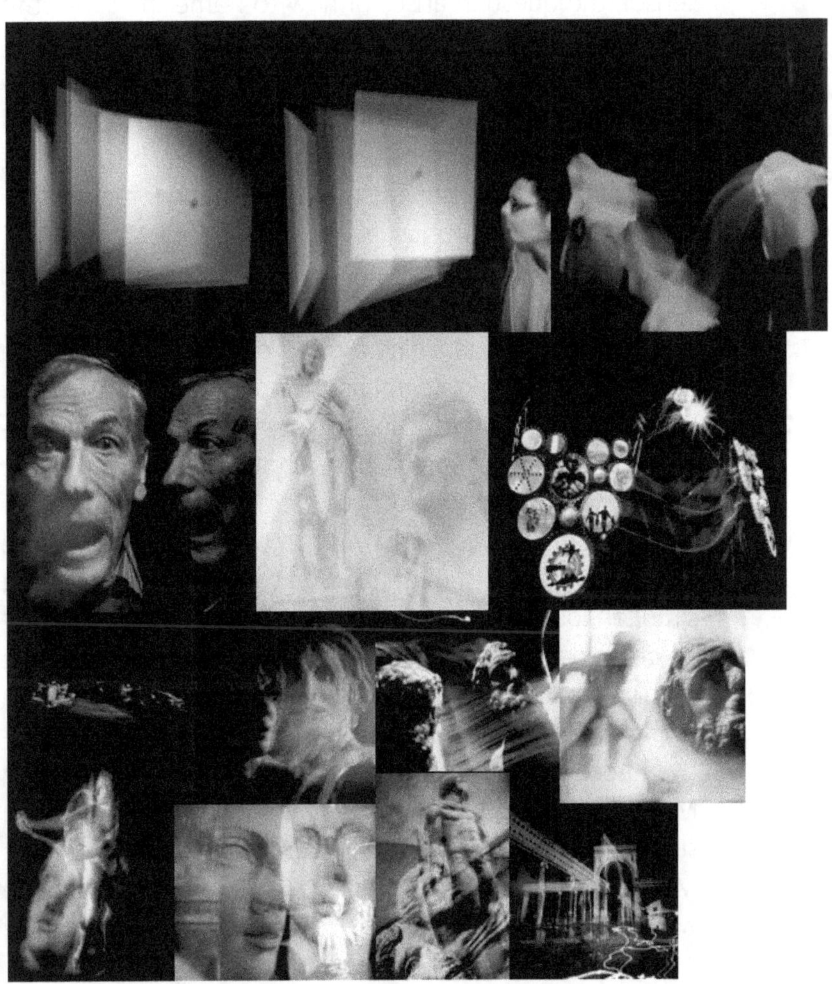

framing

Since the birth of photography, when we place ourselves behind the lens, or pinhole that lets light in towards the sensor, the question arises of how to frame the subject to be 'immortalized'. Gradually the methods have become increasingly sophisticated, ranging from shooting from below or even from below ground level, up to the now widespread method of shooting from above using a drone; but shooting at eye level still remains the most interesting for communicating according to our usual visual perspective.

It is exactly the same situation with Photodynamism, but with the possibility of having multiple 'images' in the same photograph, thus obtaining a piece of work that is not the result of several photographs juxtaposed (as can already be done with multi-exposures, diptychs, triptychs and others), but the expression that the photographer gives to the subject with multi-perspectives, dematerializations and re-materializations. The work thus composed assumes a value that is not just the sum of two or more images represented simultaneously, but has a multiplicative and exponential value derived from the characteristics of FoTotempismo itself; in this way the various framing methods of instant photography and others, are grouped in a single work and creativity becomes infinite. In the mythological image depicting Marsyas (img.185), the author has framed and composed the subject with the intention of making him confront himself; Marsyas, after losing the challenge with Apollo, looks as if he wants to say: *"but who made me accept this challenge!?"*; as we know, the loser's punishment was to be skinned alive.

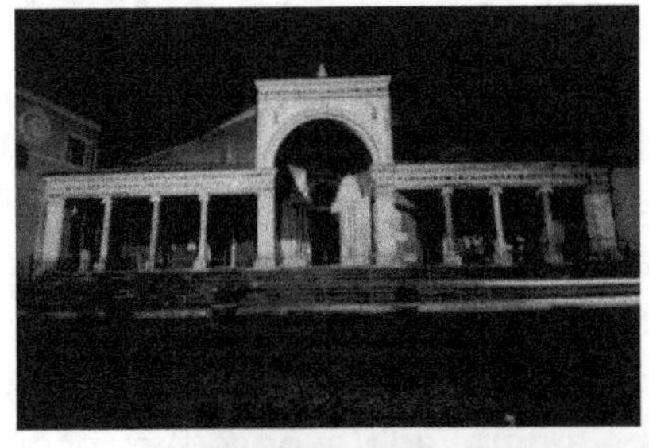

img.182

Cathedral dei Cosmati in Civita Castellana (VT)

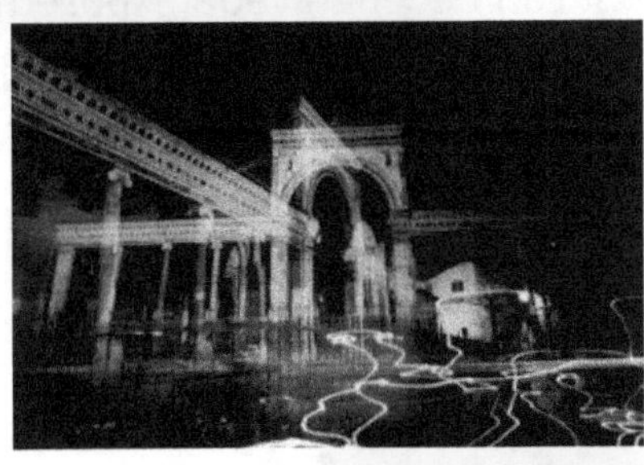

img.183

Cathedral dei Cosmati In FoTotempismo

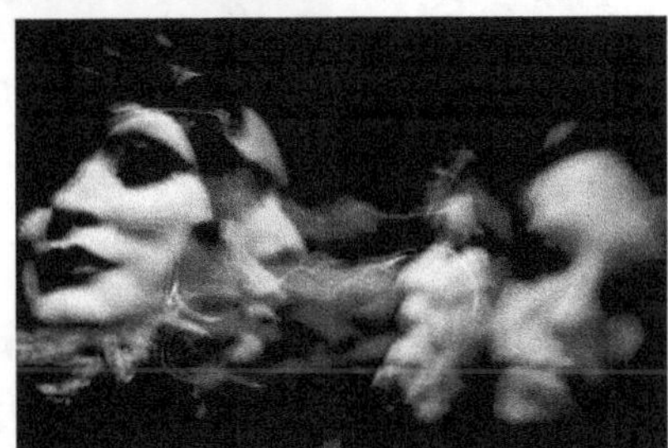

img.184

Portrait with mask

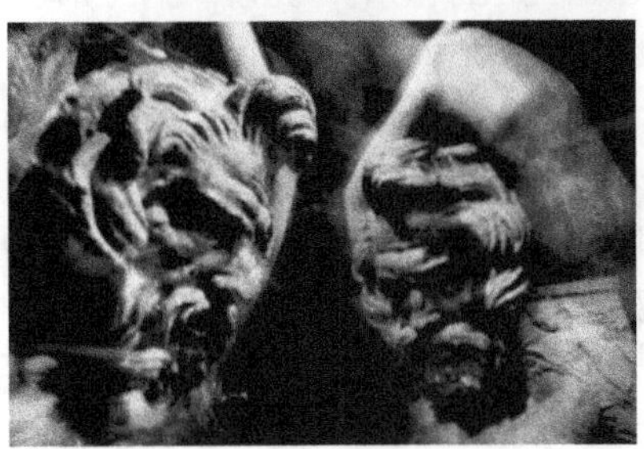

img.185

Marsyas (sculpture)

dark backgrounds

The first experimental images were made with the subject more illuminated than the rest of the scene, which immediately gave good results. The reason for greater success with a dark background is that, where there is darkness (dark area) the sensor is not 'engraved' by the light, so it can be 'engraved' (exposed) a second time. In this way, by exposing the subject to more light than the background, and positioning it to the left of the sensor, or elsewhere, depending on the composition, there remains space for the trails of dematerialization, re-materialization and for the allocation of other perspectives. It is not necessary for the backdrop to be exclusively black, it can also be grey or other colours, thus generating effects to be discovered. In the studio this situation can be managed using various backdrops and various types of lighting; the best results are obtained with spot lighting focused on the subject. However, conditions in the field are different and here dark backgrounds are favoured. Nighttime conditions are excellent for photographing subjects in their natural situations, such as: street scenes, portraits, nightlife, landscape, architecture and others. Equally good are the lighting conditions inside museums and environments that, with the lighting they are equipped with (windows or lamps directed on the statues), offer large areas in shadow but with the subject illuminated. Setting the exposure for the subject in these situations gives good results.

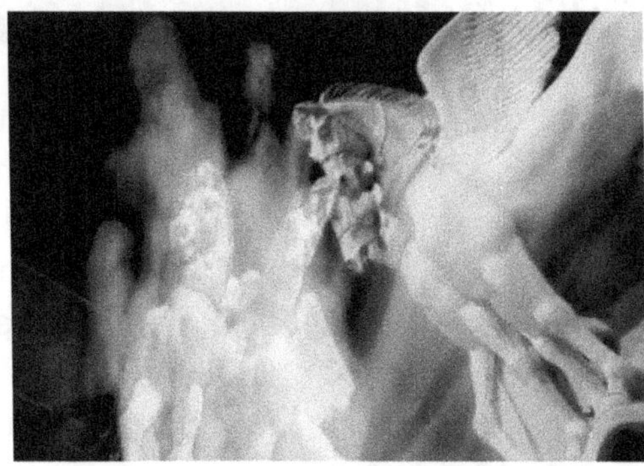

img.186

Winged Horses
in FoTotempismo

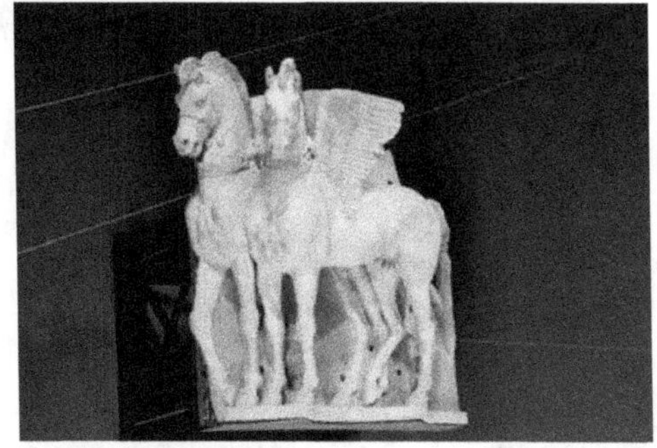

img.187

Winged Horses
(Tarquinia VT)

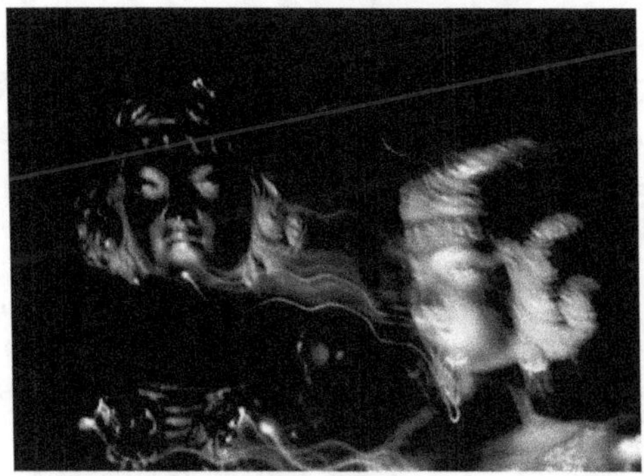

img.188

Sculpture
in FoTotempismo

light backgrounds

With the experience gained by photographing with dark backgrounds, we can progress to producing images in FoTotempismo using light backgrounds. Even in this circumstance all the methodology and techniques examined so far are valid. It is sometimes easier when the subject is also light in colour and the background is uniform; however, nonhomogeneous backgrounds are not to be underestimated, which, when properly managed are able to offer amazing images. In image 189 the white marble statue of the *Resting Satyr* is portrayed, who located in a white niche with its natural shading made the ideal set for a pleasing fototempistic composition, as can be seen in image 190.

Other conditions can be seen in image 191, in which the dark-coloured bronze statuettes stand out from the uniform light background.

Also in this situation, by appropriately managing: sensor sensitivity, apertures, exposure times and movement of the author/camera a very expressive image was composed (img.192). So, while increasing the difficulties, with due will and experience, excellent results in various lighting conditions and scenarios can be achieved. From here, awareness of the importance of research becomes more evident, and such knowledge leads to the use of FoTotempismo in all circumstances, representing all the known photographic genres.

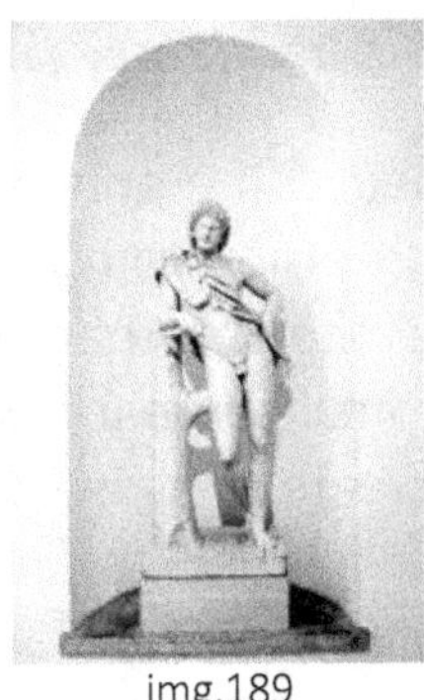

img.189

Resting Satyr

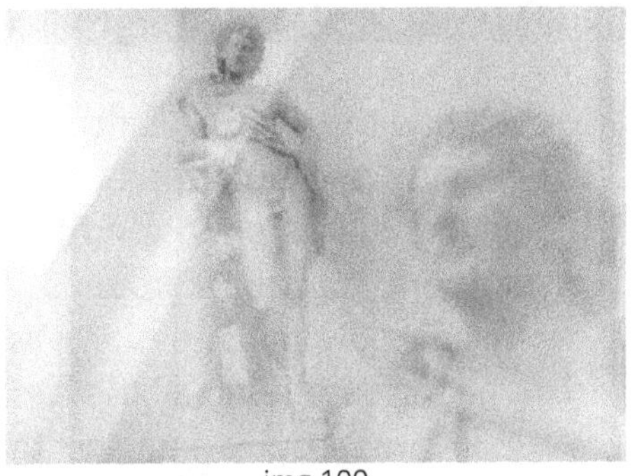

img.190

Resting Satyr (FoTotempismo)

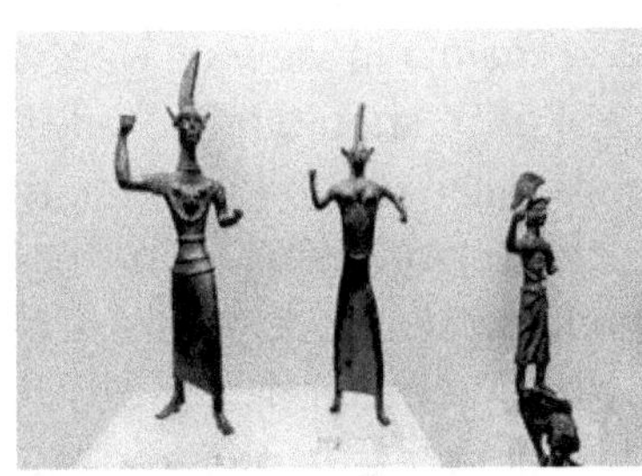

img.191

Minerva fighting

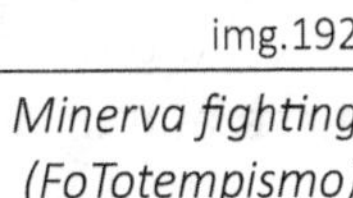

img.192

Minerva fighting (FoTotempismo)

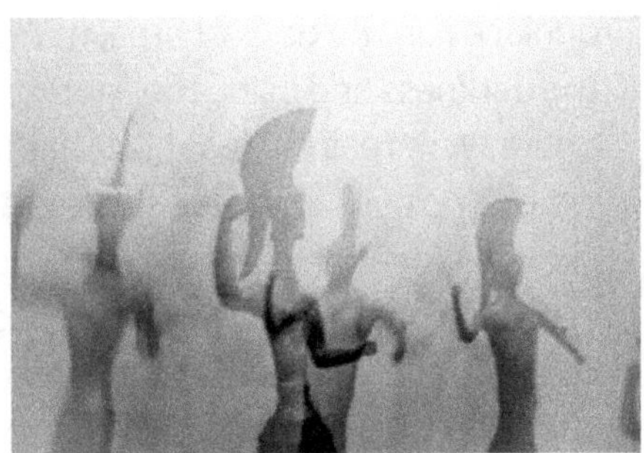

dark or light backgrounds?

Provided with the experience described in the previous pages, we now explore the application of fototempistic action with backgrounds and scenarios that are the sum of dark and light backgrounds. As a first approach we have seen how much easier it is to create images with dark backgrounds and a little less with light backgrounds (img.196). It is easy to imagine that with both light and dark backgrounds (img.193- 195) we are going to complicate matters. In these circumstances, even better planning is needed for the composition of the image, building it according to the typology of the subject, of the involvement of the background and mainly in view of what we wish to communicate. First of all, it should be noted that the dark background portions will never be so black that nothing is visible, similarly, the bright areas will never be so white that there is no shadow. Therefore, aware of this fact and of the results previously obtained, it is possible to bring out the light or the darkness in the image we wish to compose.

So where the subject will appear mainly dark we will frame or place it in the darkest area, making its image emerge from the darkness and using the lighter areas to create the atmosphere. Whereas if the subject has light enough components we can position it where there is a light background; in this circumstance the subject can be positioned or framed even in a dark background area depending on the discretion of the author. All this does not prevent the author also from choosing situations other than those described.

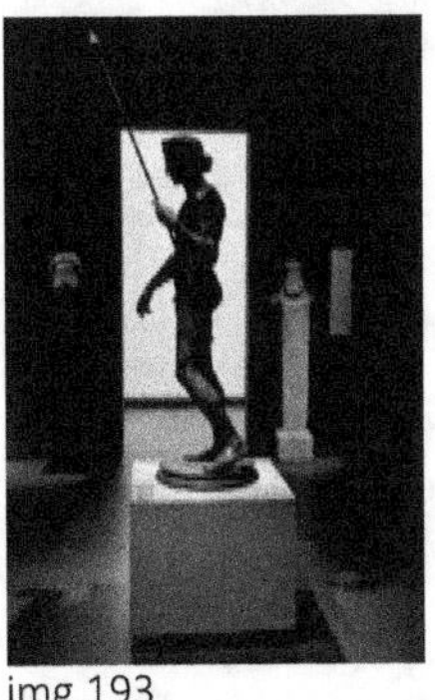

img.193

'Dionysus' (still photo)

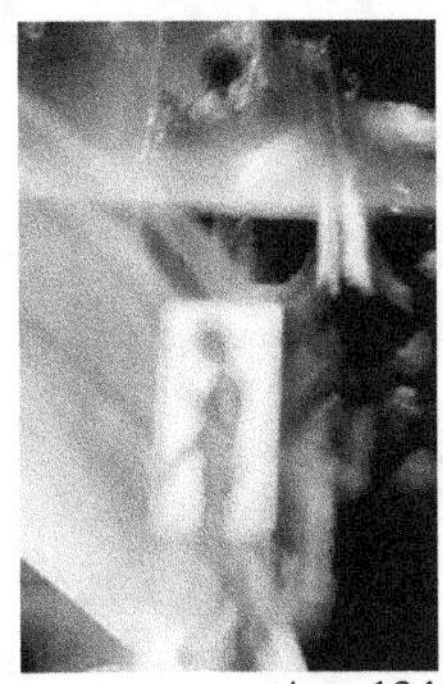

img.194

'Dionysus' (FoTotempismo)

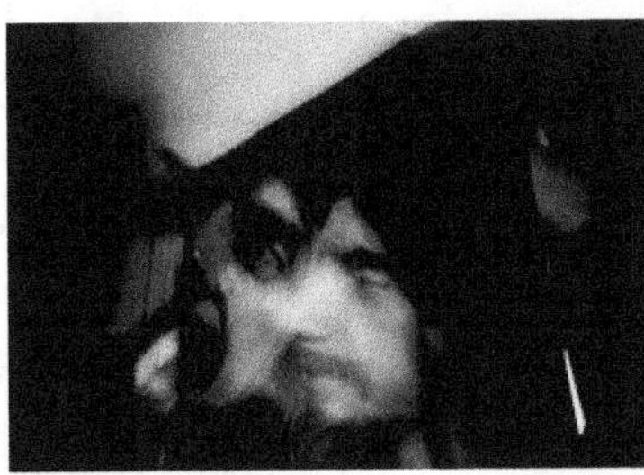

img.195

Portrait (FoTotempismo)

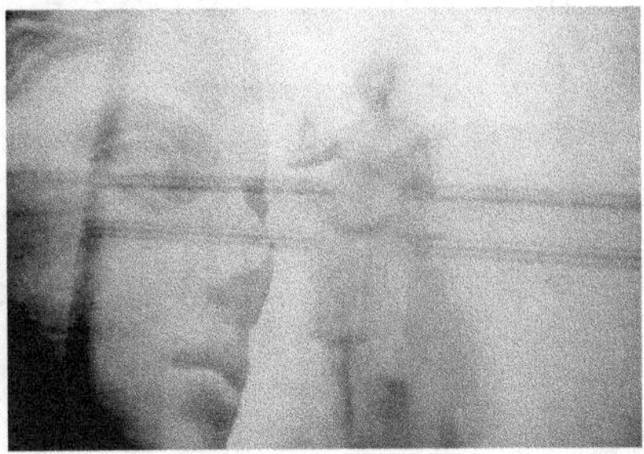

img.196

FoTotempismo on a light background

Shooting in FoTotempismo in full light is the most complicated procedure, but it is also one that can offer some really fascinating images.

Images 197 and 198 are still photos of the two perspectives then represented in image 201 in FoTotempismo. With careful examination of image 201, on the right you can see the arch and the waterfall descending, in the centre of the image the sparkling froth is generated from the top of the waterfall with the green vegetation on the left, while on the left above, shot with a long focal length of the zoom, there is the waterfall.

Among the subjects which give excellent results in the open air, there is: modern architecture, structures with oblique lighting, portraits in full sun on shaded foliage, even urban subjects in foggy or hazy climatic conditions. Images 199 and 200 show exercises to highlight the main difficulties, even in this case the author's creativity is that which generates the best emotion.

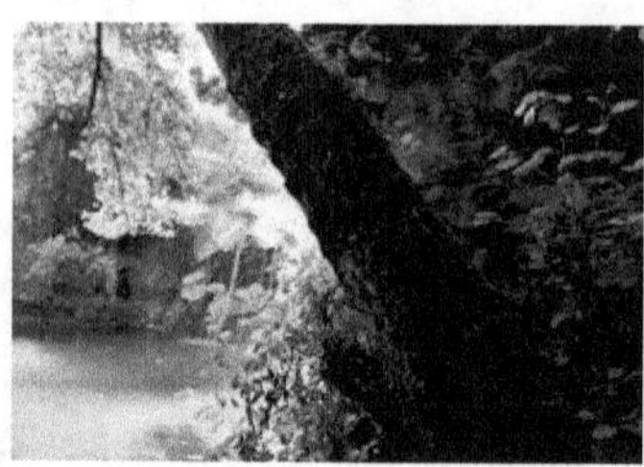

img.197

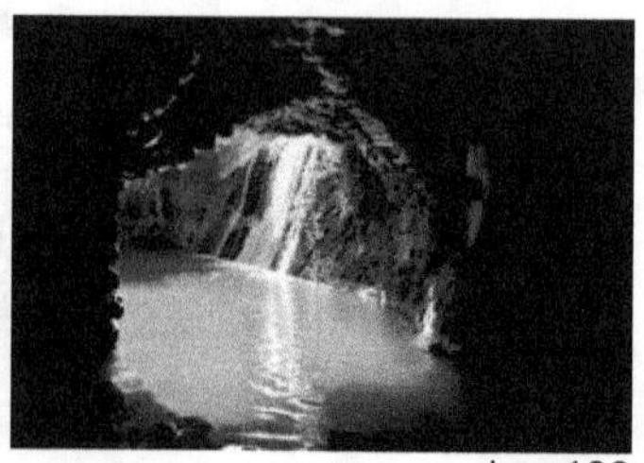

img.198

Still shots of the waterfall from both perspectives

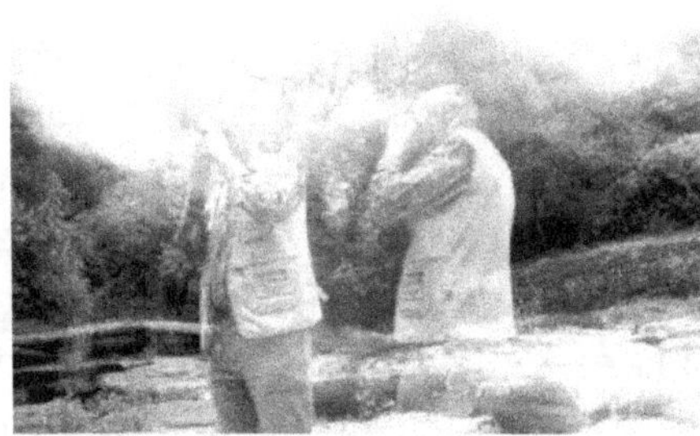

img.199

*Portrait in full light in
FoTotempismo*

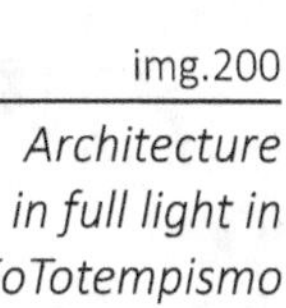
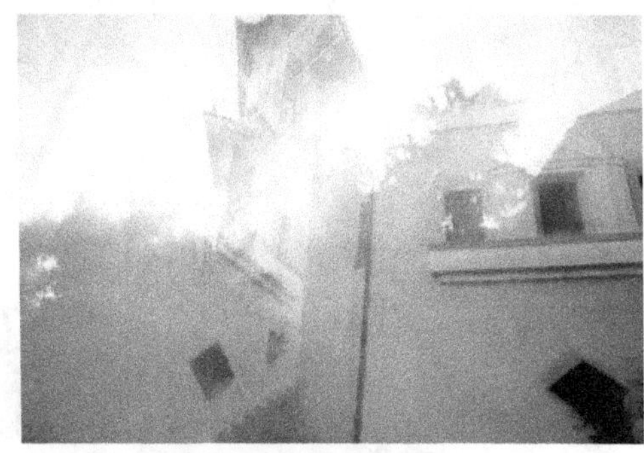

img.200

*Architecture
in full light in
FoTotempismo*

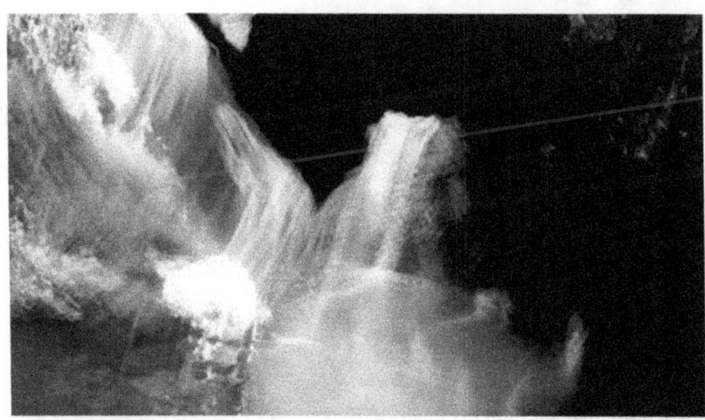

img.201

Waterfall in FoTotempismo in full light corresponding to img. 197, 198

The choice of how to chromatically compose the work has always, since the appearance of colour in photography, fascinated both the author and the observer. With fototempistic images other factors come into play, even if consistency to the idea decided upon at the beginning of the project remains essential, which will create the impression for the desired message. In the following images two cases will be examined: in the case of images 202, 203 & 204 the author's considerations for the final

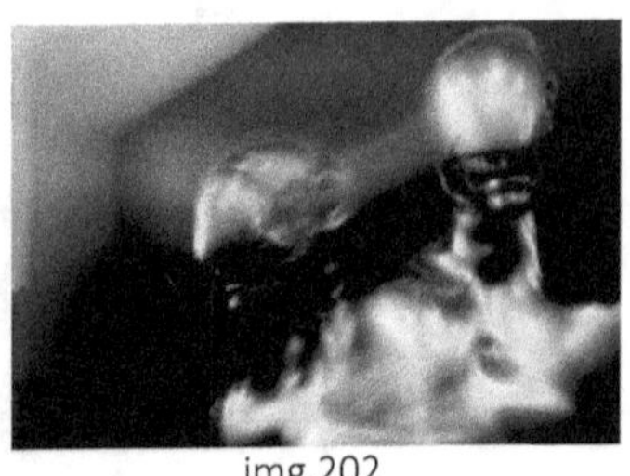

img.202

Natural colour image

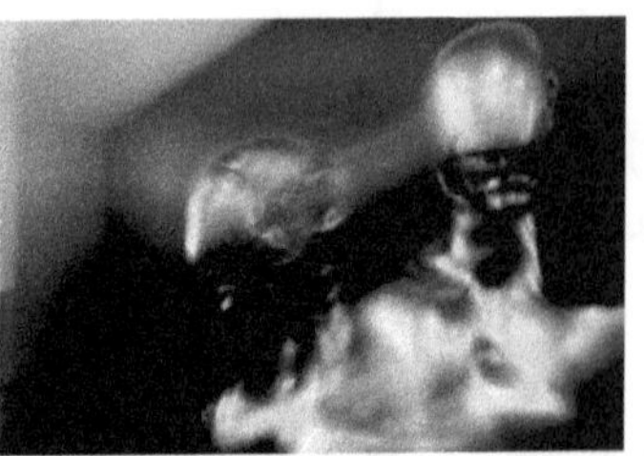

img.203

Black/white image

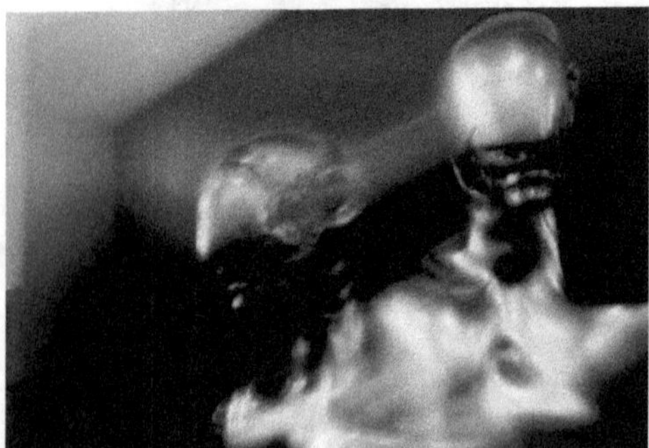

img.204

desaturated image

work in choosing between: colour, B/W and desaturated led to choosing one in full colour to increase tensions, incisiveness and strength of the message to be transmitted. In contrast, for images 205, 206 & 207, the final choice for the work was the desaturated one; in fact, wishing the subject to represent the 'Rebuke of the Eternal Father on the World', the image in colour reinforced too strongly the tensions created by FoTotempismo and the one in B/W made them too far from reality, therefore the desaturated one was chosen, which best expressed the calmness of the reproach, as intended by the author.

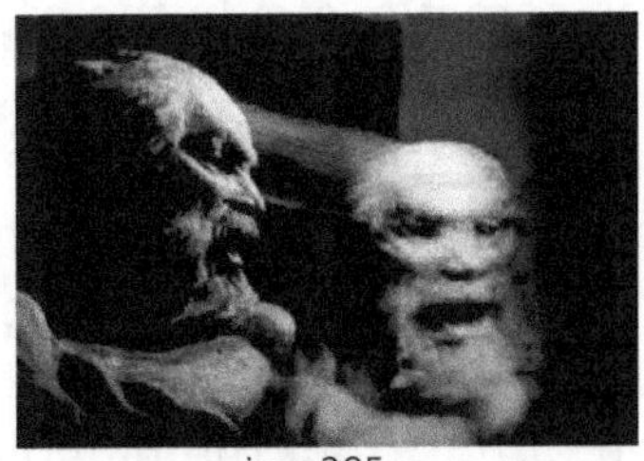

img.205

natural colour image

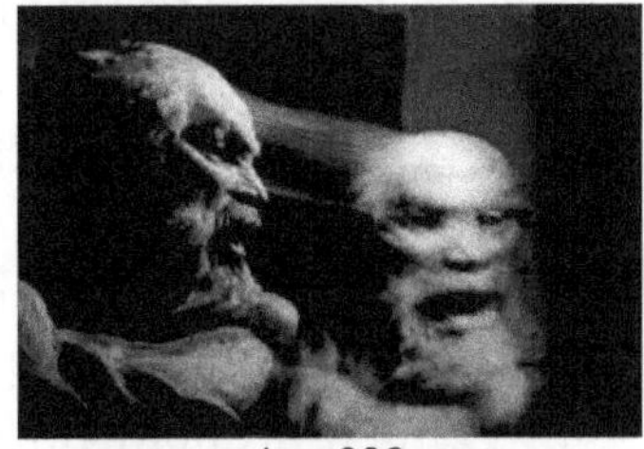

img.206

black/white image

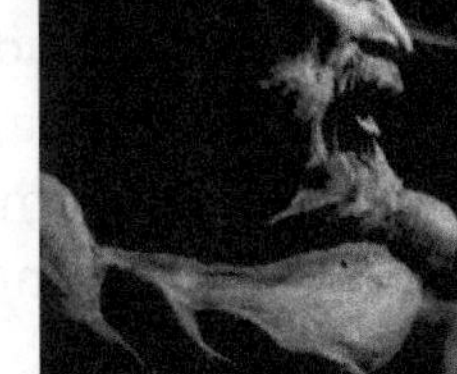

img.207

desaturated image

Which tools to use

Each discipline that generates art uses a type of instrument suitable for the purpose: brush, spatula, chisel, pen and others, so too FoTotempismo uses a tool which serves to shape the images on the photosensitive area, exactly like other disciplines do on: canvas, paper, stone, metal, ceramic, etc. In the case of FoTotempismo the primary tool is a container with a *pinhole* (from the Greek *stenos opaios*, narrow hole), i.e. small hole capable of conveying the light thus projecting an image onto a surface. Certainly this container that at first was a simple box into which no light entered, if not from the pinhole, has gradually improved up to the present day, and has now reached extremely high levels with the current cameras. Today these tools are sophisticated, with many lenses capable of regulating the amount of light, the opening time of the 'pinhole', automatic focus, varying focal lengths, vibration dampening, and still other technologically advanced functions and features managed with programmed algorithms, which automatically and autonomously provide images that the 'photographic community' expects.
But even a simple 'lens', achieved with a very small

FoTotempismo

hole made on the lens cover of a camera, may be suitable for taking pictures in FoTotempismo.

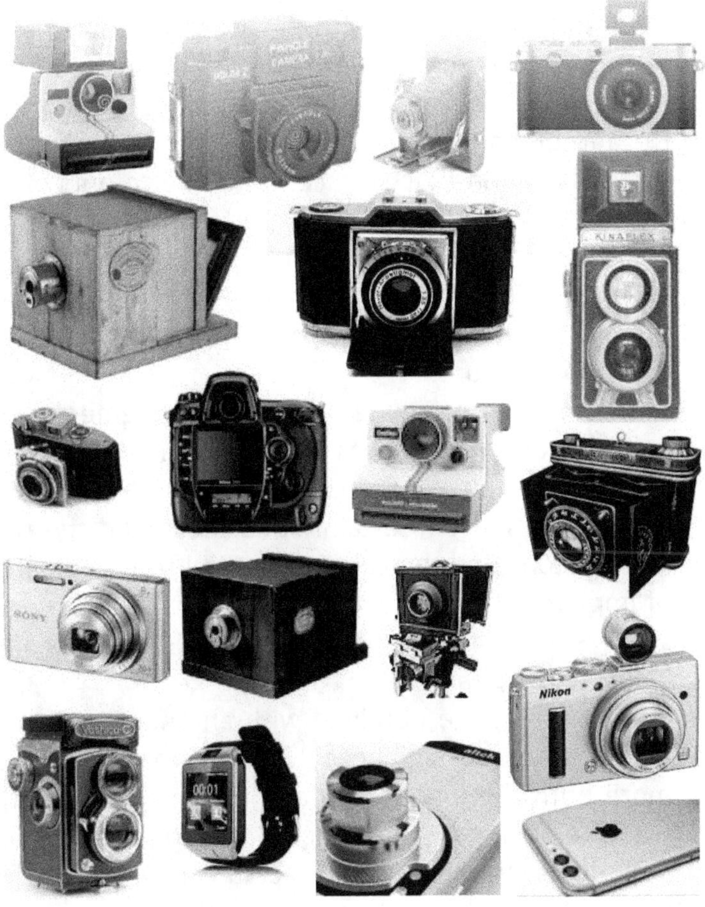

the sensors

On which materials to leave the 'Sign'

As already mentioned, with the 'Gesture' that characterizes each discipline, it leaves its 'mark' on the surface or within its substance. Thus it is with FoTotempismo, the author leaves their 'Sign' with a personal 'Gesture' on the light-sensitive surface, using the colours of the light itself. Many types of support and light-sensitive chemical materials were used in pre-digital times and it will certainly not be the material on which to leave the mark that will limit the fototempistic concept, not even in the future.

FoTotempismo originated in the era of cameras with a digital sensor and it was with them that the first image was created, but it is not for this that it is limited to the sensor. Certainly this shortened the time needed to refine the concept, but all the parameters of implementation are identical, both using analogue sensors (films, plates, polaroid, emulsion papers of all kinds) and digital.

Indeed the image obtained with an analogue sensor assumes a more significant value, emphasizing even more both the uniqueness and the originality of the work, removing all the temptations from the artefact that digital can induce. In fact the development of

FoTotempismo

both the analogue sensor and analogue printing allows only minimum variations without altering too much the image obtained in the shooting phase.

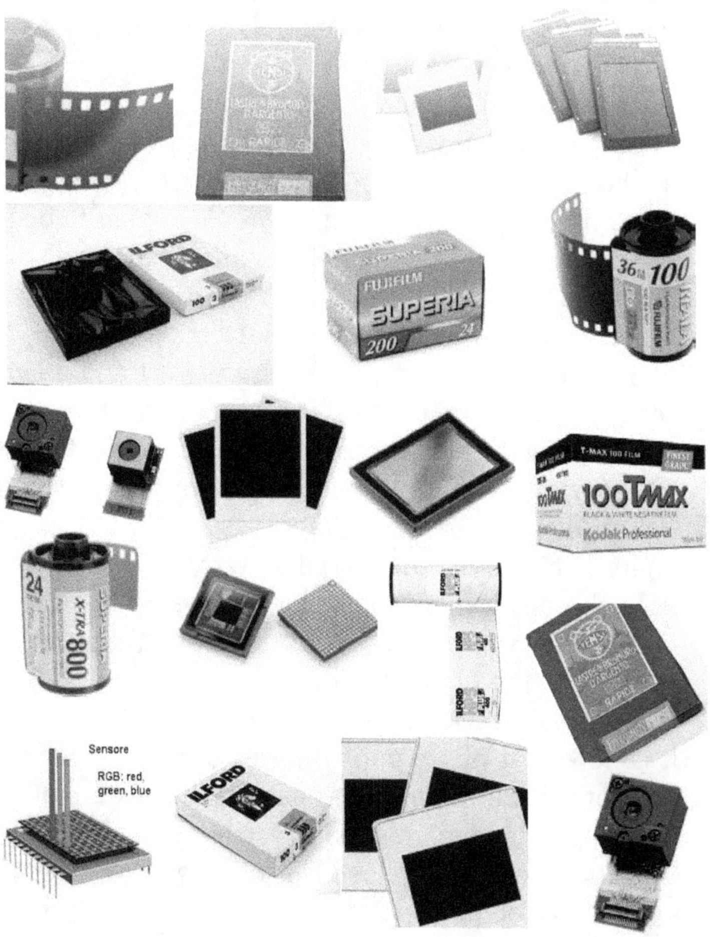

the impression
in Photography and Painting

At the conclusion of this journey I want to add just a few lines to confirm indisputably photography as an artistic discipline.

It is common opinion that, unlike painting, the photographer must have a subject to shoot to obtain a photographic image. On hasty examination, as is customary for human beings, it would appear to be so, but on careful examination, the same need can also be observed in painting.

We consider that a camera system is needed for photography consisting of an optical part and a light-sensitive part, called the sensor, which stores and sends the information of the framed subject to its memory; the whole is a technical-chemical system and now also silicon-based digital.

There is also a carbon-based system in nature which uses the same dynamic, namely: an eye in place of the photographic lens, a light sensitive retina and a memory in the brain of man.

Therefore, the two systems are 'equivalent'.

It is here that photography makes use of the manual skills of the photographer as painting makes use of the artisan painter's manual skills.

Yes, that's exactly it, just like photography needs a subject, so too does painting.

We humans take it for granted that a painter 'creates' an image, in that, despite not having the subject in their visual orbit manages to represent an image of

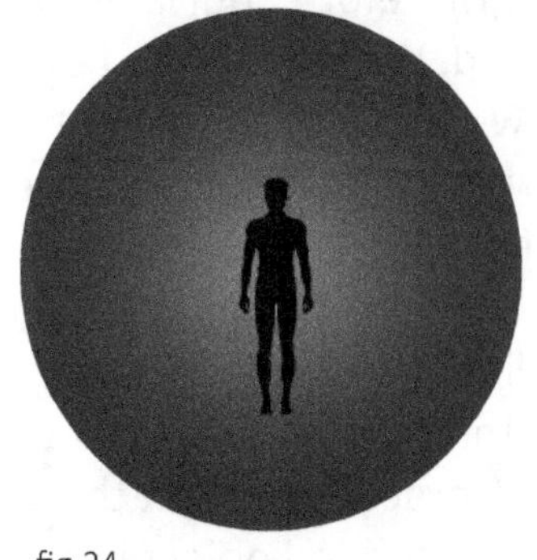

fig.24

Blind person in a sphere

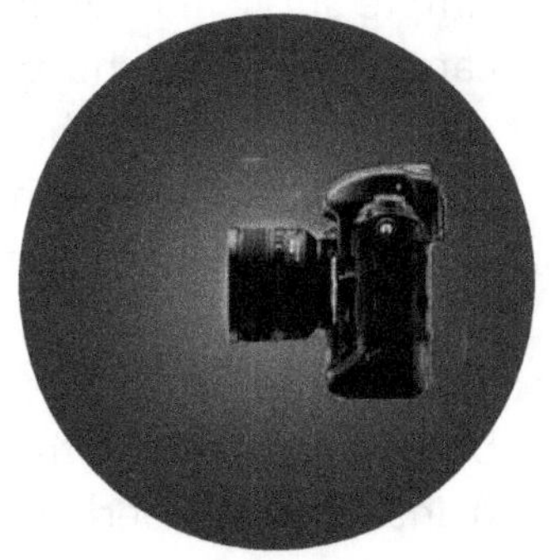

fig.25

Camera with closed shutter

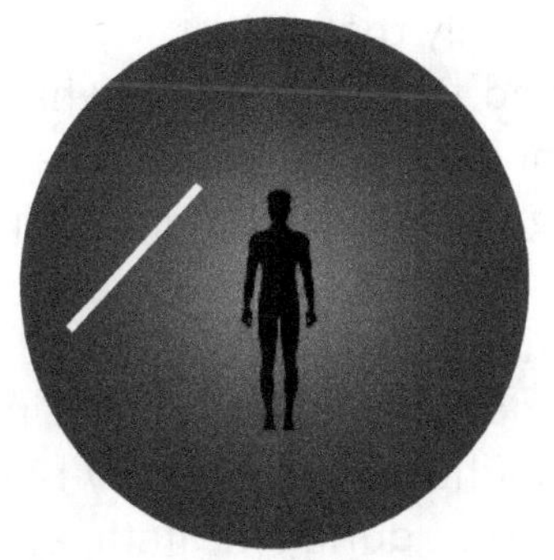

fig.26

A white line in the sphere

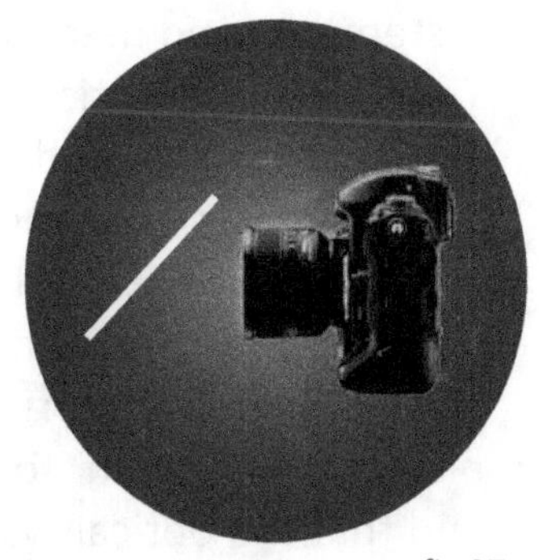

fig.27

A white line in the sphere

'Reality' or in any case attributable to it.

This is absolutely false.

To explain it, let us consider the human being born without sight but with all the organs activated by a simple surgical intervention, therefore equivalent to a camera with the shutter closed. We submit the human subject to surgery that allows them to see and at the same time we place them within a dark sphere where all visual sensations are the same as before, that is, without any message.

For hypothesis, in this condition we place a canvas, a brush and paints in front of the person. What can they paint? Nothing, perhaps only inexact or abstract things.

The next step is to bring an line-shaped object into the sphere and ask the 'painter' to depict something. They will only be able to depict an object that was seen.

This happens because their optical and mnemonic system saw and memorized only that object.

Therefore, the 'artisan' hand will only depict what it has seen and stored without adding anything else, just like a camera shooting system consisting of lens-sensor-memory would do; therefore also the painter needs a subject-imprint as in photography.

Here is where the myriad amount of images comes into play that have been stored in the human memory-brain and that the optical system sent during its lifetime.

At this point the 'painter' expresses these with craftsmanship on canvas or other supports, even mixing the various images memorized to combine them fantastically with each other, thus manifesting artistic expression.

The photographer does the same thing; their tool is not the brush but the camera, they assimilate the images, as the painter did on 'coming out of the sphere', and they gradually impress them onto the film-sensor by processing them mentally before shooting, as the painter does to express an artistic concept.

In conclusion, only the instrument changes between photography and painting and the way of using it to make a simple image or an artistic expression.

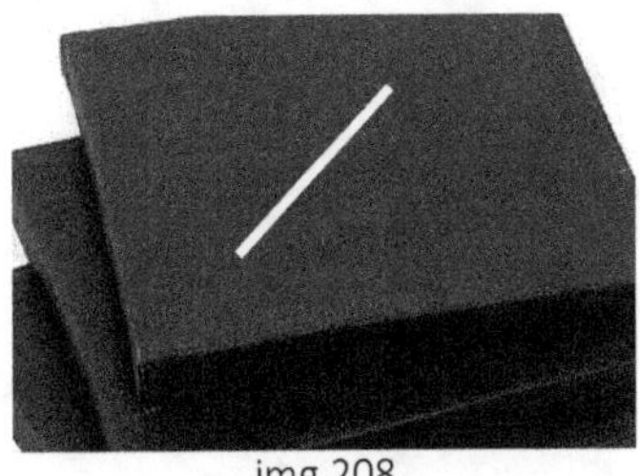

img.208

Line painted by man

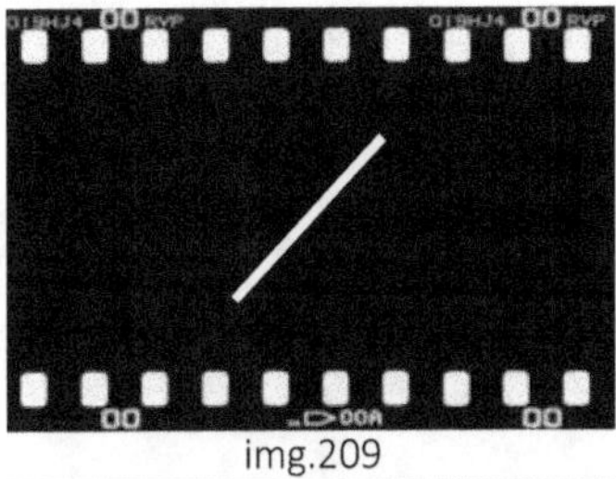

img.209

Line photographed by man

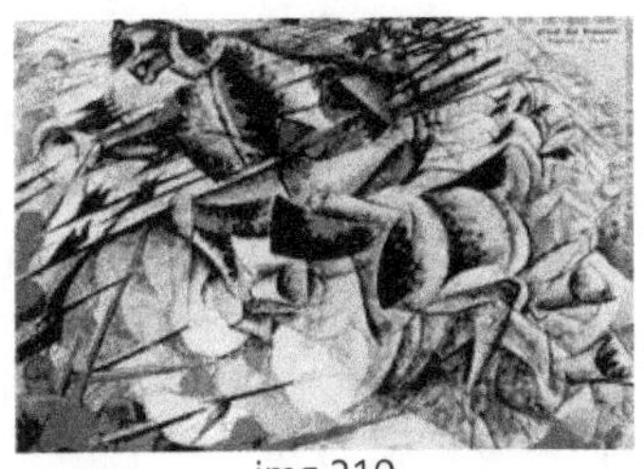

img.210

A painting of evolved man

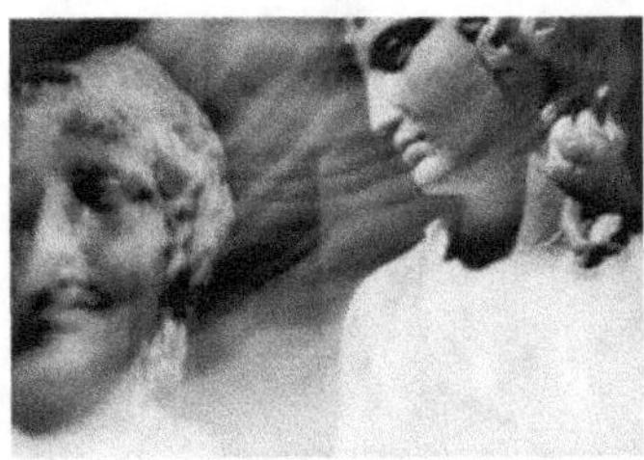

img.211

A photograph of evolved man

Bibliography

Boccioni U. *Pittura, scultura, futuriste: dinamismo plastico*, Edizioni futuriste di "Poesia", Milano 1914.

Florenskij P. A. (Misler N.) *Lo spazio e il tempo nell'arte*, Adelphi Editore, 4ª ediz.,Milano 1995.

Crispolti E. *Storia e critica del futurismo*, Editori Laterza, Bari 1986.

Krauss, R. E. *Teoria e storia della fotografia*, Edizione italiana a cura di Elio Grazioli, Pearson Italia S.p.a., Milano 1996.

Schwarz A. *Man Ray*. Ediz. illustrata, Giunti Editore, Firenze 1998.

Calvenzi G. *Italia, ritratto di un paese in sessant'anni di fotografia,* Contrasto, Roma 2003.

Barthes R. *La camera chiara. Nota sulla fotografia,* Einaudi, Torino 2003.

Flusser V. *Per una filosofia della fotografia* Pearson Italia S.p.a., Milano 2006.

Vaccari F. *Dialoghi, Verso uno statuto delle immagini contemporanee,* Campanelli Vito, Lulu.com, Bari 2016.

Di Lauro G. *Identità fotografiche. Processi di costruzione della realtà attraverso l'immagine*, Passerino Editore, Gaeta (LT) 2019.

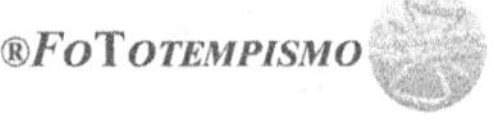

ENZO TRIFOLELLI
beyond photographer
®FOTOTEMPISMO

index

Thanks to

Gianpiero Ascoli
my friend;
I want to thank you for having accompanied me on this journey of discovery and in-depth study of the concept of FoTotempismo, without you this book would not have been possible.

Thanks to Silvio Mencarelli
for his precious advice and support for the publication.

Thanks also to:

Studio Luciano Zuccaccia for their support and editorial help
'Heros and Heroines' for having stimulated the research
IL CASTELLO Publishers
Ass. Cult. *IL CASTELLO*
Centro Immagine Soriano nel Cimino
NuovaFrontieraFotografica
Selettronic S.C.A R.L.
Roberto Salbitani
Claudio Limiti
Gianni Amadei
Vincenzo Pacelli
Giuliano Zappi
Marco Scataglini
Irene Pacelli
Giulia Pacelli
All the people pictured
The students of my workshops

In addition, my thanks also go to all
those whose contribution have made
it possible to arrive at this volume.

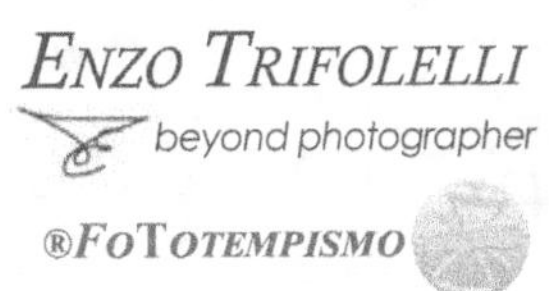

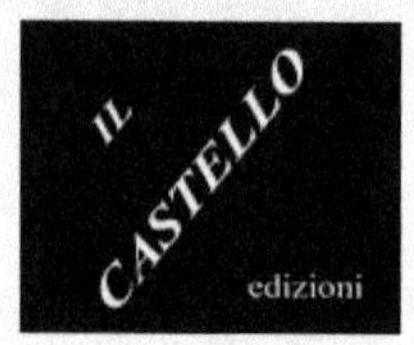

Published by	Edizioni IL CASTELLO Via Roma, 46/b 01038 Soriano nel Cimino (VT) Italy
Text	Enzo Trifolelli
Photographic concept	®FoTotempismo
Consultation	Gianpiero Ascoli, Silvio Mencarelli
Images	Enzo Trifolelli and others

Contacts	www.enzotrifolelli.com info@enzotrifolelli.com
First edition	English by Julie Anne Hobson, January 2021
Printed	PressUP - Nepi (VT) Italy
Cover photo	by E. Trifolelli 'il Padre' (the Father), sculpture by Gianluca Bagliani
Produced	in partnership with Selettronic S.C.A R.L.

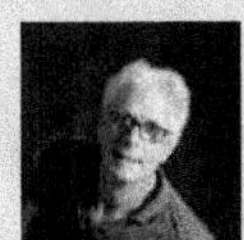 

ENZO TRIFOLELLI
®*FoTotempismo*

He was born in Bassano in Teverina (VT) in 1951.
In 2009 he became the promoter and founder of the Centre for Photographic Study and Research of Tuscia. In 2011 he published the photographic account The PALIO, the volume was awarded a medal by the President of the Italian Republic Giorgio Napolitano.
In 2010 he defined his idea-concept which he named FoTotempismo, thus introducing the 'Gesture' and the 'Sign' into photography.
The first exhibition in FoTotempismo was in 2012 with *Pierrot and our society*. In 2014 the traveling exhibition *'and then ...'* was inaugurated in Fiuggi with the relative photo book. In July of the same year he defined the manifesto of the *NuovaFrontieraFotografica* and completed it with the collaboration of Gianpiero Ascoli, Marco Scataglini and Anna Maria Staccini, later published on 22 July 2017 on the occasion of *SorianoImmagine2017*. In 2016 he exhibited at MIA Photo Fair in Milan and there presented the book the *Awakening of the Statues I*, in the same year he participated in the Milan Photo Festival. In March 2017 he presented the book the *Awakening of the Statues* II with relative exhibition. In July of the same year he produced and curated the *SorianoImmagine2017* photographic review, *'Space-time' from the Etruscans to the Nuova Frontiera Fotografica* with 21 exhibitions in nine locations. In 2018 workshops, exhibitions and displays were held in museums, including the Civic City and Diocesan Museum of Acquapendente. In 2019 he received the *Scrapante Prize*; he also presented the photographic exhibition and the book *the Awakening of the Etruscans* at the National Etruscan Museum of Villa Giulia MiBAC in Rome. In July of the same year he produced and curated the *SorianoImmagine2019* photographic review *'Space-time' from the Etruscans to the Nuova Frontiera Fotografica* with 21 exhibitions in nine locations.

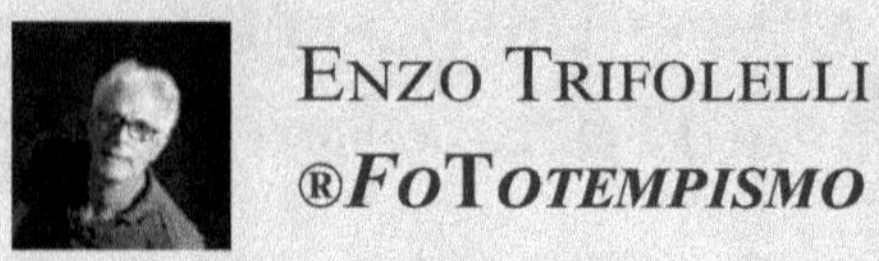 

Enzo Trifolelli
®*FoTotempismo*

Individual Publications

The Palio / Il Palio, edizione Il Castello, Soriano nel Cimino, 2011

Images, edizione Il Castello, Soriano nel Cimino, 2011

Pierrot / Pierrot, edizione Il Castello, Soriano nel Cimino, 2012

and then… / E poi…, edizione Il Castello, Soriano nel Cimino, 2014

L'urlo, edizione Il Castello, Soriano nel Cimino, 2014

The scream, edizione Il Castello, Soriano nel Cimino, 2014

the Awakening of Statues I / Il Risveglio delle Statue I, edizione Il Castello, Soriano nel Cimino, 2016

the Awakening of Statues II / Il Risveglio delle Statue II, edizione Il Castello, Soriano nel Cimino, 2017

the Awakening of Etruscans I / Il Risveglio degli Etruschi I, edizione Il Castello, Soriano nel Cimino, 2019

the Return of ETruscans I / Il Ritorno degli ETruschi I, edizione Il Castello, Soriano nel Cimino 2019

ETruscan Love / Amore ETrusco, edizione Il Castello, Soriano nel Cimino, 2020

www.ingramcontent.com/pod-product-compliance
Lightning Source LLC
Chambersburg PA
CBHW061520120726

48001CB00004B/1370